CHRISTA WOLF was born in Landsberg, Warthe, in 1929. She studied German at Jena and Leipzig Universities and has worked as an editor, lecturer, journalist and critic. The winner of many literary prizes, including the Georg-Buchner Prize of the German Academy for Language and Poetry, she has written short stories, essays, film scripts and four other novels, three of which are also published by Virago. They are *The Quest for Christa T.*, *A Model Childhood* and *No Place on Earth*.

Christa Wolf is a committed socialist of independent temper and for several years she was a member of the central committee of the East German Writers' Union. One of the most important writers to come out of Eastern Europe, her earlier novels reflect her preoccupation with the personal suppressions and official silences under Nazism, and with the events in Germany which followed the war.

In 1982 she was awarded a guest lectureship at the University of Frankfurt, where in May she gave a series of five 'Lectures on Poetics'. These related to studies and travels undertaken in Greece in 1980. The fifth 'lecture' was a draft of *Cassandra*, which she then revised and expanded for publication. It is presented here along with the lectures which originally accompanied it.

CASSANDRA

Cassandra

BY CHRISTA WOLF

A NOVEL AND FOUR ESSAYS

TRANSLATED FROM THE GERMAN

BY JAN VAN HEURCK

Published by VIRAGO PRESS Limited 1984
41 William IV Street, London WC2N 4DB

Translation copyright © 1984
by Farrar, Straus and Giroux, Inc.
Originally published in German
in two volumes under the titles
Voraussetzungen einer Erzählung: Kassandra and
Kassandra, Erzählung © 1983 by Hermann Luchterhand
Verlag GmbH & Co KG, Darmstadt und Neuwied

British Library Cataloguing in Publication Data
Wolf, Christa
  Cassandra.
  I. Title   II. Voraussetzungen einer
  Erzählung: Kassandra. *English*
  833'.914   PT2685.036

ISBN 0-86068-568-3
ISBN 0-86068-573-X Pbk

Printed in Great Britain by litho at
The Anchor Press, Tiptree, Essex

CONTENTS

TRANSLATOR'S NOTE

In 1980 East German author Christa Wolf took a trip to Greece accompanied by her husband, Gerhard. In 1982 she was awarded a guest lectureship at the University of Frankfurt, where in May she delivered a series of five "Lectures on Poetics" relating to her Greek travels and studies. The fifth "lecture" was a draft of the novel *Cassandra*, which she then revised and expanded for publication. The four introductory lectures were published separately in Germany under the title *Conditions of a Narrative: Cassandra; The Frankfurt Lectures on Poetics* (*Voraussetzungen einer Erzählung: Kassandra*). This volume presents the novel first, followed by its companion lectures, which illuminate its background and implications.

CASSANDRA

It was here. This is where she stood. These stone lions looked at her; now they no longer have heads. This fortress—once impregnable, now a pile of stones—was the last thing she saw. A long-forgotten enemy demolished it, so did the centuries, sun, rain, wind. The sky is still the same, a deep blue block, high, vast. Nearby, the giant fitted-stone walls which, today as in the past, point the way to the gate, where no trace of blood can be seen seeping out from beneath. Point the way into the darkness. Into the slaughterhouse. And alone.

Keeping step with the story, I make my way into death.

Here I end my days, helpless, and nothing, nothing I could have done or not done, willed or thought, could have led me to a different goal. Deeper than any other feeling, deeper even than my fear, this imbues, etches, poisons me: the indifference of the celestials to us of earth. Unavailing the venture to set our little warmth against their icy chill. Vain our attempt to evade their atrocities, long have I known that. But a couple of nights ago on the sea crossing, when storms threatened to smash our ship from every direction; when no one could hold on unless he was lashed down; when I found Marpessa secretly untying the knots which bound her and the twins to each other and to the mast, and being attached to a longer rope than the others, I threw myself at her unhesitatingly and unthinkingly to prevent her from abandoning the lives of her children and mine to the indifferent elements, so that I could surrender them to mad people instead; when, shrinking from her gaze, I crouched again in my place beside the whimpering, spewing Agamemnon—I could only marvel at the durable stuff of those cords that bind us to life. I saw that Marpessa, who, as once in the past, would not talk to me, was better prepared for what we are suffering now than I, the seeress; for I derived joy from everything I saw —joy, not hope!—and lived on in order to see.

Strange how every person's weapons—Marpessa's silence, Agamemnon's blustering—must always remain unchanged. I, to be sure, have gradually put down my weapons; that was what proved possible for me in the way of change.

Why did I want the gift of prophecy, come what may?

To speak with my voice: the ultimate. I did not want anything more, anything different. If need be, I could prove that, but to whom? To the foreigners, impudent and reserved at the same time, who are standing around the chariot? Enough to make you laugh if anything still can: that my proneness to justify myself should have gone down only just before I did.

Marpessa does not speak. I will not see the children again. She is hiding them from me underneath her shawl.

The same sky over Mycenae as over Troy, only empty. Shiny like enamel, inaccessible, polished clean. Something in me matches the emptiness of the sky above the enemy land. So far, everything that has befallen me has struck an answering chord. This is the secret that encircles and holds me together; I have never been able to talk of it with anyone. Only here, at the uttermost rim of my life, can I name it to myself: There is something of everyone in me, so I have belonged completely to no one, and I have even understood their hatred for me. Once "in the past" —yes, that's the magic word—I tried to talk about it to Myrine, in hints and broken phrases. Not to obtain relief, there was no relief; but because I believed I owed it to her. Troy's end was in sight, we were lost. Aeneas had pulled out with his people.

Myrine despised him. And I tried to tell her—no, not just that I understood Aeneas; that I *knew* him. As if I were he. As if I were crouching inside him, feeding in thought on his traitorous resolves. "Traitorous," said Myrine, angrily raining ax blows on the undergrowth in the trench surrounding the citadel, not listening to me, perhaps not even understanding what I said, for since I was imprisoned in the basket I speak softly. It is not my voice that suffered, as they all thought. It is the tone. The tone of annunciation is gone. Happily gone.

Myrine shrieked. Strange that I, who am not yet old myself, must speak of almost everyone I knew in the past tense. Not of Aeneas, no. Aeneas is alive. But must a man who lives when all men die be a coward? Was it more than policy that moved him to retreat with the last men to Mount Ida, his native territory, rather than lead them to death? After all, a few of us must survive (Myrine denied that): who better than Aeneas and his people?

Why not me, along with him? The question was not asked. He, who tried to ask it, ended by taking it back. Just as I, alas, had to suppress what I could have said to him only now. In turn, I stayed alive long enough at least to think it. Will stay alive, for another few hours. I will not ask for the dagger which I know Marpessa is carrying on her. Which her eyes alone offered me a short time ago when we saw the wife, the queen. Which my eyes alone declined. Who knows me better than Marpessa? No one anymore. It is past noon. What I grasp between now and evening will perish with me. Will it perish? Once a thought comes into the world, does it live on in someone else? Inside our trusty chariot driver, who finds us a nuisance?

"She's laughing," I hear the women say; they do not know that I speak their language. They draw from me shuddering; everywhere I get the same reaction. Myrine, seeing me smile as I talked of Aeneas, shrieked: Unteachable, that's what I was. I laid my hand on the nape of her neck until she was still, and from the wall beside the Scaean Gate both of us watched the sun sink into the sea. We knew it was the last time we would stand together this way.

I am testing for pain. I am probing my memory the way a doctor probes a limb to see whether it has atrophied. Perhaps pain dies before we die. That information, if true, must be passed on; but to whom? Of those here who speak my language, there is none who will not die with me. I make the pain test and think about the goodbyes. Each one was different. In the end we identified each other by whether or not we knew this was goodbye. Sometimes we just raised our hands lightly. Sometimes we embraced. Aeneas and I did not touch each other anymore. It seems to me that his eyes, whose color I could not fathom, were above me for an infinite time. Sometimes we continued to talk, the way I talked with Myrine, so that at last the name was named which we had kept silent so long: Penthesilea.

I talked of how I had seen her, Myrine, march through this gate three or four years before beside Penthesilea and her armored band. Of my rush of irreconcilable feelings—amazement, compassion, admiration, horror, embarrassment, and yes, even an infamous amusement: how they found release in a laughing fit which distressed me and which Penthesilea was never able to pardon me for, hypersensitive as she was. Myrine confirmed the fact. Penthesilea was offended. This and nothing else was the reason for her coldness toward me. And I confessed to Myrine that my bids for reconciliation were halfhearted, even though I knew that Penthesilea was going to fall in battle. "How could you know that!" Myrine asked me with a trace of her former violence; but I was no longer jealous of Penthesilea. The dead are not jealous of each other. "She fell in battle because she wanted to fall. Why else do you think she came to Troy? And I had reason to keep close watch on her, so I saw how it was." Myrine was silent. What had always enchanted me more than anything else about her was her hatred for my prophecies, which I never uttered in her presence, to be sure; but they were always reported to her promptly, including the passing mention of my certainty that I was going to be killed. She would not let me get away with that, unlike the others. Where did I get the right to make such pronouncements? I did not answer, closed my eyes in happiness. At last, after such a long time, my body again. Once again the hot stab through my insides. Once again the utter weakness for someone. How she tore into me. So I had not cared for Penthesilea, the man-killing warrior woman, eh? she asked. Well, did I think that she, Myrine, had killed fewer men than her commander in chief? When in fact she had most likely killed more, after Penthesilea's death, in order to avenge her?

Yes, my pony, but that was something else again.

That was your clenched defiance and your blazing grief for Penthesilea, don't you think I understood that? Then there was her deep shrinking shyness, her fear of being touched, which I never infringed until the moment when I was allowed to wind her blond mane around my hand and so found out how very much I had felt like doing that for so long. Your smile in the moment of my death, I thought; and because I no longer abstained from any caress, I left the terror behind for a long time. Now it approaches me darkly once again.

Myrine got into my blood the moment I saw her, bright, daring, ardent beside the dark, self-consuming Penthesilea. Joy-giver or pain-giver, I could not let her go; but I do not wish she was beside me now. I rejoiced to see her, a woman, put on her weapons—she was the only one to do so—when the men of Troy brought the Greeks' horse into the city against my objections. I strengthened her resolve to keep watch beside the monster while I stayed with her, unarmed. I rejoiced, perversely again, to see her hurl herself at the first Greek to come up out of the wooden steed around midnight. Rejoiced—yes, rejoiced! —to see her fall and die from a single blow. Because I was laughing they spared me as the lives of madmen are spared.

I had not yet seen enough.

I do not want to speak anymore. All the vanities and habits

have been gutted; the places inside me where they could have grown back are laid waste. I feel no more sorry for myself than for others. I no longer want to prove anything. The laughter of this queen when Agamemnon stepped onto the red carpet went beyond all proof.

Who will find a voice again, and when?

It will be one whose skull is split by a pain. And until then, until his coming, nothing will be heard but bellows and commands and whimpers and the "yes, sirs" of those who obey. The helplessness of the victors who silently prowl around the vehicle, passing each other my name. Old men, women, children. Their helplessness at the atrocity of the victory. At its aftermath, which I can already see in their blind eyes. Stricken blind indeed. Everything they have to know will unfold right before their eyes, and they will see nothing. That is just how it is.

Now I can put to use a skill I have practiced all my life: to conquer my feelings by thought. In the past it was love I had to conquer; now fear. It assailed me when the chariot, dragged slowly up the mountain by weary horses, came to a stop between the somber walls. Outside this final gate. When the sky opened and sunlight fell on the stone lions, which looked away past me and everything, and always will look away. Of course I know what fear is, but this is something different. Perhaps it is cropping up in me for the first time only to be killed again at once. Now the inner core is being razed.

My curiosity—about myself as well as about others—is fully at liberty now. When I recognized this I shrieked out loud. It was during the crossing; I was wretched like all the others, buffeted by the heavy sea, drenched to the skin by the spurting foam, disturbed by the wailing and exhalations of the other Trojan women, who were not kindly disposed toward me: for everyone always knew who I was. I was never permitted to lose myself in their midst. I wished for that too late; I did too much in my past life to make myself known. Self-reproaches, too, prevent the important questions from coming together. Now the question grew like fruit inside the peel, and when it detached itself and lay before me, I shrieked aloud, with pain or bliss.

Why did I want the gift of prophecy, come what may?

As it happened, on that stormy night King Agamemnon the "Most Resolute" (ye gods!) grabbed me out of the tangle of other bodies; my cry coincided with this moment and required no further explanation. I, I was the one who had stirred up Poseidon against him, he shrieked at me, out of his head with fear; for had he not sacrificed three of his best horses to the god before the crossing? "And Athena?" I asked coldly. "What did you sacrifice to her?" I saw him turn pale. All men are self-centered children. (What about Aeneas? Nonsense. Aeneas is an adult.) What, mockery, in the eyes of a woman? They cannot stand that. The victorious king would have killed me—that is what I wanted him to do—if he had not still been afraid of me as well. The man has always taken me for a witch. He wanted me to pacify Poseidon! He thrust me to the bow, jerked my arms up in the posture he considered suitable for an incantation. I moved my lips. You poor wretch, what does it matter to you whether you drown here or are murdered at home?

If Clytemnestra was the woman I thought she was, she could not share the throne with this nonentity. —She *is* the woman I thought she was. Besides that, she is racked with hatred. Most likely the weakling treated her vilely while he still controlled her, the way they all do. I not only know men but women as well, which is more difficult; and so I know that the queen cannot spare my life. A short time ago her glances told me so.

When did my hatred disappear? Oh yes, it is gone, my plump juicy hate. I know one name that could awaken it, but I prefer to leave that name unthought as yet. If only I could. If only I could wipe out the name, not merely from my memory, but from the memory of all men living. If I could burn it out of our heads—I would not have lived in vain. Achilles.

If only my mother had not come to mind just now, Hecuba, aboard another ship headed toward other shores with Odysseus.

Who can help the thoughts that come into his head? Her crazed face as they dragged her away. Her mouth. My mother called down on the Greeks the most hideous curse ever uttered in human history. It will come true, one must only know how to wait. I called out to her that her curse would be fulfilled. Her last word was my name, a scream of triumph. When I stepped into the ship, everything in me was dumb.

That night the storm abated soon after I "charmed" it. Not only my fellow captives, but also the Greeks—even the crude, avid oarsmen—drew back from me, shy and deferential. I told Agamemnon I would lose my power if he forced me into his bed. He let me go. His potency was already long gone; the girl who lived with him in his tent for the last year betrayed it to me. He had threatened that if she did this—betrayed his un-utterable secret—he would find a pretext to have her stoned to death by his troops. Suddenly I understood his exquisite cruelty in battle, just as I understood why his silence deepened the farther we got from Nauplion along the long, dusty road through the plains of Argos, and the closer we came to his citadel: Mycenae. The closer we came to his wife, to whom he had never given a reason to be merciful if he showed any weakness. Who knows what misery she may spare him if she murders him.

They do not know how to live; this is the real disaster, the truly fatal danger—I came to understand that only little by little. I, the seeress! Priam's daughter. How long I was blind to the obvious: that I had to choose between my birth and my office. How long I feared the dread I must arouse in my people if I were to perform that office, come what may. The same dread that has now hurried ahead of me over the sea. The people here —naïve if I compare them with the Trojans, for they have not experienced war—are exhibiting their feelings, fingering the chariot, the foreign objects, the plundered weapons, even the horses. Not me. The chariot driver, who seems ashamed of his countrymen, told them my name. I saw the same thing I am used to seeing: their dread. "They are not the best people, of course," says the chariot driver. "They stayed at home." The women approach again. They appraise me unabashed, peer under the shawl I have drawn over my head and shoulders. They bicker about whether I am beautiful; the older ones claim I am, the younger say no.

Beautiful? I, the terrible one. I who wanted Troy to fall.

Rumor, which overruns the seas, will also precede me into time. Panthous the Greek will turn out to be right. "But you are lying, my dear," he said to me while we performed the pre-scribed passes at the shrine of Apollo, readying the ceremony. "You are lying when you prophesy we are all doomed. Prophesy-ing our destruction, you immortalize yourself. You need that more than you need a snug life in the present. Your name will go on. And you know it."

I could not slap his face yet a second time. Panthous was jealous, spiteful, and sharp-tongued. But was he right? In any case, he made me think the unheard-of: The world could go on after our destruction. I did not let him see how that unnerved me. Why had I allowed myself to suppose that the human race would be wiped out along with us? Did I not know how the female slaves from the conquered tribe were always forced to increase the fertility of the victors? Was it the overweening pride of a king's daughter that made me implicate all the Trojan women—not to mention the men—in the death of our house? It took me a long time and much labor to distinguish between qualities in ourselves that we know and those that are inborn and virtually unrecognizable. Affable, modest, unassuming—that was the image I had of myself, which survived every catastrophe virtually intact. Not only that: Whenever it survived, the catas-trophe lay behind me. Did I gravely wound the self-esteem of my family in order to preserve my own—because to be honest, proud, and truth-loving was a part of this image? Did I pay them back for injuries they had inflicted on me by the inflexible way I spoke the truth? I believe that this is what Panthous the Greek thought about me. It took me a long time to notice, but he knew and detested himself, and sought relief by attributing one cause and one alone to every act or omission: self-love. He was absolutely convinced of a world order in which it was impossible to serve oneself and others at the same time. Never, never was there a breach in his aloneness. But he had no right —I know that today—to regard me as like himself. At first perhaps he was right to think me like him, on one score—what Marpessa called my pride. I lived on to experience the happiness of becoming myself and being more useful to others because of it. I do know that only a few people notice when someone changes. Hecuba, my mother, knew me when I was young and ceased to concern herself with me. "This child does not need me," she said. I admired and hated her for it. Priam, my father, needed me.

When I turn around I see Marpessa smiling. Now that things have taken a grave turn, I hardly see her without a smile. "Marpessa, the children will not be allowed to live; they're mine. You will, I think." "I know," she says. She does not say whether she wants to live or not. They will have to drag the children away from her. Perhaps they will have to break her arms. Not because they are mine, but because they are children. "I'll be the first to go, Marpessa. Right after the king." Marpessa answers: "I know." "Your pride, Marpessa, overshadows even mine." And she, smiling, replies: "That's how it must be, mistress."

How many years it has been since she called me mistress. Where she led me I was not mistress, not priestess. That I was allowed that experience makes dying easier for me. Easier? Do I know what I am saying?

I will never know whether this woman whose love I courted loved me. At first it may be that I did it from coquetry: in the past something in me wanted to please. Later I did it because I wanted to know her. She served me to the point of self-abandon, and so she must have needed to exercise reserve.

When the fear ebbs away, as it is doing just now, remote thoughts come to mind. Why did the prisoners from Mycenae describe their Lion Gate as even more gigantic than it looks to me? Why did they portray the cyclopean walls as more immense than they are, their people as more violent and avid for vengeance? They talked gladly and extravagantly about their home, like all captives. Not one ever asked me why I was gathering such exact intelligence about the enemy land. And why, in fact, did I do so, at a time when even to me it seemed certain that we were winning? We were supposed to smite the enemy, not to know him! What impelled me to know him, when I could reveal to no one my shocking discovery: They are like us!? Was I trying to find out where I was going to die? Was I thinking about dying? Wasn't I swollen with triumph like all of us?

How quickly and completely we forget.

War gives its people their shape. I do not want to remember them that way, as they were made and shattered by war. I gave a crack on the mouth to that minstrel who went on singing the glory of Priam until the end: the undignified, flattering wretch. No. I will not forget my confused, wayward father. But neither will I forget the father I loved more than anyone else when I was a child. Who was not too particular about reality. Who could live in fantasy worlds. Who did not have clearly in view the contingencies that maintained his nation, or those that threatened him. This made him less than the ideal king, but he was the husband of the ideal queen; that gave him special privileges. I can still see him: Night after night he used to go in to my often-pregnant mother, who sat in her megaron, in her wooden armchair, which closely resembled a throne, where the king, smiling amiably, drew up a stool. This is the earliest picture I remember, for I, Father's favorite and interested in politics like none of my numerous siblings, was allowed to sit with them and listen to what they were saying; often seated in Priam's lap, my hand in the crook of his shoulder (the place I love best on Aeneas), which was very vulnerable and where I myself saw the Greek spear run him through. It was I, who forever afterward confused with the ascetic, clean odor of my father the names of foreign princes, kings, and cities; the goods we traded or trans-ported through the Hellespont on our famous ships; the figures of our income and the debates about their expenditure. (Now those princes are fallen, the cities impoverished or destroyed, the goods spoiled or plundered.) It was I, I of all his children my father believed, who betrayed our city and betrayed him.

Nothing left to describe the world but the language of the past. The language of the present has shriveled to the words that describe this dismal fortress. The language of the future has only one sentence left for me: Today I will be killed.

What does the man want? Is he speaking to me? "I must be hungry," he says. Not I, he is the one who is hungry; he wants to stable the horses and go home at last, to his family, who sur-round him impatiently. I am to follow his queen, he says. Quietly enter the fortress with the two guards, who are attending me for my protection, not to keep watch on me. I will have to terrify him. "Yes," I say to him, "I am going. Only not now, not yet. Leave me here a little while yet. The reason is, you know" (I say to him, trying to spare him): "When I enter this gate I am as good as dead."

The same old story: Not the crime but its heralding turns men pale and furious. I know that from my own example. Know that we would rather punish the one who names the deed than the one who commits it. In this respect, as in everything else, we are all alike. The difference lies in whether we know it.

It was hard for me to learn that, because I was accustomed to being the exception and did not want to be lumped under the same roof with everyone else. That is why I struck Panthous on the evening of the day he consecrated me as a priestess; when he said to me: "Tough luck for you, little Cassandra, that you are your father's favorite daughter. You know that Polyxena would make a more suitable priestess. She prepared herself, whereas you are relying on his support. And, it seems"—I thought his smile impudent when he said that—"you are also relying on your dreams."

I slapped his face for that. He gave me a penetrating look, but all he said was: "And now you are relying on the fact that although I am the chief priest, I am, after all, only a Greek."

What he said was true, but not completely, for less than he could imagine was I guided by self-interest. (Yes, I know, unbeknown to us even our self-interest is guided by something!) The dream of the night before came unsummoned, and it troubled me deeply. It was Apollo who came to me, I saw that at once despite his distant resemblance to Panthous; although I could hardly have said wherein the resemblance consisted. Most likely in the expression of his eyes, which I called "cruel" then but merely "clear-headed" later on; referring to Panthous, for I never saw Apollo again! I saw Apollo bathed in radiant light the way Panthous taught me to see him. The sun god with his lyre, his blue although cruel eyes, his bronzed skin. Apollo, the god of the seers. Who knew what I ardently desired: the gift of prophecy, and conferred it on me with a casual gesture which I did not dare to feel was disappointing; whereupon he approached me as a man. I believed it was only due to my awful terror that he transformed himself into a wolf surrounded by mice and spat furiously into my mouth when he was unable to overpower me. So that when I awoke in horror I had an unspeakably loathsome taste on my tongue, and in the middle of the night I fled out of the temple precinct, where I was required to sleep at that time, into the citadel, into the palace, into the room, into my mother's bed. For me it was a precious moment when Hecuba's face twisted with concern for me; but she had herself under control. "A wolf?" she asked coolly. "Why a wolf? How did you come to think of that? And where did you get the mice from? Who told you that?"

Apollo Lykeios. The voice of Parthena, the wetnurse. The god of the wolves and the mice: she knew dark stories about him which she whispered to me and which I was not supposed to repeat to anyone. I would never have thought that this ambivalent god could be identical to our unimpeachable Apollo in the temple. Only Marpessa, Parthena's daughter and the same age I was, knew about the stories and kept silent as I did. My mother did not insist that I name names, for she was less troubled by the wolf shape of the sun god than by my fear to unite with him.

It was an honor for a mortal woman if a god wanted to lie with her, was it not? Yes, it was. And the fact that the god I had appointed myself to serve wanted to possess me completely: wasn't that natural? Yes of course. So, what was wrong? I should never, never have told Hecuba this dream! She would not leave off asking me prying questions.

Had I not sat one year before with the other girls in the temple grounds of Athena just after I bled for the first time—hadn't I been forced to sit there? I thought as I had thought at the time, and the skin of my scalp crawled with dreadful shame just as it had done a year before—and hadn't everything followed its predetermined course? Even now I could point out the cypress tree under which I sat, provided that the Greeks have not set fire to it; I could describe the shape of the loose row of clouds from the Hellespont. "Loose row." Absurd, ridiculous words: I cannot waste any more time on them. I will simply think of the scent of olives and tamarisks. Close my eyes, I can't go on; but I could. I opened them a crack and let in the legs of men. Dozens of men's legs clad in sandals; you would not believe how different they all were, and all repulsive. In a single day I had enough of men's legs to last me a lifetime; no one suspected. I felt their looks on my face, on my breast. Not once did I look around at the other girls, they did not look at me. We had nothing to do with each other; it was up to the men to select and deflower us. For a long time before I went to sleep I heard the snapping of fingers and the single phrase uttered with so many different intonations: "Come on." All around me the emptiness grew. One by one the other girls had been taken away: the daughters of the officers, the palace scribes, the potters, the craftsmen, the charioteers, and the tenant farmers.

I had known emptiness since my earliest childhood. I experienced two kinds of shame: that of being elect and that of being left on the shelf. Yes, I would become a priestess at any cost.

At noon, when Aeneas came, it struck me that for a long time now I had picked out his figure from every crowd. He came straight over to me. "Forgive me," he said, "I could not come before now." As if we had had an appointment. He lifted me up—no, I got up myself; but we disagreed about that now and again. We went into a remote corner of the temple precinct and, without noticing it, crossed over the boundary beyond which one may not speak. It was not due to pride that I never said a word to the women about Aeneas when we gradually came to speak about our feelings; and not only due to shyness, although of course that played a part. I always held back; I never showed my inner self as other women did. I know that because of this I never broke down the barrier between us completely. The unspoken name of Aeneas stood between me and the women, who as the war dragged on came to fear their increasingly savage menfolk as much as the enemy, and who could not know whose side I was really on if I would tell them no details: no details, for example, about that afternoon at the boundary of the temple precinct when we two, Aeneas and I, both knew what was expected of us; for we had both been instructed by my mother, Hecuba. That afternoon, when neither of us felt capable of living up to these expectations. When each of us felt to blame for our failure. My nurse and my mother and Herophile the priestess had impressed on me the duties of consummation, but they had not reckoned on the fact that the sudden intervention of love can obstruct these duties; so not knowing which way to turn, I burst into tears at his uncertainty, even though his uncertainty could only be due to my awkwardness. We were young, young. As he kissed, stroked, and touched me, I would have done whatever he wanted; but he seemed to want nothing. He asked me to forgive him for something, but I did not understand what. Toward evening I fell asleep. I still remember dreaming about a ship that carried Aeneas away from our coast across calm blue water, and about a huge fire which interposed itself between the voyagers and us, who stayed behind, as the ship moved away toward the horizon. The sea was burning. I can still see this dream-image today, no matter how many grimmer pictures of reality have veiled it since. I would like to know—what am I thinking! like to know? I? but yes, the words are true—I would like to know what unrest, unremarked by me, already caused such dreams amid peace, amid happiness: for believe it or not, we used to talk of happiness and peace!

I woke up screaming. Aeneas, stirred awake, could not quiet me and carried me to my mother. Not until later, not until I felt compelled to examine these events day and night until they gradually lost their keen edge, did I wonder at how my mother asked him whether everything had gone all right, and how he, Aeneas, curtly answered "Yes." And how Hecuba thereupon thanked him. That was the strangest part of all, and humiliating, although I did not know why. And she sent him away. Put me to bed like a child after administering a potion which made me feel good and dissolved all questions and all dreams.

It is hard to put into words what signs tell us infallibly when we must not reflect further about an event. Aeneas vanished from my view, the first instance of what became a pattern. Aeneas remained a glowing point inside me; his name a sharp stab that I inflicted on myself as often as I could. But I would not allow myself to understand the enigmatic sentence of Parthena, my nurse, when she took leave of me—for now I was an adult—and gave me her daughter Marpessa as a maidservant. In a tone half respectful, half hate-filled, she murmured to herself: "So the old lady has gotten her way again even if this time, maybe, it's for her little daughter's good." And then she, too, asked me if everything had gone all right. And I told her my dream as I had always done. For the first time I saw a human being turn pale at my words. (What did that really feel like? Frightening? Exciting? Did it give me an appetite for more?

Later on, they accused me of needing to see people turn pale. Is that true?)

"Cybele, help!" whispered Parthena, my nurse. These were the same words she spoke when she died—shortly after the destruction of Troy and before the sea crossing, I believe. Yes, when all we captives were rounded up on the naked shore in the terrible storms of autumn, the quaking storms at the end of the world. "Cybele, help!" moaned the old woman. But it was her daughter Marpessa who helped her, giving her a potion which put Parthena to sleep, never more to awaken.

Who was Cybele?

The nurse recoiled. I could see that she was forbidden to speak that name. She knew, and I knew too, that Hecuba must be obeyed. Today it seems to me incredible how her orders affected me; I can hardly remember that I once rebelled against them in high dudgeon. All she had ever wanted was to protect me, she told me afterward. But she had underestimated me, she said. By that time I had seen Cybele.

No matter how often I walked that way in later years, alone and with the other women, I have never forgotten how I felt when Marpessa led me to Mount Ida one evening at twilight—I had always had the mountain in full view, secretly loved it as my own, walked there countless times, thought I knew it—and how Marpessa, leading the way, dived into a shrub-covered fold in the ground. How she crossed through a small grove of fig trees on paths where only goats clambered, and how we suddenly stood surrounded by young oak trees, before the sanctuary of the unknown goddess where a band of brown-skinned, slender-limbed women danced in homage. Among them I saw slave women from the palace, women from the settlements beyond the walls of the citadel, and also Parthena the nurse, who crouched outside the cave entrance, under the willow tree whose roots dangled into the opening of the cave like the pubic hair of a woman: she seemed to be directing the train of dancers with movements of her massive body. Marpessa slid into the circle, which did not even notice my arrival—a new and actually painful experience for me. They gradually increased their tempo, intensified their rhythm, moved faster, more demandingly, more turbulently; hurled individual dancers out of the circle, among them Marpessa, my reserved Marpessa!; drove them to gestures which offended my modesty; until, beside themselves, they shook, went into howling contortions, sank into an ecstasy in which they saw things invisible to the rest of us, and finally one after another sagged and collapsed in exhaustion. Marpessa was one of the last.

I fled in awe and terror, wandered around for a long time, came home late at night, found my bed ready, a meal prepared, Marpessa waiting beside the bed. And next morning in the palace, the same unruffled faces as always.

What was happening? What kind of place did I live in? How many realities were there in Troy besides mine, which I had thought was the only one? Who fixed the boundary between visible and invisible? And who allowed the ground to be shaken where I had walked so securely? "I know who Cybele is!" I shrieked at my mother. "So," said Hecuba. "That's fine, then." No questions about who had taken me there. No investigation. No punishment. Did my mother show a trace of relief, even weakness? What was that to me, a mother who showed weakness? Did she perhaps intend to confide her worries to me? Then I withdrew. Evaded the touch of real people as I would do for a long time to come. Needed and demanded to be unapproachable. Became a priestess. Yes. She got to know me sooner than I did her, after all.

"The queen," my father said to me in one of our intimate hours, "Hecuba dominates only those who can be dominated. She loves the indomitable ones." All at once I saw my father in a different light. Surely Hecuba must love him? No doubt of it. Did that mean he was indomitable? Ah. Once upon a time our parents were young, too. As the war went on, baring everyone's entrails, the picture changed. Priam became increasingly unapproachable and obstinate, yet controllable all the same; only it was no longer Hecuba who could control him. Hecuba grew softer, yet could not be swayed. Grief for his sons killed Priam before he was pierced by the enemy spear. Hecuba, forced open by pain, grew more compassionate and more alive with each year of woe.

Like me. Never was I more alive than now, in the hour of my death.

What do I mean by alive? What I mean by alive—not to shrink from what is most difficult: to change one's image of oneself. "Words," said Panthous in the days when he was still my fencing partner. "Nothing but words, Cassandra. A human being changes nothing, so why himself of all things, why of all things his image of himself?"

If I grope my way back along the thread of my life, which is rolled up inside me—I skip over the war, a black block; slowly, longingly backtrack to the prewar years; the time as a priestess, a white block; farther back: the girl—here I am caught by the very word "girl," and caught all the more by her form. By the beautiful image. I have always been caught by images more than by words. Probably that is strange, and incompatible with my vocation; but I can no longer pursue my vocation. The last thing in my life will be a picture, not a word. Words die before pictures.

Mortal fear.

What will it be like? Will I be overcome by weakness? Will my body take control of my thinking? Will the mortal fear simply reoccupy, with a powerful thrust, all the positions I have wrested from my ignorance, my comfortableness, my pride, my cowardice, laziness, shame? Will it successfully sweep away even the resolution I sought and formulated on the way here: that I will not lose consciousness until the end?

When our ships—how stupid! I mean *their* ships—moored in the bay of Nauplion during a calm while the water was smooth as glass and the sun, plump and gorged with blood, was sinking behind the chain of mountains; when my Trojan women sought consolation in inconsolable weeping, as if they had become truly captives only now, when they set foot in the foreign land; in the days following, on the dusty, hot, arduous path through the stronghold of Tiryns and the filthy market towns of Argos, met and accompanied by the abuse of the women and old men who gathered; but especially on the last stretch climbing up through dry land toward this terrible stone pile, the fortress of Mycenae, our destination, which loomed overhead, sinister but still remote; when even Marpessa moaned aloud; when the king himself, irresolute Agamemnon, instead of urging haste as one would have expected, ordered one rest stop after another and each time sat down silently beside me in the shade of an olive (olive, tenderest tree . . .), where he drank and offered me wine in a way that offended no one in his retinue; when my heart, which I had stopped feeling long ago, grew smaller, firmer, harder with each rest stop, a smarting stone from which I could not wring another drop of moisture: *then* my resolution was formed, smelted, tempered, forged, and cast like a spear. I will continue a witness even if there is no longer one single human being left to demand my testimony.

I did not want to give myself the chance to ponder this resolution again. But isn't it the kind of remedy that causes a worse ill than it is meant to combat? Has not this tried and tested remedy already brought about a renewal of my old, forgotten malady: inner division, so that I watch myself, see myself sitting in this accursed Greek chariot trembling with fear beneath my shawl? Will I split myself in two until the end before the ax splits me, for the sake of consciousness? In order not to writhe with fear, not to bellow like an animal—and who should know better than I how animals bellow when they are sacrificed! Will I, until the end, until that ax— Will I still, when my head, my neck, is already— Will I—?

Why do I simply refuse to allow myself this relapse into creatureliness? What is holding me back? Who is there left to see me? Do I, the unbeliever, still see myself as the focus of a god's gazes, as I did when a child, a girl, a priestess? Will that never pass?

Wherever I look or cast my thoughts, there is no god, no judgment, only myself. Who is it that makes my self-judgment so severe, into death and beyond?

What if that, too, is prescribed? What if that, too, is worked by strings that are out of my hands, like the movements of the girl I was, ideal image, image of longing: the bright young figure in the clear landscape, gay, candid, hopeful, trusting herself and others, deserving what they conferred on her, free; oh, free? In reality: captive. Steered, guided, and driven to the goal others set. How humiliating (a word from the old days). They all knew. Panthous too. Panthous the Greek was in on the secret. He did not twitch an eyelash as he handed over the staff and the fillet to the candidate designated by Hecuba. So he did not believe that I had dreamed of Apollo? But of course he did. "Of course, of course, little Cassandra." The awkward thing was, he did not believe in dreams.

On the day when I announced calmly, "Troy will fall," he cried, "At last!" because I did not cite a dream as proof. He shared in my knowledge, but he did not care. He, the Greek, was not anxious for Troy, only for his own life, which he felt had lasted long enough anyhow (so he said). For a long time he had been carrying around the device to end it. But he did not use it. Died in torment in order to live one day longer. Panthous. It seems we never really knew him.

Of course Parthena, my nurse, knew what was going on behind the scenes, too. Knew how I was chosen priestess. Marpessa knew it through her. But it was she (how long it has been since I thought of that) who handed me the key to my dream and my life. "If Apollo spits into your mouth," she told me solemnly, "that means you have the gift to predict the future. But no one will believe you."

The gift of prophecy. So that was it. A hot terror. I had

dreamed of it. Believe me, not believe me—they would see. After all, in the long run it was impossible for people not to believe a person who proves she is right.

I had even won over Hecuba, my skeptical mother. Now she recalled a story about my early childhood; Parthena, my nurse, was made to spread it around; by no means were dreams our only clue. On our second birthday my twin brother, Helenus, and I fell asleep in the sacred grove of the Thymbraian Apollo, left alone by our parents, poorly tended by our nurse, who had fallen asleep, no doubt a little dazed from the heavy sweet wine. When Hecuba came to look for us, she saw to her horror that the sacred serpents of the temple had approached us and were licking at our ears. She drove away the serpents with vigorous handclapping, at the same time waking the nurse and the children. But ever since then she had known: The god had given these two children of hers the gift of prophecy. "Is it really true?" people asked, and the more often Parthena the nurse told the story, the more firmly she believed it. I still remember that Hecuba's zeal left a flat taste in my mouth; I felt that she was going a little too far. But all the same she confirmed what I dearly wanted to believe: I, Cassandra, and none other of the twelve daughters of Priam and Hecuba, had been appointed prophetess by the god himself. What was more natural than that I should also serve him as a priestess at his shrine?

Polyxena . . . I built my career at your expense; you were no worse than I, no less suited to the post. I wanted to tell you that before they dragged you away to be a sacrificial victim, as they are doing to me now. Polyxena, even if we had exchanged lives, our deaths would have been the same. Is that a consolation? Did you need consolation? Do I need it? You looked at me (did you still see me?). I said nothing. They dragged you away, to the grave of depraved Achilles. Achilles the brute.

Oh, if only these humans did not know love.

Oh, if only I had strangled him with my own hands on that first day of the war—may his name be accursed and forgotten—

instead of looking on while he, Achilles, strangled my brother Troilus. Remorse eats away at me, it will not ease, Polyxena. Panthous the Greek held me back. "They're too much for you," he said. "I know them." He knew them. And me. I would not strangle any man. Polyxena, let me enjoy my belated confessions —I fell to him, had already fallen to him when it was not yet decided which of us he would dedicate priestess: you or me. Never, my dear one, did we speak of it. Everything was said in glances, half-spoken phrases. How could I have said to you what I was scarcely able to think: "Let me have the office of priestess; you do not need it." That is what I thought, I swear to you. I did not see that you needed it just as I did, only for the opposite reason. You had your lovers, that is what I thought. I was alone. After all, I used to run into them at daybreak coming out of your bedchamber. After all, I could not help seeing how beautiful you were, how you were growing more beautiful, you with your curly dark-blond hair—the only one of Hecuba's daughters whose hair was not black. Whoever could have been your father? wondered the nurses and the palace servants. No—you had no hope of becoming Priam's favorite daughter. You did not envy me that post; that infuriated me. I was not in a position to wonder why you wanted to be priestess. To wonder whether you might not possibly want something quite different from the office than I did. Not dignity, distance, and a substitute for pleasures that were denied me, but rather, protection from yourself, from the multitude of your lovers, from the fate already prepared for you. You with your gray eyes. You with your narrow head, the white oval of your face, your hairline sharp as if it were cut with a knife. With that torrent of hair which every man had to dip his hands into. You with whom no man who saw you could help but fall in love. What do I mean, fall in love! Fall prey. And not only every man, many women, too. Marpessa among them I believe, when she came out of exile and never looked at a man again. Even "fall prey" is too feeble a term for the frenzy of love, the madness, that gripped many a man, including Achilles the brute—and without your doing any-thing to cause it, that one must concede . . . Polyxena. Yes, it is quite possible that I was mistaken in the dark corridor at night; for if the shadow I saw creeping out your door was Aeneas's shadow, why should you, whose every action was per-formed openly, have sworn to me much later that Aeneas had never, never been with you? But how silly I was. How could it have been Aeneas, coming from one woman only to clutch at another's breast, and then run away!

Ah, Polyxena. The way you used to move. Brisk and im-petuous, at the same time graceful. The way a priestess is not supposed to move. "Why ever not!" said Panthous, and he flaunted his knowledge (of deeper authority than mine) of the nature of his god Apollo, whom after all he had served at the god's central shrine in Delphi on the Greek mainland. "Why not be graceful, little Cassandra? Apollo is also the god of the Muses, is he not?" He knew how to insult me, that Greek. He managed to convey that he regarded as barbaric the crude pro-file which we peoples of Asia Minor gave his god.

Which did not mean that he considered me an unsuitable priestess. Beyond doubt, he said, certain of my character traits cut me out for the priesthood. Which traits? Well, my desire to exercise influence over people; how else could a woman hold a position of power? Second: my ardent desire to be on familiar terms with the deity. And of course my aversion to the approaches of mortal men.

Panthous the Greek behaved as if he was unaware of the wound in my heart; as if he did not care that he was instilling in this heart a very subtle, very secret animosity toward him, the Chief Priest, of which I myself was scarcely conscious. After all, he was the one who taught me my Greek. And taught me the art of receiving a man, too. One night when I, the newly dedi-cated priestess, had to keep vigil by the god's image, he came to me. Skillfully, almost without hurting me and almost tenderly, he did what Aeneas (I thought of him) had been unwilling or unable to do. It seemed not to surprise him that I was untouched, or that I had such a great fear of physical pain. He never mentioned a word about that night to anyone, not even me. But I was at a loss as to how I could harbor hatred and gratitude toward one and the same man.

I have a pale memory of that time; I felt nothing. For a whole year Polyxena did not speak to me. Priam was preparing for war. I held aloof. I played the priestess. I thought, To be grown up consists in this game: to lose oneself. I did not permit disappointment. I did not allow myself the slightest mistake when I led the procession of maidens to the statue of the god. As I had expected, I was trained to lead the chorus; I succeeded at everything. At first I feared I would be punished when a wolf or even a troop of mice appeared to me during prayers instead of the radiant form of the god with the lyre; but soon I found that absolutely nothing happened if I abandoned myself pleasurably to my apparitions. When Panthous came to me too, I had to envision the other man, Aeneas, in order to convert my disgust to pleasure. Upheld by the respect of the Trojans, I lived in semblance more than ever. I still remember how my life drained out of me. I can't do it, I often thought as I sat on the city wall staring into space without seeing; but I could not bring myself to wonder what it was that placed me under such strain when my existence was so easy.

I saw nothing. Overtaxed by the gift of sight, I was blind. I saw only what was there, next to nothing. The course of the god's year and the demands of the palace determined my life. You could also say they weighed it down. I did not know it could be different. I lived between events which ostensibly comprised the history of the royal house. Events that aroused the craving for more and more new events, and finally for war.

I believe that was the first thing I really *saw*.

Rumors about the SECOND SHIP were slow to reach me. My heart bitter with renunciation, I had moved away from the great circle of my brothers and sisters, their friends and young slaves, who used to mock and criticize, whisper or loudly discuss, in the evening, the resolves the assembly reached during the day. I was not forbidden to continue my old indolent life on my free evenings, to sit around under the trees and shrubs in the inner courtyards of the citadel, to give myself to the familiar and well-loved sounds of water rippling through earthenware pipes, to surrender to the hour in which the sky grows yellow and the houses radiate outward the daylight they have absorbed; to let wash over me the never-changing murmur, whispers, and prattle of my brothers and sisters, of the teachers, nurses, and domestic slaves. I forbade it to myself after I became a priestess. After I was convinced that Polyxena had blackened my character to my brothers and sisters (which she did not so much as dream of doing, she told me later, and I could not help but believe her). After I was convinced that my idle brothers and sisters, some of whom liked gossip and family discord, had run me down to their heart's content. I wanted to be privileged above them all, but I could not bear to have them envy me.

All this, the Troy of my childhood, no longer exists except inside my head. I will rebuild it there while I still have time, I will not forget a single stone, a single incidence of light, a single laugh, a single cry. It shall be kept faithfully inside me, however short the time may be. Now I have learned to see what is not, how hard the lesson was.

Helenus. Oh, Helenus, identical in appearance, different in kind. The image of me—if I had been a man. If only I were! I thought in despair when they made you the oracle—not me! not me! "Oh, be glad, Sister. What a thankless job, to be a soothsayer." Well (he said), he would observe Calchas's instructions to the letter. Helenus was no seer. He did not have the gift, he needed the ritual. All the thoughtlessness which may have been intended for us both had gone to him. All the melancholy to me. How I longed to be in his place. What was the priestess compared to the diviner! How greedily I watched him when he donned women's clothing to inspect the animal entrails at the altar stone. How he struggled to choke down his disgust at the smell of blood, the steaming viscera which I was quite used to because from early childhood I had had the chore of disemboweling small animals for the kitchen. If only I were he. If only I could exchange my sex for his. If only I could deny it, conceal it. Yes, really, that is how I felt. Scarcely glancing at the intestines, liver, maw of the young bull, I watched the excited, gaping faces of the people who clustered around the sacrificial victim and the priest, waiting for his words as for food and drink. My brother churned out lame, conventional bulletins about sun and rain, good and bad harvests, the breeding of livestock and children. How differently I would have spoken, I would have laid down the law in quite a different tone; I would have liked to teach them something quite, quite different, those unsuspecting, easily satisfied people—namely . . . Namely? What would I have taught them then? Panthous, who kept an eye on me in those days, asked me the question point-blank. What else would I have talked about besides weather, the fertility of the soil, cattle pests, diseases. Did I want to tear the people out of their familiar round where they felt comfortable and looked for nothing else? To which I arrogantly replied: "Because they don't know anything else. Because this sort of question is all they are allowed."

"All they are allowed by whom? The gods? Circumstances? The king? And who are you to force other questions on them? Leave everything as it is, Cassandra, I'm giving you good advice." When he did not come to me at night for a long spell, I missed him sorely. Not him, "it." And when he was lying on top of me—Aeneas, no one but Aeneas. Of course. The Greek noticed many things because he kept his reserve: So let him see this, too, for all I cared. But nothing in heaven or earth could have forced me to reveal my secret. My envy of Helenus ended as everything ends: when, I do not know. My zeal to impart new questions to mankind subsided, disappeared. I kept my secret. There are secrets that ravage you, others that make you stronger.

This was one of the bad kind. Who knows how far it might have driven me if Aeneas had not really been there one day?

What are the Mycenaean women saying as they crowd around me? "She's smiling," they say. So I am smiling? Do I even know what that is anymore: to smile? The last time I smiled was when Aeneas passed me headed toward Mount Ida with his handful of people, carrying his father, old Anchises, on his back. It did not matter that he failed to recognize me when he looked for me among the crowd of women captives. I saw he was getting away, and smiled.

What does that old, emaciated woman want from me; what is she screaming? She is screaming that in time my laughter will pass. "Yes," I say. "I know that. And soon."

Now a guard intervenes to prevent the native population from holding any contact with slaves. So quick he is. That is something that always amazed me about the Greeks: they do what has to be done, quickly. And thoroughly. How long it would have taken our young palace Trojans, given to irony as they were, to understand the prohibition against associating with slaves. And to obey it! There would have been no question of obeying. Even Eumelos failed when it came to that point. "People like us are trying to save you," he said to me bitterly, "and you all sneak off behind my back and slit your own throats." In his way he was right. He wanted us to be the kind of people you need in a war. He wanted us to become like the enemy in order to defeat him. That did not suit us. We wanted to be like ourselves, inconsistent: that was the word Panthous tagged us with. Shrugged his shoulders, resigned. "It won't work, Cassandra," he said. "That's not the way you wage war against the Greeks." He must have known what he was talking about. After all, he had run away from the consistency of the Greeks, had he not? He did not talk about it. He kept his true concerns to himself. You had to reconstruct his motives from reports, rumors, and observation.

One thing struck me early on: his fear of pain. His hypersensitivity. He never risked physical combat. But it occurs to me that I was noted for my endurance of pain. For my ability to hold my hand over the flame longer than anyone else, without grimacing, without crying. I noticed that Panthous used to walk away when I did that. I attributed it to sympathy for me. It was overstimulated nerves. Much later I realized that a person's attitude to pain reveals more about his future than almost any other sign I know. When did my own haughty attitude to pain break down? When the war started, of course. When I saw the fear of the men. For what was their fear of battle if not the fear of physical pain? The curious tricks they used to deny the fear or run away from the pain, from the battle. Yet the fear of the Greeks seemed to surpass our own by far. "Naturally," said Panthous. "They are fighting on foreign soil. You are fighting at home." So what was he doing among us, this foreigner? You could not ask him.

This much was known: Panthous was a prize that Cousin Lampos brought back on the FIRST SHIP. That is how the palace referred to the enterprise once a second and a third ship had followed the first and it was decided at last to withdraw the common folk's term, "ship to Delphi," from circulation and substitute neutral designations. That is how Anchises, Aeneas's father, explained it to the king's daughter, the priestess, when he taught me the history of Troy: short and to the point. "Just you listen, girl." (Anchises's long head. The high, completely bald skull. The multitude of wrinkles running the breadth of his forehead. The thick eyebrows. The bright crafty gaze. The mobile features. The forceful chin. The irascible mouth, often gaping or twisted with laughter, more often in a grin. The slender, powerful hands with their nails worn down by toil: Aeneas's hands.) "So listen now. It's really very simple. Some-one (your father, for all I know, although I doubt he had the idea himself, I'd bet it was Calchas)—someone, I say, sends a cousin of the royal family, this Lampos, who makes a very serviceable port administrator, but as a king's envoy on a delicate assignment?—sends Lampos with a ship on a top-secret mission to Greece. He's foolish—or let's say imprudent—enough to order the people to cheer as the ship leaves harbor." "Me too, Anchises," I said. "Held on my nurse's arm. Light, cheers, banners, sparkling water, and an enormous ship: my earliest memory." "We've hit on the point already. An enormous ship. Permit me to smile. A modest little ship, I would almost say: a boat. Because the thing is, if we had been in a position to furnish an enormous ship, we would not have sent it to Greece of all places. Because in that case we would not have needed these pushy Greeks, or to have paid our respects to their oracle. We would not have entered into negotiations about our heredi- tary right: access to the Hellespont. Well then, to sum up the result: The Greeks did not agree on terms, Lampos brought rich offerings to Delphi which we could barely afford; Panthous saw him there, became part of his retinue, came back here with him. So when the ship sailed in, there were spoils of a kind, to show the cheering crowd. And our palace scribes, who as you must know are a breed unto themselves, have belatedly re- christened this the FIRST SHIP, bragging about an enterprise that halfway miscarried."

Oi, oi. But Anchises's stringent clearheadedness never lacked for kind of poetry either; I could not resist that. Besides, he himself had been one of the leaders of the SECOND SHIP, and so was undeniably an authority. But altogether a different story was heard in the inner courts, where we quarreled about nothing as heatedly as the FIRST SHIP. Hector, the eldest of my brothers, then a strongly built young man with a rather too soft disposi- tion, categorically denied that Operation One had been success- ful in any way. Cousin Lampos was not sent to the Delphic oracle to haul away a priest, he said. "No? Why was he sent then?" Hector had the story, half-officially, from the priests: Lampos was supposed to ask the Pythia whether the hill upon which Troy stood was still under a curse; that is, whether the city and its wall, which was just then undergoing fundamental repair, were secure! What a monstrous idea! As far as we younger ones were concerned, Troy, the city, and everything its name implied, had grown out of this hill, Ate, and we could not imagine it being anywhere else on earth but here, in view of Mount Ida, before the glittering plain and the sea gulf with its natural harbor. And the wall, both protective and confining, had grown along with the city: in ancient times the gods themselves, Apollo, Poseidon, had helped to build it so that it would be indestructible, impregnable. Those were the things we said, and as I listened avidly, I also heard the rejoinder: What! Suppose Cousin Lampos simply forgot to ask the Pythia about Troy's paramount concerns because of a passion for Panthous, priest of Apollo? So that the wall, made fast without the blessing of the mighty oracle, was by no means impregnable, but on the contrary, vulnerable? With the Scaean Gate as its vulnerable point? And what about Panthous? Had he perhaps followed our rather unprepossessing cousin across the sea voluntarily, not as a captive? And Priam had been weak enough to dedicate the foreigner as the priest of Apollo, which after all could mean nothing else but that we acknowledged the sovereignty of Delphi in matters of religion? Or at least in matters concerning this one god, Apollo?

All this was so incredible. So ridiculous. Such a poor invention that I, a child, could only beg them to spare me any more. Yet the subject nagged at me, made me so keen for every scrap of conversation where it flared up that again and again I felt impelled to force my way into the circle of my elders, to sneak between Hector's already powerful thighs, crouch there leaning against him, and drink in every word. It was not my birth that made me a Trojan, it was the stories told in the inner courts. I stopped being one when I was caged in the basket, as I heard the whisper of the mouths at the peephole. Now that Troy no longer exists, I am one again: a Trojan woman. And nothing more.

To whom can I tell that?

Yes. My familiarity with the inner courts, with every impulse that stirred there and touched me, the perfect pitch with which I could gauge the whispers which ceaselessly filled them—that was the one advantage I had over Panthous the Greek, at least in the beginning. Did I not even ask him once why he was here —that is there, in Troy? "Out of curiosity, my dear," he said in the flippant tone he had acquired. But could anyone leave the oracle at Delphi, the center of the world, from curiosity? "Ah, my little infidel!" he said. "If only you knew what it was like, that center." Often he saddled me with names that did not fit me until later on. When I really got to know Troy, *my* center, I understood what he meant. It was not curiosity that would have driven me away, but horror. But where was there a place left to go, and in what ship?

I really do not know why Panthous preoccupies me so. Is it that some word, linked to his name, is trying to free itself from depths to which I have not descended? Or is it an image? An image from long, long ago that is floating and that perhaps I can capture if I let my attention wander quietly where it will. I look downhill. What looks like a procession of people, their faces uplifted, densely packed in the narrow street below me. Threatening, avid, wild. Get it in focus. Get it in focus. Yes: the still, white center. A boy clad all in white, leading the young white bull by a cord. The untouchable white spot in all the turbulence. And the heated face of my nurse, holding me on her arm. And Panthous. But I do not see that, I know it: Panthous at the head of the procession, little more than a boy himself, very young, they say very handsome. And he will lead the crowd to the Scaean Gate and slaughter the bull, but release the boy. Henceforth the god Apollo, protector of the city, wanted no more boy sacrifices, he said. "Boy sacrifice," that's the term. I never saw another boy sacrifice in Troy, although . . . Priam, my father, needed Panthous in order to abolish this sacrifice. And when the Greeks charged the Scaean Gate in the ninth year of the war and threatened to capture it—the gate where the Greek had kept a boy from being sacrificed—then people said: "Panthous the traitor." My innocent, credulous people. In the end I no longer liked Panthous. I did not like the thing in me which he had been able to seduce.

Who lives will see. It occurs to me that secretly I am tracking the story of my fear. Or more precisely, the story of its unbridling, more precisely still: of its setting free. Yes, it's true, fear too can be set free, and that shows that it belongs with everything and everyone who is oppressed. The king's daughter is not afraid, for fear is weakness and weakness can be amended by iron discipline. The madwoman is afraid, she is mad with fear. The captive is supposed to be afraid. The free woman learns to lay aside her unimportant fears and not to fear the one big important fear because she is no longer too proud to share it with others. —Formulas, granted.

No doubt people are right when they say that the closer you come to death, the closer and brighter are the pictures of childhood and youth. An eternity has passed since I looked at them. How difficult it was after all—almost impossible—to see the SECOND SHIP for what Hecuba exclaimed it really was: a game of fear. What was at stake? Was it so important for them to send men like Anchises, like Calchas the seer on the ship? Anchises, who had grown old by the time he returned. Calchas, who did not come back at all. All right, so there was the matter of the king's sister Hesione. "Hesione," my father Priam said in the assembly, speaking in a lachrymose, pathetic tone, "Hesione, the king's sister, held by the Spartan Telamon, who has taken her by force." The men in the council looked perplexed. "Now, now, 'held,'" mocked Hecuba, "'taken by force.'" After all, Hesione was not being treated like a humble captive in Sparta, was she? If our information was correct, had Telamon not made her his wife? Made her the queen? That wasn't the point, he said. "A king who does not try to win back his sister when she is abducted loses face." "Oh," said Hecuba sarcastically. That was all that was said in public. They quarreled in their megaron, and the worst part was that my father sent me out. His ambivalent feelings transferred themselves to me, condensed into a sensation which seemed to reside in my navel: a vibrating tension which Parthena, my nurse, taught me to call "fear." "You mustn't be so afraid, little daughter. The child has too much imagination."

Banners, waving, cheers, sparkling water, gleaming oars—50 *oars*, the palace scribes entered on their clay tablets; they did not know how to do anything but count—as the SECOND SHIP left port. Those who stayed behind shouted inflammatory slogans to the men who stood on board the ship: "The king's sister or death!" Beside me stood Aeneas, who shouted up to his father: "Hesione or death!" I was horrified and knew that I was not allowed to be horrified. Aeneas was acting in the interests of the royal family, of which I was a member, when he wished death upon his father for the sake of a woman who just happened to be the king's sister. I suppressed my horror and forced myself to admire Aeneas. It was then that my ambivalent feelings began. So did Aeneas's—he told me later. He told me that the longer the action to recapture the strange woman continued, the more indifferent he became to her fate, indeed the more he downright detested her; while at the same time his concern for his father grew and grew. I had no way of knowing that. It was then—yes, it must have been then that those dreams began in which Aeneas appeared to me, in which I felt pleasure when he threatened me. Dreams which tormented me and drove me into a state of indelible guilt, a desperate self-estrangement. Oh yes, no doubt I could supply some particulars about the origin of dependency and fear. But no one is going to ask me.

I wanted to become a priestess. I wanted the gift of prophecy, come what may.

We swiftly varied our mistaken judgments to avoid seeing the sinister reality behind the glorious façade. One example enraged me when I was still capable of feeling enraged: All the Trojans had cheered just as I did when the SECOND SHIP set sail, yet later they insisted that this ship was the beginning of our downfall. How could they have forgotten so quickly what they had learned at the knees of their mothers and nurses just as I did: The chain of events ruinous to our city stretched back to remotest antiquity. Destruction, rebuilding, and destruction again, under the sovereignty of a shifting succession of kings, most of them luckless. So what made people hope, what made us all hope that this particular king, my father Priam specifically, would break the chain of misfortune; that he would be the one to restore the Golden Age? Why are we carried away by the very wishes that are grounded in error? The thing they resented most about me later on was my refusal to give in to their disastrous wishful thinking. This refusal (not the Greeks) cost me my father, mother, brothers and sisters, friends, my people. And won me what? No, I will postpone thinking of my joys until I need to.

When the SECOND SHIP returned at last, without the king's sister of course (suddenly everyone was saying "of course"!), and without Calchas the seer either; when the people gathered in the harbor, disappointed and it seemed to me almost hostile, grumbling because they had learned that the Spartan had laughed at the Trojans' demand; when the dark shadow appeared on my father's brow—I cried in public for the last time. Hecuba, who did not exult to see her dire prediction confirmed, reprimanded me for it, not harshly, but firmly. One did not cry over political events. Tears clouded one's reasoning powers. If our opponent gave in to his feelings—if he laughed!—so much the worse for him. It had been clear to everyone who had all his wits about him that we would not see my father's sister again. Naturally the common people attached high-flown expectations, and suffered inevitable disappointments, at every ship that came and went. Their rulers had to control themselves. I rebelled against my mother's rules. In retrospect I see she took me seriously. My father only looked to me for consolation. I never again cried in public. And less and less often in private.

There was still the question of Calchas the seer. Where was

he? Had he died on the journey? No. Had he been killed? Not that either. So he was held hostage by the Greeks? Let the people believe that if they liked (and in fact they did believe it for a time): no harm in confirming the bad reputation of the Greeks. Different tidings ran through the corridors of the palace. When they were reported to me I clenched my fists and resentfully refused to believe it. Marpessa stuck to her story. It was the truth, she said, they had talked about it in the council. And not only that, in the king and queen's bedchamber, too. What, Calchas had gone over to the Greeks? Our highly respected seer, who was privy to the innermost state secrets, was a deserter? "Yes, that's it exactly." The report had to be false. Furious, I went to Hecuba, unburdened my conscience without thinking about what I was doing, forced my mother to take action. Marpessa vanished from sight. Parthena, my nurse, appeared with tear-stained, reproachful eyes. A ring of silence descended around me. The palace, the place I called home, drew away from me; the inner courtyards I loved stopped speaking to me. I was alone with my justice.

The first cycle.

It was Aeneas—Aeneas, whom I always believed because the gods neglected to give him the ability to lie—who confirmed it all, word for word: Yes, Calchas the seer had stayed with the Greeks by his own wish. Aeneas had this on reliable evidence, from Anchises, his father, who had aged by many years. Calchas the seer was afraid that now that the SECOND SHIP had failed, the Trojans would call him to account for the favorable prophecies he had made before it sailed: so hopelessly banal were the reasons for far-reaching decisions! And the odd thing about it, Anchises had told Aeneas, was that the royal family had forced Calchas to make these favorable predictions. Without benefit of a seer.

I had known from the beginning that Marpessa was telling the truth. "Not only that," I heard myself tell Aeneas, "I myself knew from the start." The voice that said this was a stranger's voice, and of course today I know—I have known for a long time—that it was no accident that this strange voice which had stuck in my throat many times already in the past should speak out of me for the first time in Aeneas's presence. I set it free deliberately so that it would not tear me apart; I had no control over what happened next. "I knew it, I knew it": over and over in this alien, high-pitched, moaning voice from which I had to get away to safety; so that I had to cling to Aeneas, who was shocked but held his ground. Held his ground, oh, Aeneas. Tottering, limbs shaking, I clung to him; each of my fingers followed its own inclinations, gripped and tore at his clothing; my mouth, as it expelled the cry, also produced a foam that settled on my lips and chin; and my legs, which were as much out of my control as all my other limbs, jerked and danced with a disreputable, unseemly delight that I myself did not feel in the least. They were out of control, everything in me was out of control, I was uncontrollable. Four men could scarcely hold me.

Strange to say, a spark of triumph lit my way into the darkness where I tumbled at last: strange to those who do not know what cunning compacts link illness to suppressed manifestations. So this was the seizure; and for a while my life divided itself into the time before the seizure and the time after the seizure—a chronology which soon became invalid like almost all those which followed. For weeks I could not stand up or stir a limb. Wanted to be unable to stand or stir. "Let Marpessa come": that was the first order I was able to give. Above me Hecuba's mouth said: "No." Then I let myself sink back into the darkness. In some way I had control of the rising and sinking of this hard, heavy structure, my consciousness. The undecided part was: Would I—who, I?—rise to the surface again? I kept myself in suspension, a pain-free state. Once when I bobbed up, it was Marpessa's face that hung over me, her hand that bathed my temples with diluted wine. That was painful, for in this case I had to stay. Marpessa had grown thin and pale and silent like me. I did not lose consciousness completely again. I consented to be helped. I got well, as people call it. I longed for the office of the priesthood the way a shipwrecked sailor longs for land. I did not want the world the way it was, but I wanted to serve devotedly the gods who ruled it. My wish held a contradiction. I gave myself some time before I noticed it; I have always granted myself these times of partial blindness. To become seeing all of a sudden—that would have destroyed me.

For example, it was not until that dark, stormy night on the sea voyage here, when everything was coming to an end, that I was able to ask Marpessa what they did to her when they took her away. "Nothing special," she said. "They sent me to the stables." "To the stables!" "Yes." As a horsemaid among the stablehands drawn from a dozen tribes. Everyone knew what things were like in the stables. I could imagine why Marpessa never let a man near her again. When I entrusted her with my twins, that was a kind of atonement which could neither increase her devotion to me nor soften her implacability. She always let me feel that there was no way I could make amends to her. The fact that she understood me made things worse. The palace scribe and the young slave girl, Hecuba's servant, from whom Marpessa had learned the truth about Calchas the seer, had left with the next prisoner transport which King Priam sent to the King of the Hittites. After that no one spoke the name of Calchas, either in praise or in blame.

How often what I fervently desired has fallen to me when I no longer desired it. Marpessa has freely expressed her affection for me ever since I was raped right before her eyes by Ajax, whom the Greeks call Ajax the Lesser. If I am not mistaken I heard her cry: "Take me!" But she understands perfectly well that I no longer court anyone's love or friendship. No.

One should not strive to unite the incompatible. Hecuba warned me about that early on; to no avail, of course. "Your father," she said, "wants it all, and all at the same time. He wants the Greeks to pay for permission to bring their goods through our Hellespont: right. He thinks that in return they should respect King Priam: wrong. Why should it hurt him that they laugh at him when they think they are superior? Let them laugh, as long as they pay. And you, Cassandra," Hecuba said to me, "make sure that you do not burrow too deep into your father's soul."

I am very tired. I have not had a solid sleep for weeks. Incredible, but I could fall asleep now. After all, I can no longer afford to postpone anything, not even sleep. It's not good to be overtired when you die. People say that the dead sleep, but it isn't true. Their eyes stand open. The wide-open eyes of my dead brothers, which I closed, beginning with Troilus. The eyes of Penthesilea staring at Achilles, Achilles the brute, they must have driven him crazy. My father's open, dead eyes. I did not see the eyes of my sister Polyxena in death. When they dragged her away to Achilles' grave, she had the look that only dead people have. Is it a consolation that Aeneas's eyes will not find death but sleep for many nights to come? Not a consolation. A knowledge. The only words I have left are uncolored by hope or dread.

When the queen walked out the gate a little while ago, I let myself feel a last tiny hope that I could get her to spare the children's lives. All I had to do was to look into her eyes. She was doing what she had to do. She did not make things as they are, she is adapting to things as they are. Either she gets rid of her husband, this empty-headed ninny, and makes a good job of it, or she gives up herself: her life, her sovereignty, her lover—who, if I interpret the figure in the background correctly, also looks to be a self-centered ninny, but young, handsome, smooth-fleshed. She indicated to me with a shrug of her shoulders that what was happening had nothing to do with me personally. In different times nothing would have prevented us from calling each other sister. That is what I read in my adversary's face, where Agamemnon, the imbecile, was meant to see love and devotion and the joy of reunion; and in fact he did see them. Whereupon he stumbled up the red carpet like an ox to the slaughterhouse. Both of us had this same thought, and the same smile appeared in the corners of Clytemnestra's mouth as in mine. Not cruel. Painful. Pain that fate did not put us on the same side. I credit her with knowing that she, too, will be stricken with the blindness that comes with power. She, too, will fail to see the signs. Her house, too, will fall.

It took me a long time to understand that. Not everyone could see what I saw. Not everyone perceived the naked, meaningless shape of events. I thought they were making fun of me; but they believed what they were saying. There must be a meaning in that. What if we were ants. The entire race plunges blindly into the ditch, drowns, forms the bridge for the few survivors who are the germ of the new race. Like ants we walk into every fire. Every water. Every river of blood. Simply in order not to have to see. To see what, then? Ourselves.

As if I had unchained a boat in calm water, it drifts incessantly in the current, first forward, then back. When I was a child. When I was a child I had a brother named Aisakos whom I loved more than anything, and he loved me. The only thing he loved more than me was his beautiful young wife, Asterope, and when she died in childbirth, he could no longer live either and he jumped off the cliffs into the sea; but his guards rescued him time after time. Until once he really did sink under the waves and was not found until a black diving bird with a red throat appeared at the place where he had dived into the sea. Calchas, the interpreter of omens, recognized the transformed shape of Aisakos, and the bird was immediately taken under public protection. I alone—how could I forget it; that was the first time!—I alone spent days and nights writhing in my bed, convulsed with weeping. Even if I could have believed (but I did not) that my brother Aisakos was a bird; that the goddess Artemis, who was credited with some peculiar behavior, had transformed him, thus granting his most heartfelt desire—I did not want a bird in place of my brother. I wanted him, Aisakos, the sturdy, warm-skinned man with the curly brown hair who used to treat me differently from all my brothers in the palace. Who used to carry me on his shoulders, not just through all the courtyards, but also through the streets of the city that had been built around the citadel; which now is destroyed like the citadel; and where all the people used to greet him who now are dead or captive. Who used to call me "my poor little sister" and to take me out into open country where the sea breeze swept through the olive trees, making the leaves glint silver so that it hurt me to look at them. Who finally took me along to the village on the slopes of Mount Ida where he had his home: for although his father was Priam, his mother was Arisbe. Back then she seemed to me ancient and sinister, too. I saw her white eyes flash out of the darkness of a small room hung with herbs while Asterope, Aisakos's slender young wife, greeted her husband with a smile that cut into my flesh. I wanted him back, skin, hair, and all, I screamed: "Him, him, him, him." Aisakos. Moreover, I never wanted to have a child; but I did not say that, I only thought it.

Yes, it was then that I heard them say for the first time: "She is out of her mind." Hecuba, my mother, pressed my twitching, quaking shoulders against the wall with arms that had a man's strength. Forever the twitching of my limbs, forever the cold hard wall against them, life against death, my mother's strength against my weakness; forever a slave woman holding my head and forever the bitter brown juice which Parthena, my nurse, poured down my throat; forever the heavy sleep and the dreams. The child of Asterope and Aisakos who had died with his mother at birth was growing inside me. When it was fully developed I did not want to bring it into the world, so I spit it out, and it was a toad. It disgusted me. Merops, the ancient interpreter of dreams, listened to me attentively. Then he recommended to Hecuba that she remove from her daughter's proximity all men who resembled Aisakos. What could he be thinking of, I was told Hecuba asked the old man in fury. He shrugged his shoulders and went away. Priam sat down by my bed and discussed affairs of state with me in all seriousness. It was a shame, he said, a crying shame, that I could not take his place and sit in the high-backed chair at the council next morning dressed in his clothes. I loved my father even more than usual when he worried about me. Everyone in the palace knew that he took problems personally; I considered that a strength; everyone else considered it a weakness. Then it became a weakness.

The sequence of images moves with frantic speed through my tired head; words cannot keep up with them. Strange, the similarity of the tracks in my memory, no matter how varied the recollections that lead to them. These figures which light up over and over like signal fires. Priam, Aisakos, Aeneas, Paris. Yes. Paris. Paris and Operation THIRD SHIP, each of whose presuppositions and consequences is clear to me, whereas at the time I was all but lost in impenetrable chaos. The THIRD SHIP. They were fitting out the ship at the very time I was preparing for my dedication as a priestess. Perhaps this explains why I identified with the ship, why I secretly connected my fate with the ship's fate. What would I have given to be able to sail with it. Not just because I knew that this time Aeneas would accompany his father Anchises on the journey; not just because the goal of the expedition blurred over and over whenever one tried to get a clear look at it, and so left ample scope for miraculous expectations—no: I was stirred up, ready for anything because of the gradual, toilsome disclosure of the most delicate points of our family history; because of the unexpected appearance of a long-lost, unknown brother. I cared—once again I cared far too much—for the strange young man who turned up all of a sudden to take part in the festival games played in memory of a nameless brother who died as a child. I did not have to know who he was in order to tremble at the sight of him; his beauty burned me unbearably; I closed my eyes so as not to be exposed to it any longer. I wanted him to win all the competitions! He did win them all: the boxing match, the first footrace, then the

second, which my envious brothers had forced more than asked
him to run. I placed the wreath on his head, I would not let
them refuse me that right. My whole being went out to him.
He did not notice. His face seemed veiled as if only his body
were present and obedient to his wishes, not his mind. He was a
stranger to himself. Now that I think of it, that did not change,
no, that did not change. But was this self-estrangement of a
prince the key to a great war? I fear that is how people will
explain it. They need personal reasons of that kind.

I was in the middle of the arena, and so I only heard reports
of what was going on outside meanwhile: The royal guards were
sealing off all the exits—for the first time we heard that a young
officer named Eumelos had distinguished himself by his caution
and consistency during this action—and strict controls were
being used. Inside, I saw from close up how Hector and
Deiphobus, my two eldest brothers, charged the stranger with
drawn swords; he looked more amazed than frightened. Did he
really not understand that the order of the victors in the games
was pre-established; that he had violated a law? He did not
understand.

Then a piercing voice rose above the threatening hum that
swelled through the arena: "Priam! This man is your son." And
in the same moment—who knows why—I knew that it was the
truth. Only then came the gesture from my father that im-
mobilized my brothers' swords. My rigid mother nodded after
the old shepherd had showed her some swaddling clothes. And
the stranger's modest reply when the king asked him his name:
"Paris." Suppressed laughter from my sisters and brothers: Our
new brother was called "bag," "pouch." Yes, the old shepherd
said, named after the bag in which he had carried the wee infant
son of the king and queen around in the mountains. He produced the bag; it was as old as he, if not older. Then, in one of
those abrupt reversals which are typical (*were* typical) of public
events in Troy, the triumphal procession to the palace with
Paris at the center. Hold on. Didn't this procession resemble

the other one, centered on the white-clad boy sacrifice? Once again I was mute amid the excitedly chattering crowd of my sisters; galled and sore, torn open.

I was desperate to find out all about it this time, because it had to do with Paris. I believe I actually said so. How embarrassing. Well. Later I no longer believed that events owed it to me to reveal themselves. In those early years I used to chase after them. Tacitly assuming that all doors and all mouths would spring open to King Priam's daughter. But the place I came to had no doors, only animal hides stretched across the entrances of cavelike dwellings. Moreover, my training in good manners prevented me from subjecting to a pressing interrogation the three midwives, ancient and shaggy crones, who had pulled Paris (and indeed almost all of Hecuba's children) from his mother's womb. I would have turned around and gone home if it had not been for Marpessa, who had led me there; I would have been ashamed to have her see me. This was the first time I had a close view of the cave dwellings along the steep bank of our river, the Scamander; of the motley folk encamped at the entrances, dotting the bank, washing their clothes in the river; heaven knows what they lived on. I walked through their midst as if through an aisle of silence that did not feel threatening, only alien; whereas Marpessa hurled greetings in every direction, and from every side cries greeted her. Among them the obscene phrases of men, which she would have answered sharply in the citadel; but here she gave a laughing retort. Can the king's daughter envy a slave girl? Well might I ask such questions. I still do. I saw that the most beautiful thing about Marpessa was the way she walked. She moved her legs with a vigorous motion from the hip, effortlessly, her back erect. Her dark hair worn up in two braids. She also knew the girl who looked after the three ancient mothers. Oenone, a young creature of conspicuous charm even for this area, famed for the beauty of its women. "By the Scamander": That was a byword among the young men of the palace when the time came to have their first girl. I had picked it up from my brothers.

Proudly I told the three midwives my real name; Marpessa had advised me against it. What, were these three old women trying to make a fool of me? Oh, the three old sluts. "A son of Priam?" Ha, they had brought dozens of them into the world, they said. "Nineteen," I corrected them: in those days I still set store by family honor. The old crones disputed the number, even debated among themselves. "But they don't know how to count," Oenone protested, laughing. Oenone, Oenone, hadn't I heard that name before? Who was it that said it? A man's voice. Paris. Hadn't I already run into her in the palace? Whenever I left the boundaries of the citadel I got into unfathomable, often mortifying situations like this. More harshly than necessary I asked the mothers their opinion: Why, of the dozens of Priam's sons, was one in particular not supposed to have been reared? Not reared? The three old hypocrites seemed not even to know what the word meant. Oh no, certainly not. Not in their time. Not that they knew of. Until I heard one of them murmur almost dreamily: "Yes, if only Aisakos were alive!" "Aisakos?" I pursued it quick as a flash. Silence multiplied by three. Oenone too was silent. Marpessa was silent. She was— what am I thinking, she *is!*—the most silent person in my life.

It was the same at the palace. A palace of silence. Hecuba, stifling her rage, was silent. Parthena the nurse, showing her fear openly, was silent. I learned a lot by observing the various types of silence. Only much later did I learn silence myself; what a useful weapon. I turned and twisted the only word I knew: Aisakos, until suddenly one night a second name dropped out of it: Arisbe. Hadn't she been Aisakos's mother? Was she still alive?

For the first time I had experience of a lesson that I often put to the test later on: Forgotten people know about each other. Not quite by chance I met the clever Briseis—daughter of the renegade seer Calchas, who had turned into one of the forgotten overnight—outside the gates of Troy at the great autumn market, which was a flourishing center of east-west trade; and stupidly asked her whether she still knew who I was.

Who did not know who I was? Briseis had set out her particularly glowing textile goods. She, who even in the past had been highly independent and impulsive, left her customers standing while she described to me, readily and impersonally, where I might find Arisbe: at the same market, in the potters' row. I went there, questioned no one, looked at people's faces: Arisbe looked like an older Aisakos. Scarcely had I approached her than she murmured that I should visit her in her hut at such-and-such a spot at the foot of Mount Ida. So she had been told that I was coming. So my every step was being observed. I did not even notice Priam's guards, who were following me; I was a stupid young thing. The first time they were pointed out to me —by Panthous the Greek, of course—I got on my high horse, ran to my father: encountered the king, the mask. Men keeping watch on me? he asked. Wherever did I get such an idea? The young lads were there to protect me. He, not I, must be allowed to decide whether I needed them. Those who had nothing to hide had no reason to fear the eye of the king.

As far as I know I was alone when I went to visit Arisbe.

Once again this by-world, counterworld in the environs of the city which, unlike the stone world of palace and town, grew rankly and proliferated like a plant, lush, carefree, as if it did not need the palace, as if it lived with its back turned to the palace, and to me, too. People knew who I was, greeted me imperturbably, but I returned their greeting a shade too quickly. It humiliated me to go there seeking information the palace denied me. "Denied": I thought of it that way for a long time until I understood that they could not deny what they did not have. They did not even understand the questions to which I was seeking an answer, questions which increasingly were destroying my intimate relations with the palace, with my family. I realized this too late. The alien being who wanted to know had already eaten its way too deep inside me; I could no longer get rid of it.

Arisbe's hut: how wretched, how small. Was this where big strong Aisakos had lived? The aromatic fragrances, the clusters of herbs along ceiling and walls, a steaming brew on the open fire in the center of the room. The flames flickered and smoked; apart from that there was darkness. Arisbe was neither friendly nor unfriendly; but I was accustomed to friendliness and still needed it. Unhesitatingly she gave me the information I asked for. Yes: It was Aisakos my half-brother, the divinely blessed seer, who had prophesied, before the birth of the boy they called Paris: A curse lies on this child. Aisakos! That same innocuous Aisakos who used to carry me around on his shoulders? Arisbe, unperturbed, went on. But of course the decisive turn had been Hecuba's dream. By Arisbe's account, shortly before Paris was born Hecuba had dreamed that she was giving birth to a stick of firewood from which countless burning serpents crept forth. Calchas the seer interpreted this to mean: The child whom Hecuba was to bear would set fire to all Troy.

Outrageous tidings. What kind of place was I living in, then?

Arisbe, the massive woman at the fire who stirred the stinking pot, continued in her trumpet-like voice: Of course Calchas's interpretation did not go unchallenged. She herself was also consulted about this dream of the pregnant queen. "By whom?" I interjected hastily, and she replied in passing: "By Hecuba." After thorough deliberation, she said, she had succeeded in giving the dream a different twist. "Namely?" I asked abruptly. I felt as if I myself were dreaming. Hecuba, my mother, had had frightening dreams, had bypassed the official oracle to consult the former concubine of her husband, the king? Were they all crazy? Or changelings, as I had so often feared when I was a child? "Namely," said Arisbe, "that this child could be intended to restore her rights to the snake goddess as guardian of the hearth fire in every home." My scalp crawled: I must be listening to something dangerous. Arisbe smiled, then her resemblance to Aisakos became painful. She did not know, she said, whether her interpretation had pleased King Priam. With this enigmatic remark she sent me away. How much had to come to pass before this hut became my true home.

Now I had to apply to my father, after all. Things had reached such a pass that I had to have myself announced first like everyone else. One of the young men who had been following me around for weeks now stood silent and in plain view outside Priam's door. What was his name? Eumelos? "Yes," said Priam. "A capable man." He put on a busy air. For the first time it occurred to me that the intimacy between us was based, as is so often the case between men and women, on the fact that I knew him and he did not know me. He knew his ideal of me; that was supposed to hold still. I had always liked to see him working at full swing; but not insecure, and hiding his insecurity behind bustling activity. Challengingly I mentioned Arisbe's name. Priam snapped: Was his daughter plotting against him? There had already been one female intrigue in the palace, back in the days before Paris was born. One faction had implored him to get rid of the dangerous child. The other, Hecuba among them of course, wanted to save it on the grounds that this particular son was destined for higher things. "Higher things! That meant he was destined to pretend to his father's throne, what else?"

This sentence tore a veil from my eyes. At last I understood the taciturn or disconcerted looks I had picked up as a child, the ring of rejection—indeed of abhorrence—surrounding my father, which I deliberately broke through: his favorite daughter! The estrangement from my mother, the hardening of Hecuba. And so? Paris was alive. "Yes," said Priam. "The shepherd could not bear to kill him. I'll bet he was bribed by the women. No matter. Better that Troy should fall than that my miraculous son should die."

I was puzzled. Why was he ruffling up his feathers? And why should Troy fall if Paris lived? And was the king really not able to tell the difference between the tongue of an infant and the dog's tongue which the shepherd brought him as evidence that the child was dead? A flustered messenger announced the arrival of Menelaus, King of Sparta. So it was his ship that we had seen approaching since dawn. Hecuba entered on state business, seemed not to see me. "Menelaus. Do you know about it? Maybe it's not such a bad thing."

I left. While the palace was doing its best to welcome the guest who, strange to say, had come to offer sacrifice at two of our hero graves in order to halt the plague in Sparta; while the temples of all the gods were getting ready for state ceremonies, I was nursing my cross-grained satisfaction. With satisfaction I felt the coldness spreading through me. I did not yet know that not to feel is never a step forward, scarcely a relief. How long it was before feelings once again flooded the desolate rooms of my soul. My rebirth restored the present to me, what people call life, but not only that. It also opened up the past to me, a past that was new, undistorted by hurt feelings, likes and dislikes, and all the luxury emotions that belonged to Priam's daughter. I sat swollen with triumph at the banquet in the place where it behooved me to sit in the ranks of my brothers and sisters. Anyone who had been deceived as I had owed them nothing more. I had had a right to know, I more than anyone. In future I had to know more than they did in order to punish them. Become a priestess in order to gain power? Ye gods. You had to drive me to this extremity to wring this simple sentence from me. What a hard time sentences have had till the end, when they tackle me. How much faster and more easily the sentences get through when they are aimed at others. Arisbe told me so point-blank one time. "When was that, Marpessa?"

"In the middle of the war," she says. We women had been meeting for a long time already, outside the caves on the slopes of Mount Ida in the evening. The ancient midwives were still alive, too, and used to cackle with their toothless mouths; and even you smiled back then, Marpessa, at my expense. I was the only one who did not laugh. My old sense of injury swelled inside me. Then Arisbe said that instead of making faces I ought to be delighted that there were people who told me their opinion bluntly. What other daughter from a powerful family was so lucky? "Quite true," I said, "so let it pass." I believe I loved Arisbe's sense of humor more than anything. It was an unforgettable sight when her powerful body crouched on the rotting tree trunk in front of the cave while she beat time for us with her stick. Who would believe us, Marpessa, if we told them that in the middle of the war we used to meet regularly outside the fortress on paths known to no one but us initiates? That we, far better informed than any other group in Troy, used to discuss the situation, confer about measures (and carry them out, too); but also to cook, eat, drink, laugh together, sing, play games, learn? Always months came when the Greeks, entrenched behind their seafront palisades, did not attack. It even proved possible to hold the Great Market outside the gates of Troy, under the noses of the Greek fleet. And not seldom one of their princes—Menelaus, Agamemnon, Odysseus, or one of the two Ajaxes—would turn up among the stalls and booths, grab at our wares, which often were unfamiliar to him, and buy fabrics, leather goods, utensils, and spices for himself or his wife. When Clytemnestra appeared a little while ago, I recognized her at once by her dress. A slave was carrying the fabric for this dress in the wake of the unhappy Agamemnon the first time I saw him at our market. Something about his manner displeased me at once. He pushed his way imperiously to the front of Arisbe's stall, slid the ceramics back and forth choosily, and broke one of the most beautiful vases, which he paid for in haste at a word from Arisbe; then fled with his retinue amid the laughter of the onlookers. He had seen that I had seen him.

"He will take revenge, that one," I said to Arisbe; and it troubled me deeply that the great and famous commander in chief of the Greek fleet was a weakling who lacked self-esteem. How much better it is to have a strong enemy. Sometimes a minor trait throws light on great events. Suddenly it was clear to me that the report by a Greek deserter (which Priam had ordered not to be circulated further lest our people regard the enemy as a monster) might and must be true: This same

Agamemnon had caused his own daughter, a young girl named Iphigenia, to be sacrificed on the altar of the goddess Artemis before his fleet crossed over. How often I was compelled to think of Iphigenia all through the war years. The only conversation I consented to have with this man was about his daughter. It was on board the ship, the day after the storm. I was standing at the stern, he was beside me. Deep blue sky and the line of white foam which the ship left in the smooth blue-green sea. I asked Agamemnon point-blank about Iphigenia. He wept, but not the way people weep from grief: from fear and weakness. He had to do it, he said. "Had to do what?" I asked coldly. I wanted him to say it. He squirmed. He had to sacrifice her, he said. That was not what I wanted to hear: but of course murderers and butchers do not know words like "murder" and "butcher." How far I had removed myself from them even in my speech. "Your Calchas" (Agamemnon said accusingly) "absolutely demanded this sacrifice from me if we were to have favorable winds." "And you believed him," I said. "Maybe I didn't," he whined. "No, I didn't. It was the others, the princes. They were all envious of me, the commander in chief. They were all spiteful. What can a leader do against a host of superstitious men?" "Leave me in peace," I said. The vengeance of Clytemnestra rose up huge before me.

Long ago, after my first encounter with this man of ill omen, I told Arisbe: "No priest could have gotten Priam to make such a sacrifice." Arisbe stared at me wide-eyed; then I thought of Paris. Was it the same thing? Was it really the same thing: to have an infant child killed secretly, or to butcher a grown girl in public? And did I fail to see that it was the same thing because not I the daughter was affected but Paris the son? "You're slow on the uptake, my dear," said Arisbe.

I was slow on the uptake. My privileges intruded between me and the most necessary insights; so did my attachment to my own family, which did not depend on the privileges I enjoyed. I was almost shocked to find I felt embarrassed by the

haughty, affected behavior of the royal family when we walked
in solemn procession, in company with our guest Menelaus, to
bring Pallas Athena her new robe. Beside me walked Panthous;
I saw him smile mockingly. "Are you laughing at the king?" I
asked him sharply. Then for the first time I saw something like
fear in his eyes. And I saw that he had a very fragile body
topped by a somewhat overlarge head. I understood why he
used to call me "little Cassandra." At that very moment he
stopped doing so. Just as he stopped visiting me at night. For
a long time no one visited me at night. I suffered of course,
hated myself for the dreams in which I found a perverse relief,
until all this extravagant emotion revealed itself for what it was:
nonsense, and dissolved away.

Easy to think like that, but what else shall I do now that
it's all behind me? The transition from the world of the palace
to the world of the mountains and woods was also the transition from tragedy to burlesque, whose essence is that you do not
treat yourself as tragic. Important, yes, and why not? But you
do not treat yourself as tragic the way the upper echelons in the
palace do. The way they must. How else could they persuade
themselves that they have a right to their selfishness? How
else could they heighten their enjoyment further than by letting it unfold against a background of tragedy? I certainly con-
tributed my bit; all the more credibly because I did it my own
way. Madness invading the banquet—what could be more
grisly, and hence more stimulating to the appetite? I am not
ashamed. Not anymore. But neither have I been able to forget
it. I was sitting at the royal banquet on the eve of Menelaus's
departure, which was also the eve of departure for the THIRD
SHIP. On my right was Hector, whom my brothers and sisters
and I dubbed "the Dim Cloud" among ourselves; on my left,
stubbornly silent, Polyxena. Across from me sat my charming
young brother Troilus with clever Briseis, daughter of the renegade Calchas: the couple had placed themselves under my protection—mine of all people's—which flattered my vanity. At the

head of the table were Priam, Hecuba, and Menelaus our guest: henceforth no one was supposed to call him our "guest-friend." What? Who had forbidden that! "Eumelos," I heard. Eumelos? Who is Eumelos? Oh yes, that man in the council who was now the head of the palace guard. Since when did an officer decide the use of words? Ever since those who styled themselves the "king's party" began to regard the Spartan Menelaus not as our guest-friend but as a spy or a provocateur. As our future enemy. Ever since they had surrounded him with a "security net." A new word. In exchange for it we gave away the old word "guest-friend." What do words matter? All of a sudden those of us who persisted in saying "guest-friend"—including me—found themselves under suspicion. But the palace guard was a small band of men in dress uniform who surrounded the king only on high feast days. This would change, and change radically, Eumelos promised. Who? Eumelos. Those who did not yet know the name were eyed askance. Eumelos, son of a lowly scribe and a slave woman from Crete. Whom everyone—everyone within radius of the palace—was suddenly calling "capable." A capable man in the right post. But the capable man had created this post for himself. And so what? Wasn't it always the way! Eumelos's remarks circulated among the civil servants. Tasteless remarks; I exchanged sarcastic comments about them with my brother Troilus and his Briseis. Now I met young men on the streets of Troy wearing the insignia of the palace guard, who behaved differently than our young men were accustomed to behave. Presumptuous. My laughter died away. "I am foolish enough to think that some men are following me," I said to Panthous. "They are foolish enough to follow you," said Panthous. "At least when you come to see me." Panthous the Greek was placed under surveillance, suspected of conspiring with Menelaus the Greek. Anyone who came near him fell into the net. Including me. It seemed incredible: the sky grew dark. Ominous, the empty space that had formed around me.

At the banquet in the evening you could tell the different groups apart just by looking: that was something new. Troy had changed while I was not looking. Hecuba, my mother, was not on Eumelos's side. I saw how her face grew stony whenever he approached her. Aeneas's dearly loved father, Anchises, seemed to be the leader of the opposition party. He spoke amiably and candidly with the exasperated Menelaus. Priam seemed to want to please everyone. But Paris, my beloved brother Paris, already belonged to Eumelos. The slender handsome youth, devoted to the bulky man with a horse face.

Inevitably I have given Paris a lot of thought. Now that I come to think of it, he always hankered for attention. Had to push to get ahead. How his face had changed; it was strained now, a tightening around the nose gave it a strange distorted look. His blond locks among the dark heads of Hecuba's other sons and daughters. Eumelos silenced the whispers about Paris's uncertain parentage by proclaiming that Paris was indeed of royal blood, for he was the son of our revered Queen Hecuba and a god: Apollo. We were all embarrassed by the affected way Paris moved his head whenever anyone alluded to his divine parentage; for in the palace it went without saying that a claim like the divine descent of a human being was intended metaphorically. After all, who did not know that the children born after the ceremonial deflowering of the women in the temple were all divinely descended? Moreover, the palace guard adopted a threatening posture if anyone—be it Hector himself, the heir to the throne—made fun of Paris by continuing to use his nickname: "Pouch, Pouch." But ridicule was our favorite party game. So did this mean that we were not allowed to make fun of the plan to hang the dilapidated shepherd's pouch in which the shepherd had carried Paris inside the temple of Apollo along with the god's bow and lyre? No. The priestess Herophile, that thin-lipped, leather-cheeked woman who could not stand me, put a stop to this blasphemy. But Eumelos's troop did manage to arrange for a stuffed she-bear to be set up outside the south gate, through which Paris had reentered Troy, in token that a she-bear had suckled the royal child Paris when his parents exposed him.

And then there was the way my poor brother needed so many girls. Obviously, all my brothers took the girls they found attractive. In happy times the palace used to run a benevolent commentary on the love affairs of the royal sons; and the girls, generally from the lower classes and slaves to boot, felt neither insulted nor particularly elevated by my brothers' desire for them. Hector, for one, exercised restraint, his huge sluggish body preferred to rest; that is why we all looked on with admiration at the way he trained for the war then, completely against his inclination. And it made no difference to Andromache one way or the other. How he could run—ye gods!—when Achilles the brute chased him around the stronghold.

Not one of us—no seeress, no oracle—even dimly suspected what was in store that evening. The focus of attention was not Eumelos, not Paris, not even our guest Menelaus. The eyes of the palace were trained on Briseis and Troilus, a pair of lovers if ever there was one. No one who looked their way could help smiling. Briseis was Troilus's first love, and no one could doubt him when he said she would also be his last. Briseis, not much older but more mature, seemed scarcely able to credit her good fortune; she had not been in high spirits since her father had left us. On the other hand, Oenone, the supple beauty whose most striking feature was her neck—a swan's neck crowned by a beautifully shaped head—Oenone, whom Paris had brought with him out of the mountains and who was idolized by the people in the kitchen, seemed depressed. She was serving at table, she had been assigned to the royal couple and their guest; I saw that she had to force herself to smile. In the corridor I caught her drinking a goblet of wine in one gulp. I was already beginning to quake inside, I was still suppressing it. I did not deign to look at any of the figures who were loitering in our vicinity but asked Oenone what was wrong. Wine and worry had flushed away her awe of me. Paris was sick, she said, pale-lipped, and none of her remedies could help. Oenone, who, the servants believed, had been a water nymph in her previous life, was versed in all matters of plants and their effects on the human organism; almost everyone in the palace went to her when they were sick. Paris's sickness was unknown to her and made her afraid. He loved her; she had tokens which left her in no doubt of that. But when he was lying in her arms he used to cry out another woman's name: "Helen, Helen." He said Aphrodite had promised her to him. But had anyone heard of Aphrodite, our dear goddess of love, driving a woman to a man who does not love her, who does not even know her? Who wants to possess her only because it is claimed that she is the most beautiful woman in the world? Because by possessing her he would become supreme among men?

Behind the trembling voice of Oenone I could hear plainly the hoarse, piercing voice of Eumelos, and the quaking inside me intensified. Like everyone's, my body gave me signs; but unlike others, I was not able to ignore them. Fearing disaster I reentered the banquet hall, where the one group had grown stiller and stiller while the other—those attached to Eumelos— had waxed louder and more impudent. Paris, who had drunk too much already, made Oenone give him another cup of wine, which he downed in a gulp. Then in a loud voice he addressed Menelaus the Greek, who sat next to him, on the subject of his beautiful wife, Helen. Menelaus—no longer young, balding, inclined to stoutness, and not looking for a fight—answered his host's son politely until his questions grew so bold that Hecuba, unwontedly angry, ordered her ill-mannered son to keep silent. The hall grew still as death. Only Paris leaped to his feet, shouted: What? He was to keep silent? Again? Still? Demean himself? Make himself invisible if possible? "Oh no. Those days are past. I, Paris, did not come back in order to keep silent. It is I, Paris, who will fetch the king's sister back from the enemy. But if they refuse to give her to me, I'll find another woman, more beautiful than she. Younger. Nobler. Richer. That's what I have been promised, if you all want to know!"

Never before had such silence reigned in the palace of Troy. Each person present felt that a mark was being overstepped here which had not been violated until now. No member of our family had ever dared to speak in such a way. But I, I alone saw. Or did I really "see"? What was it, then? I felt. Experienced—yes, that's the word. For it was, it is, an experience when I "see," when I "saw." Saw that the outcome of this hour was our destruction. Time stood still, I would not wish that on anyone. And the cold of the grave. The ultimate estrangement from myself and from everyone. That is how it seemed. Until finally the dreadful torment took the form of a voice; forced its way out of me, through me, dismembering me as it went; and set itself free. A whistling little voice, whistling at the end of its rope, that makes my blood run cold and my hair stand on end. Which as it swells, grows louder and more hideous, sets all my members to wriggling and rattling and hurling about. But the voice does not care. It floats above me, free, and shrieks, shrieks, shrieks. "Woe," it shrieked. "Woe, woe. Do not let the ship depart!"

Then the curtain fell before my thoughts. The abyss opened. Darkness. I fell headlong. They say I made horrifying gurgling noises, that I foamed at the mouth. At a signal from my mother the guards—Eumelos's men!—gripped me under the shoulders and dragged me out of the hall, where (they tell me) it was so quiet that people could hear my feet scraping on the floor. The temple physicians crowded around me; Oenone was not admitted. I was locked in my room, so they say. At the banquet the stricken company were told that I needed rest. I was bound to recover, the incident was trifling. Lightning swift the rumor spread among my brothers and sisters that I was mad.

It was reported to me that early the next morning the people cheered the departure of Menelaus and, at the same time, the sailing of the THIRD SHIP; and that they crowded around to receive their portion of sacrificial meat and bread. That evening the city was noisy. Not a sound penetrated the inner courtyard onto which my window looked out; all the entryways were barred. The sky I stared at from my window was impenetrably black both day and night. I did not want to eat. Parthena, my nurse, gave me little swallows of asses' milk. I did not want to feed this body. I wanted this criminal body, where the voice of death had its seat, to starve, to wither away. Lunacy: an end to the torture of pretense. Oh, I enjoyed it dreadfully, I wrapped it around me like a heavy cloak, I let it penetrate me layer by layer. It was meat and drink to me. Dark milk, bitter water, sour bread. I had gone back to being myself. But my self did not exist.

To be forced to give birth to what will destroy you: the terror beyond terror. I could not stop producing madness, a pulsating gullet that spit me out, then sucked me in, spit me out, then sucked me in. I had never worked harder than when I could not even move my little finger. I was out of breath, gasped for air, panted. My heart raced and pounded like the hearts of fighters after a match. And there *was* a fight going on inside me, I saw that all right. Two adversaries had chosen the dead landscape of my soul as their battlefield and were engaged in a life-and-death struggle. Only madness stood between me and the intolerable pain which these two would otherwise have inflicted on me, I thought. So I clung to the madness as it clung to me. In my heart of hearts, where the madness did not penetrate, something still knew about the moves and countermoves I allowed myself "higher up": there is a comic element in all madness. Those who learn to recognize and to use it have won.

Hecuba came, severe. Priam, anxious. My sisters, timid. Parthena, my nurse, sympathetic. Marpessa, reserved. No one was any use. Not to mention the solemn helplessness of Panthous. I let myself sink deeper, experimentally, in tiny thrusts. The tie that bound me to these people was very, very thin; it could tear. A hideous itch. I had to take a chance and give the monstrous apparitions an even wider berth, withdraw my senses even farther. It is not fun, I do not mean to imply that. You pay for journeys to the underworld, which is full of shapes no one is prepared to meet. I howled. Wallowed in my own filth. Scratched up my face, would not let anyone near me. I had the strength of three men—inconceivable what counterforce had subdued it until now. I climbed the cold walls of my room, from which everything had been removed but a pile of twigs. I ate with my fingers like an animal. My hair stood out matted and filthy around my head. No one, including me, knew how it would end. Oh, I was obstinate.

One day a figure entered; I bellowed at it, too. It crept into a corner and stayed there until my voice gave out. A long time after I had grown still, I heard it say: "This is not the way you can punish them." These were the first human words I had heard for such a long time, it took me an eternity to understand what they meant. Then I started bellowing again. The figure disappeared. That night, in a lucid moment, I could not decide: Had it really been there or was it, too, one of the illusory apparitions that surrounded me? The next day it came again. So it was real. It was Arisbe.

She never repeated what she had said the day before; this was her way of letting me know that she knew I had understood her. I would have liked to strangle her, but she was as strong as I was, and fearless. I noticed that Parthena, my nurse, admitted her secretly. By not betraying her presence I made it clear that I needed her. Apparently she believed it was up to me to free myself from madness. I heaped filthy abuse on her for that. She gripped the hand with which I was trying to strike her and said sternly: "Enough self-pity." I was silent at once. People did not talk to me that way.

"Come to the surface, Cassandra," she said. "Open your inner eye. Look at yourself."

I hissed at her like a cat. She left.

So I looked. Not immediately. I waited until it was night. Until I was lying on the crackling twigs, covered with a blanket which Oenone might have woven. So I was allowing names. Oenone. One of *them*. She had played a dirty trick on me, taking my beloved brother away from me, Paris, the handsome blond one. Whom I would have drawn to me if it had not been for the magical arts of this water nymph. Oenone, the filthy beast. Did it hurt? Yes. It hurt. I raised myself a tiny bit closer to the surface, to observe the pain. Groaning, I endured it. I clawed the blankets, I clung to it so that the pain would not wash me away. Hecuba. Priam. Panthous. So many names for deception. For neglect. For lack of appreciation. How I hated them. How I wanted to show them I hated them.

"Fine," said Arisbe, who was sitting there again. "And what about your part in it?"

"What do you mean, what about my part in it? Whom have I hurt? I, the weak one? What harm have I done all these people who are stronger than I am?"

"Why did you make them strong?"

I did not understand the question. The part of me that was eating and drinking again, that called itself "I" again, did not understand the question. The other part, which had been in control during the madness, was no longer being asked; "I" was suppressing it. Not without regret I let the madness go, not without dismay my inner eye saw an unknown form arising out of the dark waters as they dispersed. The gratitude I owed and showed to Arisbe held more than a grain of ingratitude and rebellion; she seemed to expect that. One day she declared she was no longer needed, and when I told her in a fit of emotion that I would never forget certain things she had done, she replied coolly: "Yes, you will." It has always upset me when other people knew more about me, or thought they knew more, than I did.

It took them a long time to make up their minds about me, Arisbe told me years later. Which should they bet on: my inclination to conform with those in power, or my craving for knowledge? "They!" So "they" existed, after all, and they were trying to "make up their minds" about me! "Don't be childish," said Arisbe. "Admit it; for too long you have been trying to have it both ways."

So that is how it was. At last I was coming back to life, I heard the others say; that meant coming back to them. Into the snare. Into the everyday world of the palace and the temple, whose customs seemed as strange and unnatural to me as if they belonged to an alien race. The first time I caught the blood of a lamb in the sacrificial vessel again at the altar of the Thymbraian Apollo, the meaning of this act completely escaped me; anxious, I believed I was taking part in a sacrilege. "You have been far away, Cassandra," said Panthous, who was observing me. "It's really a pity that when one comes back one always finds the same old thing." Apart from this moment, apart from this single sentence, he had grown more impenetrable. Quickly I realized why: It was no longer pleasant to be a Greek in Troy.

Eumelos's people were at work. They had won disciples among the palace scribes and the servants in the temple. We must be armed mentally, too, if the Greeks attacked us, they said. Mental armament consisted in defamation of the enemy (people were already talking about the "enemy" before a single Greek had boarded ship), and in distrust of those suspected of collaborating with the enemy: Panthous the Greek; Briseis, daughter of the renegade Calchas. Who often cried in my bed-chamber at night. Even if she was willing to part from Troilus in order not to put him at risk, he would not let her go. All of a sudden I was the protectress of a pair of endangered lovers. The inconceivable happened: My young brother Troilus, the king's son, was treated with hostility because he had chosen the sweetheart he wanted. "Ye-e-es," said King Priam, "too bad, too bad." Hecuba asked: "Where do you sleep when the two of them spend the night in your room?" She offered to let me come into her bedchamber. Secretly.

But what kind of place were we living in then? I must try

to remember exactly. Did anyone in Troy talk about war? No. He would have been punished. We prepared for war in all innocence and with an easy conscience. The first sign of war: We were letting the enemy govern our behavior. What did we need him for?

The return of the THIRD SHIP left me strangely cool. Care was taken to see that it arrived at night. Nevertheless, a crowd gathered, torches were raised; but who can recognize faces in dim light, who can count them, who can tell them apart? There, unmistakably, was Anchises, who still moved like a young man until a very advanced age. He seemed in more of a hurry than usual, gave no explanations, refused to let Eumelos accompany him, and disappeared into the palace. There were the young men I should have been waiting for: but for whom was I waiting, really? For Aeneas? For Paris? For which of them did my heart begin to beat faster all the same? No one could get near them. For the first time a broad cordon of Eumelos's men had been thrown around the landing stage. Paris had not come on this ship, we were told next morning at a debriefing for members of the royal family. The Spartans having refused once again to restore the king's sister to him, he had been forced (we heard) to make good his threat. He had, in short, abducted the wife of Menelaus. The wife of the King of Sparta. The most beautiful woman in Greece. Helen. He was traveling with her to Troy by a roundabout route.

Helen. The name struck us like a blow. The beautiful Helen. Anything less would not have suited my little brother. We might have known. We had known. I was witness to the scurrying back and forth between the palace and the temple priests, to the sessions of the council that went on day and night; I saw how a news report was manufactured, hard, forged, polished like a spear. At the behest of our dear goddess Aphrodite, the Trojan hero Paris had abducted Helen, the most beautiful woman in Greece, from the boastful Greeks, and so had erased the humiliation once inflicted on our mighty King Priam by the theft of his sister.

The people ran through the streets cheering. I saw a news item turn into the truth. And Priam had a new title: "our mighty king." Later, as our prospects of winning the war grew increasingly dim, we had to call him "our almighty king." "Practical reforms," said Panthous. "When you have said something long enough, you come to believe it in the end." "Yes," Anchises replied dryly, "in the *end*." I hoped at least to impede the language war. I would never say anything but "Father" or at most "King Priam." But I remember quite clearly the dead silence which used to greet such words. "You can afford to talk like that, Cassandra," I was told. It was true. What they could afford was to fear murder and homicide less than the sulky eyebrows of their king and the denunciation of Eumelos. I could afford a little foresight and a little defiance. Defiance, not courage.

How long it has been since I thought about the old days. It is true what they say, the approach of death does make your whole life pass before you. Ten years of war. That was long enough to forget completely the question of how the war started. In the middle of a war you think of nothing but how it will end. And put off living. When large numbers of people do that, it creates a vacuum within us which the war flows in to fill. What I regret more than anything else is that, in the beginning, I too gave in to the feeling that for now I was living only provisionally; that true reality still lay ahead of me: I let life pass me by. Panthous started coming to me again, now that I was regarded as cured. I detected in his lovemaking (but I ought not to use the name for the acts he performed on me, they had nothing to do with love) a new trace of subservience which I did not like; and he admitted that before my illness I had not excited him as I did now. I had changed, he said. Aeneas avoided me. "Of course," he confessed later, "you had changed."

The absent Paris was celebrated in song. Fear lurked inside me. I was not the only one. Unbidden, I interpreted for the king a dream he told at table. Two dragons were fighting.

One wore a hammered-gold breastplate, the other carried a sharp, polished spear. Thus the one was invulnerable but unarmed; the other, though armed and hate-filled, was vulnerable. They waged an eternal battle.

"You are in conflict with yourself," I said to my father. "You are holding yourself in check. You are paralyzing yourself."

"What are you saying, Priestess?" Priam replied formally. "Panthous interpreted my dream a long time ago. The dragon in golden armor is me, the king, of course. I must arm myself in order to overcome my treacherous, heavily armed foe. I have already ordered the armorers to step up production."

"Panthous!" I cried in the temple. "Well?" he said. "They are all animals, Cassandra. Half animals, half children. They will obey their appetites no matter what we do. So do we have to stand in their way, let them trample us underfoot? No. I've made my decision."

"What you decided is to feed the beast in yourself, to arouse it inside you." His cruel, masklike smile. But what did I know about this man?

You can tell when a war starts, but when does the prewar start? If there are rules about that, we should pass them on. Hand them down inscribed in clay, in stone. What would they say? Among other things they would say: Do not let your own people deceive you.

When Paris finally arrived later (strange to say on an Egyptian ship), he took a heavily veiled woman off board. The people—held back as usual now behind the cordon of Eumelos's soldiers—were silent, holding their breath. The image of the most beautiful woman lit up inside each of them, so radiant that she would blind him if he could see her. Speaking choruses sprang up, first shy, then enthusiastic. "He-len. He-len," they said. Helen did not show herself. Nor did she attend the banquet. She was exhausted by the long sea voyage. Paris, a changed man, delivered exquisite gifts given him by his host, the King of Egypt; told miraculous stories. He talked and talked, extravagant, arabesque, with swings which he seemed to consider funny. He laughed many times, he had become a man. I could not take my eyes off him. I could not catch his eyes. Where had his handsome face gotten that crooked line; what sharpness had etched his once soft features.

A sound from the streets penetrated the palace; it was like nothing we had ever heard before, it was like the threatening hum from a beehive when the bees are about to swarm. People's heads were turned by the thought that the beautiful Helen was inside the palace of their king. That night I refused myself to Panthous. Furious, he tried to take me by force. I called for Parthena, my nurse, who was nowhere nearby. Panthous left; he belched lewd insults with a twisted face. The raw flesh beneath the mask. I tried to hide from myself the sorrow that sometimes descended on me, black, from out of the sun.

Every fiber in me shut itself off, refused to recognize that there was no beautiful Helen in Troy. At a time when everyone else in the palace made it clear that they had understood. When I had run into the charming, beautiful-necked Oenone outside Paris's door at dawn, for the second time. When the swarm of legends surrounding Paris's beautiful invisible wife crumbled in embarrassment. When they all lowered their eyes whenever I spoke Helen's name—I was the only one who still did so, saying it over and over as if I could not help myself—and even volunteered to care for her when it was claimed she was still tired. My offer was turned down; and even then I did not yet want to think the unthinkable. "Really, you're enough to drive one to despair," Arisbe told me. I grasped at every straw—and a deputation from Menelaus, demanding the return of their queen in no uncertain terms, was hardly a straw. The fact that they wanted her back proved to me that she was here. There was no doubt about my feelings: I wanted Helen to return to Sparta. Yet it was clear to me that the king was bound to reject the demand. With all my heart I wanted to side with him, with Troy. I could not for the life of me see why the debate in the council went on for another whole night. Paris, his face a pale greenish hue, announced in a voice of doom: "No. We are not going to hand her over." "Come on, Paris!" I cried. "Aren't you happy?" At last his look met mine, confessed to me how he was suffering. This look gave me back my brother.

Then we all forgot the reason for the war. After the crisis in the third year, even the soldiers stopped demanding to see the beautiful Helen. It would have taken more perseverance than a man could muster to go on mouthing a name that tasted increasingly of ashes, gangrene, and decay. They let Helen go and defended their own skins. But they had needed her name in order to cheer for the war. It raised them beyond themselves. "Notice that," Aeneas's father Anchises said to us—he enjoyed teaching and, when the end of the war was in sight, forced us to ponder its beginning: "Notice that they chose a woman. A man could have provided the image of glory and riches just as well. But of beauty? A people who are fighting for beauty!" Paris himself, reluctantly it seemed, had gone to the market-place and thrown the name of the beautiful Helen to the people. They did not notice that his heart was not in it. I noticed. "Why do you speak so coldly about your ardent wife?" I asked him. "My ardent wife?" was his scornful reply. "Wake up, Sister. Ye gods: She doesn't exist."

Then my arms jerked up before I even had a chance to realize. Yes, I believed him. I had felt it for a long time, had been eaten up with fear. A seizure, I thought, still clearheaded, but already I could hear that voice saying: "Woe, woe, woe." I do not know, did I shriek it aloud or did I only whisper it? "We are lost. Woe, we are lost!"

I already knew what was going to happen next: the firm grip on my shoulders, the men's hands grabbing me, the clink of metal on metal, the odor of sweat and leather. It was a day like today, an autumn tempest gusting from the sea, driving clouds across the deep blue sky, stones underfoot, laid out just as they are here in Mycenae, the walls of houses, faces, then thicker walls, hardly any people as we approached the palace. Just like here. I felt how a captive feels looking at the citadel of Troy, and ordered myself not to forget it. I did not forget it; but I have not thought about my way there for a very long time. Why not? Maybe because I felt ashamed of my half-deliberate cunning. For when I shrieked, why did I shriek: "We are lost!"? Why not: "Trojans, there is no Helen!"? I know why not, I knew even then. The Eumelos inside me forbade me. Eumelos was waiting for me in the palace, it was he at whom I shouted: "There is no Helen!" But of course he already knew it. The people were the ones I should have told. In other words, I, the seeress, was owned by the palace. And Eumelos was fully aware of that. It enraged me that on top of everything his face could also express mockery and disdain for me. It was for his sake, whom I hated, and for the sake of my father, whom I loved, that I had avoided screaming their state secret out loud. There was a grain of calculation in my self-renunciation. Eumelos saw through me. My father did not.

King Priam felt sorry for himself. This complicated political situation, and now me to boot! He sent the guards away, which was brave of him. If I went on this way he would have no choice but to lock me up, he said wearily. At that, something inside me thought: Not now, not yet. Whatever did I want, for heaven's sake? he asked. All right, so they ought to have talked with me earlier about that confounded business with Helen. All right, so she was not here. The King of Egypt had taken her away from Paris, the stupid boy. Only everyone in the palace knew that, why didn't I? And what were we to do next? How could we get out of the thing without loss of face?

"Father," I said urgently, in a way I never spoke to him again. "No one can win a war waged for a phantom."

"Why not?" the king asked me in all seriousness. "Why not? All you have to do is make sure the army does not lose faith in the phantom," he said. "And why should there even be a war?

You always use these big words. What I think is, we'll be attacked, and what I think is, we'll defend ourselves. The Greeks will ram their heads into a stone wall and withdraw at once. After all, they won't let themselves bleed to death over a woman, no matter how beautiful she is; and I don't believe she is, anyway."

"And why wouldn't they!" I cried. "Assuming they believed Helen was with us. Suppose they were the kind of people who could never get over an insult that a woman, be she beautiful or ugly, inflicted on a king, a man?" (As I said that, I was thinking of Panthous, who seemed to hate me since I rejected him. Suppose they were all like that?)

"Don't talk rubbish," said Priam. "They want our gold. And free access to the Dardanelles." "So negotiate terms!" I suggested. "That's all we need. To negotiate over our inalienable property and rights!" I began to see that my father was already blind to all the reasons for opposing war, and that what made him blind and deaf was the declaration of the military leaders: We will win. "Father," I begged him. "At least deprive them of the pretext of Helen. Here or in Egypt, she's not worth the life of a single Trojan. Tell that to Menelaus's ambassadors, give them the gifts a host gives guests, and let them go in peace." "You must be out of your mind, child," said the king, genuinely shocked. "Don't you understand anything anymore? The honor of our house is at stake."

The honor of our house was what concerned me too, I protested. I was thickheaded. I thought that they wanted the same thing I did. So what freedom it brought me the first time I said no, no, I want something different. But on this occasion the king was right to think I meant what I said. "Child," he said, drawing me to him; I breathed the scent I loved so much. "Child. Anyone who does not side with us now is working against us." Then I promised him to keep secret what I knew about the beautiful Helen, and left unmolested. The guards in the corridor stood motionless. Eumelos bowed as I went past him. "Bravo, Cassandra," Panthous said to me in the temple. Now I hated him as he did me. It is too hard to hate oneself. There was a great deal of hate and stifled knowledge in Troy before the enemy, the Greeks, drew all our ill will upon themselves and made us close ranks against them, to begin with.

Over the winter I turned apathetic and silent. I could not say the most important thing, so it no longer occurred to me to say anything. My parents, who no doubt were keeping an eye on me, spoke noncommittally to me and each other. Briseis and Troilus, who continued to solicit my sympathy, did not understand my apathy. Nothing from Arisbe. Nothing from Aeneas. Marpessa mute. No doubt everyone began to give up on me, the inevitable fate of those who give up on themselves. Then in spring the war began as expected.

We were not allowed to call it "war." Linguistic regulations prescribed that, correctly speaking, it be called a "surprise attack." For which, strange to say, we were not in the least prepared. We did not know what we intended to do, and so we did not really try to learn the Greeks' intentions. I say "we," I started to say "we" again many years ago. I accepted my parents back in misfortune. But at the time, when the Greek fleet rose against the horizon, a dreadful sight; when our hearts sank; when our young men went laughing to meet the enemy, into certain death, with no more protection than their leather shields; then I passionately cursed all those responsible. A defensive ring! An advance line behind a fortification! Trenches! There was nothing of the sort. True, I was no military strategist, but anyone could see how our soldiers were being herded toward the enemy along the level shore to be butchered. I have never been able to get that picture out of my mind.

And then, on the very first day, my brother Troilus.

I have always tried not to remember how he died, and yet nothing in the whole war left a keener imprint. Shortly I myself am to be slaughtered, and fear fear fear forces me to think; yet even now I remember every cursed detail about my brother

Troilus's death, and this one dead man would have lasted me the rest of the war. Proud, loyal to my king, daring, trusting in Hector's vow that no Greek would ever set foot on our shores, I stayed in the temple of Apollo outside the city, from which one used to look out on the coast. I just thought "used to look out," but it should be "still look out." The temple has been spared. No Greek laid violent hands on Apollo's shrine. Whoever is standing there now looks out on the coast covered with debris, corpses, war material, which Troy once governed, and when he turns around he sees the destroyed city. Cybele, help.

Marpessa is sleeping. The children are sleeping.

Cybele, help.

That day saw the start of something that became a habit: I stood and saw. Went on standing when the other priests, including Panthous, had fled in panic toward Troy. When the uncompromising leather-cheeked old priestess Herophile fled into the interior of the temple in horror. I stood there. Saw how my brother Hector-Dim-Cloud—oh, he was wearing his leather jerkin!—smote the first Greeks who left the ships and waded through the shallow water, trying to reach the shores of Troy. My Trojans cut down the second wave of Greeks, too. Would Hector be proved right? I saw the human dolls fall to the ground, soundlessly and sufficiently far away. There was not the tiniest spark of triumph in my heart. Then indeed something quite different began; I saw it.

A formation of Greeks in close array, wearing armor and surrounding themselves with an unbroken wall of shields, stormed onto land like a single organism with a head and many limbs, while they set up a howl whose like had never been heard. Those on the outlying edges were quickly killed by the already exhausted Trojans, as no doubt it had been intended that they should be. Those toward the center slew altogether too many of our men. The core reached shore as they were meant to, and with them the core's core: the Greek hero Achilles. He was intended to get through even if all the others fell. He did get through. "So that's how it's done," I heard myself tell myself feverishly. "All for one." What now? Cunningly he did not attack Hector, whom the other Greeks took in charge. He went for the boy Troilus, who was driven toward him by well-trained men the way game is driven toward the hunter. So that's how it's done. My heart began to pound. Troilus stood his ground, faced his opponent, fought. He fought by the rules, as he had been taught was the way to fight between high-born men. He adhered faithfully to the rules of the athletic contests in which he had excelled since childhood. Troilus! I was trembling. I knew ahead of time each step he would take, each turn of his head, each design he would trace with his body. But Achilles. Achilles the brute did not respond to the boy's offer. Perhaps he did not understand it. Achilles raised his sword high above his head, gripping it with both hands, and let it whistle down on my brother. All rules fell into the dust forever. So that's how it's done.

My brother Troilus fell to the ground. Achilles the brute was on top of him. I refused to believe it, I believed it at once. I was at odds with myself as so often in the past. If I saw what I think I saw, he strangled my brother as he lay. Something happened that went beyond my conception, beyond the conception of us all. Those who could see saw it the first day: We would lose this war. This time I did not shriek. Did not go crazy. Went on standing there. Broke the clay goblet in my hand without noticing.

The worst was still to come, is still to come. Troilus, wearing light armor, had gotten up again, had wrenched himself free from Achilles' hands, began to run—ye gods, how he could run! Aimlessly at first; then—I signaled, shouted—he found the direction, ran toward me, ran to the temple. Saved. We would lose the war but this brother, who at that moment seemed the dearest of them all, was saved. I ran to him, grabbed his arm, drew him into the interior of the temple—his throat was rattling, he was collapsing—in front of the god's statue, where he was safe. The repulsed Achilles wheezed after him; I no longer needed to pay him any notice. What I needed to do was to unfasten my brother's helmet, loosen his cuirass; he was gasping for air. The old priestess Herophile, whom I never saw weep before or since, helped me. My hands flew. He who lives is not lost. Not lost to me, either. I will take care of you, Brother, I will love you, get to know you at last. "Briseis will be happy," I said into his ear.

Then Achilles the brute came. The murderer came into the temple, which darkened as he stood at the entrance. What did this man want? What was he after, wearing weapons here in the temple? Hideous moment: already I knew. Then he laughed. Every hair on my head stood on end and sheer terror came into my brother's eyes. I threw myself over him and was shoved aside as if I were not there. In what role was his enemy approaching my brother? As a murderer? As a seducer? Could such a thing be—the voluptuousness of the murderer and the lover in one? Was that allowed to exist among human beings? The fixed gaze of the victim. The capering approach of the pursuer, whom I now saw from behind, a lewd beast. Who took Troilus by the shoulders, stroked him, handled him—the defenseless boy from whom I, wretched woman, had removed the armor! Laughing, laughing all over. Gripped his neck. Moved to the throat. His plump, stubby-fingered, hairy hand on my brother's throat. Pressing, pressing. I hung on the murderer's arm, on which the veins stood out like cords. My brother's eyes were starting out of their sockets. And the gratification in Achilles' face. The naked hideous male gratification. If that exists, everything is possible. It was deathly still. I was shaken off, felt nothing. Now the enemy, the monster, raised his sword in full view of Apollo's statue and severed my brother's head from his torso. Human blood spurted onto the altar as before it had spurted from the carcasses of our sacrificial animals. Troilus, the sacrificial victim. The butcher fled with a horrid and gratified howl. Achilles the brute. I felt nothing for a long time.

Then the touch. A hand on my cheek, which for the first time in my life seemed to be where it belonged. And a look I knew. Aeneas.

Everything in the past was pale premonition, uncompleted longing. Aeneas was the reality; and faithful to reality, craving reality, I wanted to cling to it. At the moment he could do nothing here, he said. He said he was leaving. "Leave," I said. Oh, how good he was at disappearing. I did not call after him, did not follow him, and did not try to find out about him. People said he was in the mountains. Many made faces of contempt. I did not defend him. Did not talk about him. Was with him with every fiber of my body and soul. Am with him. Aeneas. Live. You are my reserve force, I will not give you up. At the end you did not understand me, you threw the snake ring into the sea in anger. But we have not gotten to that point yet. The conversation with you comes later. When I need it. Yes, I will need it.

I insisted on being heard in the council as a witness to the death of Troilus. I demanded that this war be ended at once. "And how?" the men asked me, aghast. I said. "By telling the truth about Helen. By making them offerings. Gold and other goods, whatever they want. As long as they go away. As long as the pestilential breath of their presence departs. By admitting to what they will demand we admit—that Paris gravely violated the right of hospitality, which is sacred to us all, when he abducted Helen. The Greeks must regard this action as a grievous rapine and a grievous breach of trust. So they tell their wives, their children, their slaves tales of what Paris did. And they are right. End this war."

Stalwart men turned pale as death. "She's mad," I heard them whisper. "Now she's mad." And King Priam, my father, rose slowly, dauntingly, to his feet and then roared as no one ever heard him roar. His daughter! Why must it be she of all people who spoke for the enemy here in the council of Troy? Why did she not speak for Troy instead: unequivocally, publicly and loudly, here, in the temple and in the marketplace? "I was speaking for Troy, Father." I still ventured to say softly. I could not keep from trembling. The king shook his fists, screamed: Had I forgotten so quickly the death of my brother Troilus! "Throw that person out! She is no longer my child." The hands again, the smell of fear. I was led away.

Panthous told me that after I left the council discussed the oracle circulating through the streets of Troy which said that Troy could win the war only if Troilus reached twenty years old. Now, everyone knew that Troilus was seventeen when he fell. Calchas the seer, Calchas the traitor was behind the rumor, Eumelos claimed. "So," Panthous told me, "I simply suggested that we pass a posthumous decree declaring Troilus to be twenty years old." And Eumelos supplemented the suggestion: Anyone who continued to maintain that Troilus was only seventeen when Achilles slew him would be punished. I said: "I would be the first one you'd have to punish." "So what?" said Panthous. "Why not, Cassandra?"

For the first time a chill came over me.

But King Priam put up a struggle. No (I was told he had said), insult his dead son further with lies? No. Not with his consent. So there was a time when the dead were sacred, at least to us; and I knew that time. The new time respected neither living nor dead. It took me a while to understand it. It was already inside the stronghold before the enemy came. It penetrated through every crack, how I do not know. Among us its name was Eumelos.

I was choosing the easy way out, Panthous the Greek instructed me. I had come to detest the way he used to hide behind impenetrable didacticism; but I was not inside his skin, the skin of a Greek. Once I asked him angrily whether he thought I was going to denounce him to Eumelos. "How can I know that?" he asked, and smiled. "Besides, what could you accuse me of?" We both knew that Eumelos made do without grounds. Of course he got Panthous years later, through the women. Blind, I was blind not to have seen the fear behind his game.

There is no more time left, and so self-reproach is not enough. I must ask myself what it was that made me blind. The humiliating thing is, I could have sworn I already had the answer, did have for a long time.

Should I get down out of the chariot, after all? The wickerwork where I am sitting is hard. One consolation: The willow rods that compose it grew by our river, the Scamander. Oenone took me there to gather willow wands, in the autumn after the war began. She said I should make them into a bed. "They kill the desires," Oenone said earnestly. "Did Hecuba send you?" "Arisbe," she said. Arisbe. What did that woman know about me? She herself, Oenone said, had slept on willows all the months when Paris was away. She never spoke Aeneas's name. Absentmindedly I listened to her disconsolate lament about Paris, who, she said, had been ruined by the foreign woman. What did Arisbe have in mind? Was she trying to warn me? To chastise me? I lay on the willows howling with rage. They did not help. I longed for love unbearably, a longing which only one man could appease; my dreams left no doubt about that. Once I took a very young priest into my bed. It was almost expected of me; I was training him and he revered me. I quenched his passion while I remained cold and dreamed of Aeneas. I began to pay heed to my body, which—who would have thought it!—obeyed the guidance of dreams.

It occurs to me that I had to do with willow wands twice more after that: The basket where I was imprisoned was wickerwork too, so densely woven that scarcely one ray of light got through to me. And later the women, I among them, laid suckling pigs on willow rods inside the caves, for Cybele. When I did that, I was free of the gods. Willow wands, my last seat. Without my realizing it, my hand has begun to loosen a slender wand from the weave. It is broken but hardly moves. I will continue to tug and shake it, more attentively now. I want to set it free. I want to take it with me when the time comes that I must get down.

Now his wife is butchering Agamemnon.

Presently it will be my turn.

I notice that I cannot believe what I know.

That is how it always was, how it always will be.

I did not know it would be so difficult, not even when I realized with horror that we were going to disappear without a trace: Myrine, Aeneas, I. I told him that. He was silent. It comforted me that he had no comfort to offer. When we saw each other for the last time, he wanted to give me his ring, the snake ring. My eyes said no. He threw it from the cliff into the sea. The shining arc it described in the sunlight burned into my heart. No one will ever learn these all-important things about us. The scribes' tablets, baked in the flames of Troy, transmit the palace accounts, the records of grain, urns, weapons, prisoners. There are no signs for pain, happiness, love. That seems to me an extreme misfortune.

Marpessa is singing a song to the twins. She learned it, as I did, from her mother, Parthena the nurse. It says: "When the child is sleeping, his soul, a beautiful bird, flies to the silver olive and then slowly mounts toward the setting sun." Soul, beautiful bird. I felt its movements in my breast, sometimes light as a feather's touch, sometimes violent and painful. The war gripped the men's breasts and killed the bird. Only when it reached out for my soul too did I say no. A strange notion: The movements of the soul inside me resembled the movements of the children in my body, a gentle stirring, a motion like that in a dream. The first time I felt this frail dream-motion it shook me to the core, opened the barrier inside me which had held back my love for the children of a father who had been forced on me; the love rushed out with a river of tears. I looked at my children for the last time when the thickset Agamemnon, stomping over the red carpet, disappeared behind the door of the palace. Now I will not look at them again. Marpessa has covered them, hiding them from me.

You could say that it was through them, on their account, that I lost my father. Priam the king had three devices against a disobedient daughter: He could declare her insane. He could lock her up. He could force her into an unwanted marriage. This device, to be sure, was unprecedented. Never in Troy had the daughter of a free man been forced into marriage. This was the last extremity. My father sent for Eurypylos and his army of Mysians even though everyone knew that Eurypylos wanted me for his wife in exchange. When that happened it was clear to us all: Troy was lost. Now I, Hecuba the queen, the unhappy Polyxena, all my sisters, indeed all the women in Troy, were seized by ambivalence: they had to hate Troy even while they wished it the victory.

So many brothers, so much grief. So many sisters, so much horror. Oh, the dreadful fertility of Hecuba.

When I think of Troilus, Hector, Paris, my heart bleeds. When I think of Polyxena, I feel like flying into a rage. If only nothing survived me but my hatred. If the hatred sprouted from my grave, a tree of hate that would whisper: "Achilles the brute." If they felled the tree, it would grow again. If they pinned it down, each blade of grass would take over the message: "Achilles the brute, Achilles the brute." And every minstrel who dared to sing of Achilles would die in torture on the spot. Between the brute and posterity, let there be an abyss of contempt or oblivion. Apollo, if you do exist after all, grant me this; I would not have lived in vain.

I saw how those who fought on the battlefield gradually came to believe the lies of those who knew nothing of battle, because they flattered them. There is such an accord between the two that often I was tempted to despise human nature. The women in the mountains exorcised my arrogance. Not by words. By being different, by extracting from their nature qualities I hardly dared dream of. If I still have time, I should speak of my body.

After the death of Troilus, Briseis, daughter of Calchas, almost lost her mind. Many were the women I heard shriek in those years—but the shrieks of Briseis when we buried Troilus curdled our blood. For a long time she let no one speak to her and did not speak a word herself. Her first word was a soft "yes" when I brought her the message from her father, Calchas. If the king would allow it, she wanted to go join her renegade father on the other side. I had the impression that the king was only too glad to grant her request without delay. Obviously a daughter in mourning belonged with her father who loved her, he said. King Priam, I thought, was not sorry to see the last of a woman who mourned as she did. I had already heard whispers in the palace that her grief was undermining morale. Eumelos, to be sure, was indignant. "What?" he asked insidiously. Did the king consider blood ties more important than those of the state? "Indeed I do," said Priam; he was the old Priam and I loved him. How could I not? And the fact that he cursed me in the council—didn't that show how attached he was to me? No. It would take more than that to make me disown my father, good King Priam.

As Briseis's friend, I accompanied her to the Greek camp; that too seemed reasonable to everyone except Eumelos. With us came two of my brothers and five warriors, all unarmed. Not one of us Trojans doubted that a Trojan woman who is going to her father deserves a worthy escort. But the Greeks seemed confused by us, almost anxious! Calchas, after he had greeted his daughter tenderly and warily, explained our strange reception. "Never," he said, "would one of the Greeks enter the enemy camp unarmed." "But they would have our word that they would be safe if they did that," I cried. Calchas the seer smiled. "A word! Adapt, Cassandra. The sooner the better. If I had not terrified them, they would have done in your unarmed brothers." "Terrified them, how?" "By telling them about the magical power one of our unarmed warriors possesses, especially when he is accompanied by a woman." "One of our warriors, Calchas?" "One of us Trojans, Cassandra." For the first time in my life I saw a man gutted by homesickness.

We were standing by the sea, the waves were licking our feet. I saw the heaps of weapons—spears, javelins, swords, shields—

behind the wooden wall which the Greeks had swiftly erected against us along the coast. Calchas understood my gaze, replied: "You are lost." I wanted to test him. "We could give Helen back to Menelaus," I said. Again he smiled his painful smile: "Could you really?"

A shock: He knew. Did they all know then, all the men who were swaggering up to gape at me and Briseis: the temperate Menelaus, the keenly observant Odysseus. Agamemnon, whom I instantly disliked? Diomedes of Argos, a lanky fellow. They stood and stared. "In Troy men don't look at women that way," I said in our language, which only Calchas could understand. "They certainly don't," he replied unmoved. "Get used to it." "And this is where you are taking Briseis? To these men?" "She must live," said Calchas. "Survive. Nothing more. Life at any cost."

So now I knew why Calchas was with the Greeks.

No, Calchas, I said. At any cost? Not so.

Today I think differently. I was so calm. Now everything inside me is in revolt. I will beg that terrible woman for my life. I will throw myself at her feet. "Clytemnestra, lock me up forever in your darkest dungeon. Give me barely enough to live on. But I implore you: Send me a scribe, or better yet a young slave woman with a keen memory and a powerful voice. Ordain that she may repeat to her daughter what she hears from me. That the daughter in turn may pass it on to her daughter, and so on. So that alongside the river of heroic songs this tiny rivulet, too, may reach those faraway, perhaps happier people who will live in times to come."

And could I believe that, even for one day?

Slay me, Clytemnestra. Kill me. Hurry.

Inside the citadel they are drinking. The wanton clamor I would so gladly not have heard is rising to a crescendo now. So on top of everything else the men who come to fetch me will be drunk.

We did not see the hero Achilles when we delivered Briseis

to her fate. He was her fate. He saw us from some hidden place. How my heart burned when I embraced her. With an unmoved face she stood leaning against Diomedes, whom she had just seen for the first time in her life. The ungainly lout. I pictured my delicate boyish brother Troilus. "Briseis!" I said softly, "what are you thinking of?" "He loves me," she replied. "He says he loves me." I saw him place his hand on her the way men touch slave women. The Greek men all around us laughed their booming male laughs. I was seized by a ghastly fear of the love of the Greeks.

But where was Achilles? His name was boring into me; when I mentioned it, I saw Calchas lose his look of composure at last. The mask cracked. Before me stood the Trojan I knew, the friend of my early childhood, my father's shrewd, temperate adviser. He drew me aside, paid no heed to the suspicion of the Greeks, which he aroused when he evidently confided to me a secret that was weighing on his mind. Yes, Achilles. He was a problem to Calchas, too. Achilles and the Greeks (he said) claimed that Achilles was the son of a goddess. Her name: Thetis. Well. We priests decided among ourselves not to form an opinion. Achilles gave away many weapons and much wine to ensure the spread of the legend. He threatened the grimmest punishment to anyone who dared to doubt its truth—and no doubt about it, that man had not his equal in meting out punishment. So, Calchas said, what he told me now could easily cost him his life. Namely: When the war was about to begin, Odysseus and Menelaus were assembling the Greek allies (he, Calchas, had been present at the negotiations and since then he had known what it meant to be a Greek); then they came to fetch Achilles, too. His mother, goddess or not, said that he was not at home, that he was far away, that he had left on a journey. Odysseus, who knows people and up to a certain point himself as well (which is rare)—Odysseus smelled a rat. He left the rat and Menelaus (whom all the Greeks secretly despised because he had lost Helen) with the woman, followed his keen nose, and found Achilles in a secluded room, in bed with another young man. And since the practiced, far-seeing Odysseus had tried to evade the levy himself by pretending to be mad (What, we didn't know that? Well, what *did* we know about our enemies, then?); since he would not allow another man to get off when he had to bleed, he literally dragged Achilles into the war by the scruff of his neck. It might be that he already regretted it. For Achilles was after everyone in sight: young men, whom he genuinely desired, and girls, as a proof that he was like everybody else. A fiend in battle so that everyone would see he was not a coward, he did not know what to do with himself once the fighting was done. And this was the man to whom Calchas the seer later had to turn over his daughter. Perhaps he fooled himself into thinking that among wanton men, only the most wanton could protect a woman. I saw Briseis again after the fall of Troy, when we were driven through the camp of the Greeks. I thought I had seen all the horror a human being can see. I know what I am saying: Briseis's face surpassed it all.

If only he, Achilles, had died a thousand deaths. If only I could have been present at every one.

Let the earth vomit out his ashes.

I am very tired.

On that long-ago day when we returned from the Greek camp without Briseis, I felt I had been away for a long time and very, very far. There lay my Troy, my beloved city, behind its high wall. The target, the prey. A god had given me new eyes. Suddenly I saw all the weaknesses which the Greeks could exploit. I swore to myself that never, never should a man like Achilles walk through our streets. Except for this last day of all, I was never more of a Trojan than that day. I saw that the others were feeling the same thing I did. So we came home, to the Scaean Gate. There the sentries intercepted us. We were shown into a small, dark, stinking room in the gatehouse. Eumelos's men dictated our names to an embarrassed, pompous scribe. All of us had to say who we were, even my brothers and I, whom everyone knew. I burst out laughing, was severely reprimanded. Where had we been, we were asked. "So, with the enemy. And for what purpose?"

Then I thought I was dreaming. The men were searched—even my brothers, the king's sons—pocket by pocket, seam by seam. I held the bright knife to the chest of the first man who touched me, the knife I carried on me for all eventualities, so as not to be at the mercy of the enemy. "I didn't need it over *there*," I said bitterly.

What did I mean by that, I was asked. Was I comparing a Trojan loyal to his king to the enemy? I knew the man who dared to speak this way to me: physically gone to pot, bloated, running to fat. He had tried to touch me in the past. I ruminated and said coldly: "Anyone who touches me will end up with a knife in him." The man retreated, half groveling, like a dog. Oh yes, I knew him. My father's chief scribe. Was he one of Eumelos's men? What was happening to my city, then? What was happening to my Trojans that they did not see our little band being driven through their streets? It was simple, I saw: simply not to see. I could not find their eyes. Coldly I scrutinized the backs of their heads. Had they always been so cowardly? Was there such a thing as a people who had cowardly backs of heads? I asked Eumelos, who, seemingly by chance, was waiting for us at the entrance of the palace. I got under his skin. He hectored his deputy: "But not her! One must be able to draw distinctions. Not everyone who knew Briseis the traitor, or even was her friend, is under our suspicion. But what if what Cassandra calls cowardly (exaggerating as we know she is in the habit of doing) is simply loyalty to the king? It goes without saying that you are all free."

Priam explained to me that in war everything that would apply in peace was rescinded. After all, it did not hurt Briseis what people said about her here, where she would never return. And it was helping us. "In what way?" "Inasmuch as opinions about her case differed." "In heaven's name, how can opinions differ about a case that does not exist? That was invented especially for the purpose?" "Even if that's true, once something has become public knowledge, it is real." "So. Real like Helen."

Then he threw me out for the second time. Things were beginning to add up; was I addled or something? I think so. I think in a certain sense I was. I lived through it, but it is still hard to explain it to myself. I still believed that a little will to truth, a little courage, could erase the whole misunderstanding. To call what was true, true and what was untrue, false: That was asking so little (I thought) and would have served our cause better than any lie or half-truth. For it was intolerable (I thought) to base the whole war—and our whole lives, for wasn't war our life!—on the accident of a lie. It was out of the question (I thought, although I can hardly recall it) that the rich plenty of our existence should be reduced to one pigheaded contention. After all, we need only call to mind our Trojan tradition. But what was that tradition? What did it consist in? Then I understood: In the Helen we had invented, we were defending everything that we no longer had. And the more it faded, the more real we had to say it was. Thus out of words, gestures, ceremonies, and silence there arose a second Troy, a ghostly city, where we were supposed to feel at home and live at ease. Was I the only one who saw this? Feverishly I checked the names. My father. I could no longer speak to him. My mother, who closed herself off more and more. Arisbe. Parthena the nurse. You, Marpessa. Then something, a secret fear, warned me not to look into your world before I was ready. Better to suffer but to remain where I was. Where my brothers and sisters moved about without question, as if there were solid ground beneath their feet. Where Herophile, the old leather-cheeked priestess, fervently dedicated offerings to the god Apollo, beseeching him to support our arms. Impossible that the king's daughter and a priestess should doubt the royal family and have faith in her servant girl and her nurse. You all stepped like shadows, Marpessa, to the edge of my field of vision. You became shadows. Deprived of reality. As I myself became unreal, the more I treated as real what the palace of Eumelos commanded. The palace's greatest ally in winning my allegiance was our best enemy, Achilles.

My attention, everyone's attention, focused on the monstrous crimes of this rabid beast, who with his wanton band had thrown himself on the countryside around Mount Ida—where Aeneas was! He plundered the villages, massacred the men, raped the women, cut the throats of the goats and sheep, trampled down the fields. Aeneas! I trembled with fear. One month later he entered the stronghold leading those Dardanians who had managed to save themselves. Everyone was yelling and weeping; it was my most beautiful day ever. It was always like that when he and I breathed the same air; life flowed back into the husk of my body. When I stood on the wall at evening I saw the sun again, the moon and stars; the olive trees flashing silver in the wind; the purple, metallic sheen of the sea at sunset; the shifting brown and blue tones of the plain. The fragrance of the thyme fields wafted over to me; I felt how soft the air was. Aeneas was alive. I did not have to see him, I could wait until he came to me. He was towed off to the council; there was a lively, almost cheerful bustle in the streets of Troy. A saying made the rounds, no one claimed to have invented it and everyone seemed to know it at the same moment: "If Hector is our arm, Aeneas is the soul of Troy." Thank-fires burned at all the sacrificial shrines in his honor. "But that's preposterous!" I heard him say to Herophile, our high priestess. "Are you thanking the gods for letting our land be devastated?" "We're giving thanks for your rescue, Aeneas," she said. "Nonsense. My rescue was a by-product of the enemy's devastation." "Should we extinguish the sacrificial fires? Make the gods even more angry?" "As far as I'm concerned, yes." I saw Aeneas leave the temple. The quarrel went unnoticed. The sacrifices proceeded; I helped perform the rituals as my office required: passes, gestures, words without meaning. At night Aeneas stayed in the humble accommodations assigned to the fugitives. I lay awake, tortured myself wondering whether he equated me with Herophile, the stubborn old high priestess. For my benefit—and his— I compiled the differences. To my amazement I found there was not much to choose between us for anyone looking on from the outside. The difference I took such pride in amounted to nothing more than my inner reservations. This was not enough to satisfy him, Aeneas. Was it enough for me?

After a long, desolate spell without dreams, I finally had another dream one night. It was one of those dreams which I realized at once was significant, which I did not understand immediately but did not forget. I was walking alone through a strange city; it was not Troy, but Troy was the only city I had ever seen before. My dream city was larger, more extensive. I knew it was night, yet the moon and the sun were in the sky at the same time and were struggling for dominance. I had been appointed judge (by whom it was not stated): Which of the two heavenly bodies could shine more brightly? There was something wrong about this contest, but try as I might, I could not find out what. Until finally, disheartened and anxious, I said that of course everyone knew and could see that it was the sun that shone most brightly. "Phoebus Apollo!" a voice cried in triumph, and at the same time, to my horror, Selene, the dear lady of the moon, sank to the horizon lamenting. A judgment had been passed on me; but how could I be guilty when I had done nothing but tell the truth?

Posing this question, I woke up. I told Marpessa my dream, casually and with artificial laughter. She said nothing. For many days she kept her face averted. Then she came, showed me her eyes, which it seemed to me had grown darker and deeper, and said: "The most important thing about your dream, Cassandra, was that faced with a completely perverted question, you nevertheless tried to find an answer. You should remember that when the time comes."

"Who says so? To whom did you tell my dream?"

"Arisbe," Marpessa replied, as if it were obvious, and I was silent. Had I secretly hoped to have my dream referred to her, to Arisbe? Did that mean she had authority over my dreams? I knew that the answer was already in the questions, and I felt a stirring inside me after the long freeze brought on by the first months of the war. Already spring was coming again; the Greeks had not attacked us for a long time; I left the fortress, sat on a hill above the Scamander River. What did that mean: The sun shone brighter than the moon? Was the moon ever intended to shine brighter? Who put such questions into my head? If I understood Arisbe rightly, I was entitled—perhaps even obligated—to reject them. One coil in the rope that bound me, the outermost coil, snapped, dropped away; many others remained. It was a time to draw breath, to stretch stiff joints; a blossoming of the flesh.

At the new moon Aeneas came. Strange that Marpessa was not sleeping in the anteroom as was her duty. I saw his face for only a moment as he blew out the light that swam in a pool of oil beside the door. Our recognition sign was and remained his hand on my cheek, my cheek in his hand. We said little more to each other than our names; I had never heard a more beautiful love poem. Aeneas Cassandra. Cassandra Aeneas. When my chastity encountered his shyness, our bodies went wild. I could not have dreamed what my limbs replied to the questions of his lips, or what unknown inclinations his scent would confer on me. And what a voice my throat had at its command.

But Troy's soul was destined not to stay in Troy. Very early the next morning he boarded ship with a troop of armed men; he had to put up a fight to be allowed to take his own men, the Dardanians. This was the last ship for a long time to carry goods to the coasts of the Black Sea. I believe—and I understood him yet failed to understand—that Aeneas preferred to leave rather than to stay. Admittedly, it was hard to think of him and Eumelos sitting at the same table. Stick with his father, he enjoined me. For months on end he vanished from my sight. Time seemed to slow down; in my memory it was pale and ghostly, punctuated only by the great rituals I had to help perform, and by the public oracles to which our people flocked for desperately needed comfort. My brother Helenus and Laocoön, priest of Poseidon, an estimable man, were their favorite oracles; but I could not help seeing that they were spreading empty chatter. Helenus, surprised by my indignation, did not dispute that the oracles were more or less made to order. Made to whose order? Well, the royal family's, the temple's; what was the matter with me? That was the way it had always been, for the oracles were the mouths of those who appointed them and who were divine almost as the gods themselves were divine. How rare it was that a god condescended to speak through us; after all, I must know that better than anyone. And yet how often we required the gods' counsel. So who got hurt if he, Helenus, prophesied that the Greeks would never conquer our city unless through the weakest gate, the Scaean Gate? Besides, he himself believed this was true, subjectively speaking; and it achieved the highly desirable effect of increasing the alertness of the sentries at the Scaean Gate still further. Or take Laocoön. Laocoön (he said) divined, from the entrails of the last sacrificial bull, that Troy would be threatened only if ten of the twelve white horses in our royal stables fell into the hands of the Greeks. It was unthinkable that that should occur. Yet now, as a result of the prophecy, the right interior flank of the stronghold where the stables lay was also especially secure. What in the world could I have against that?

Nothing: that was all I could say. How can I explain? Helenus was careless but not a fraud. Exactly my age, handsome, I always liked to behave condescendingly to him: my superior. What made him superior? His faith, no doubt about it. In the gods? No. His faith that we were in the right, and doubly in the right if we forced the word of the gods to come down to us. He acted and spoke in good faith, in the faith that the world was exactly as he proclaimed it. No one could inflict doubt on him; never did I see on his face so much as a shadow of that smile which by now had engraved itself into the corners of Panthous's mouth. He accepted his popularity in the way that people like: casually, as something that he had coming to him, and without placing unnecessary burdens on them or himself. He got along remarkably well with Hector and one day made the surprising prediction that Hector would carry the fame of Troy through all time to come. Andromache—Hector's wife since the beginning of the war, loyal, domestic, rather plain—was crying her eyes out. She came running to tell me her dreams; people had gotten into the habit of doing that. Hector dreamed (Andromache told me) that he was pushed out of the warm womb of a bitch, through a dreadful narrow opening, and into the world, where he was forced to change at once from a sheltered and cherished puppy into a ravening boar. The boar accosts a lion and—in the scorching sun!—is overwhelmed and torn to shreds. Her husband woke up bathed in tears, Andromache confided. He was not the kind of man heroes are made of, she said. In the gods' name, would I entreat Hecuba on his behalf: everyone knew he was her favorite son.

What a child my eldest brother was. I was angry at Hecuba for having coddled him and kept him a little boy, and I thought it right and proper that she should intervene on his behalf. To my great astonishment Anchises, Aeneas's much-loved father, was conferring with her. No doubt of it, Hecuba, my mother, had appointed him to comfort her because she could do nothing, nothing whatever for Hector; they were grooming him for the role of Chief Hero. Hector-Dim-Cloud! A number of my brothers were better suited than he to lead the battle. But Eumelos wanted to strike at the queen through her favorite son. If he failed as a hero, he and along with him his mother would become the laughingstock of the city. If he did as he was asked and led the battle, he would be killed sooner or later. Cursed Eumelos. Hecuba looked at me and said: "Cursed war." All three of us were silent. I learned that protest begins with this silence in which more than one takes part.

Anchises. If only Anchises were here. If he were with me I could bear anything. He did not allow you to fear that anything could be unbearable, no matter what happened. Yes, the unbearable did exist. But why fear it long before it arrives! Why not simply live, and if possible cheerfully? Cheerfulness, that is the word for him. Gradually I saw where he got it from: He saw through people, above all himself, but he did not feel disgusted by what he saw like Panthous; he enjoyed it. Anchises was—no, is—a free man. He thinks dispassionately even about people who wish him ill. Eumelos, for example. It would never have occurred to me to talk about Eumelos gaily and without prejudice. To understand and feel compassion for him rather than to fear and hate him. "Just consider the fact that he has no wife," Anchises said. "Y-e-e-s—you women don't suspect what that means to a man. That he has to force slave women to sleep with him. That he can smell you gloating. Oh yes, a man like that can smell what's going on around him. After all, he's after the same thing as the rest of us, he only wants to get back to where he had it good once: under your skirts. You won't let him in. So he takes revenge, it's as simple as that. A bit of responsiveness from your lot and who knows, he might be cured."

How we tore into him. So evil was a deficiency? An illness? Something that could be cured? "Well," he admitted then, "maybe for Eumelos there's no more hope." Nevertheless, he still maintained: "That man is a product of Troy just like—let's say like King Priam." Anchises used to plead the most monstrous things with a laugh, but here he was going too far. Eumelos was an aberration, I cried, a sort of accident, an oversight of the gods if there was such a thing. If there was such a thing as gods. Whereas Priam . . . "Whereas Priam does nothing more than appoint Eumelos to office," Anchises said dryly. "Is that right? Another aberration?" "Of course." "So, an accident?"

What could I say to that? Oh, how I resisted admitting that

Priam and Eumelos were a matched pair who needed each other. For weeks I avoided Anchises, until the incredible happened. The palace guard barred Hecuba the queen from taking part in the sessions of the council. Now (I thought when I heard), now order in the palace is collapsing; and I actually felt amazed that I was looking forward with joy as well as anxiety to the change that now was bound to occur. Nothing happened. They did not look at her, my mother Hecuba reported in Anchises's hut, where I arrived out of breath from running. None of the men had looked at her when they walked past her into the council. "Not even my son Hector," Hecuba said bitterly. "I stepped into his way. Eyed him from top to toe—well, you both know how I can look. 'Try to understand, Mother,' he said. 'We want to spare you. The things we have to talk about in our council, now in wartime, are no longer the concern of women.' "

"Quite right," said Anchises. "Now they are the concern of children."

Now Hecuba the queen discussed with him everything that weighed on her mind. I did not feel comfortable to see such intimacy between my mother and Aeneas's father. But I conceded to her that Anchises made everything easier. He admired Hecuba; you could see he would have admired her no less if she had not been the king's wife. He treated me like a very dear and respected daughter; but he did not talk about his son Aeneas before I spoke of him myself. His tact was as inalienable as his good cheer. He expressed his feelings not only with his mobile face but with the whole of his high, bald skull. Oenone, who loved him like a father, used to say: "His mouth is laughing, but his forehead is sad." You could not help but look at his hands, which were almost always working a piece of wood, or at least feeling it, while his eyes might suddenly listen to find out what quality or form was hidden in the wood. He never had a tree chopped down without first conferring with it at length; without first removing from it a seed or a twig which he could plant in the earth to ensure its continued existence. He knew everything there was to know about wood and trees. And the figures he carved when we sat around together, he then gave away like a prize; they became a sign by which we could recognize each other. If you entered a house and found one of Anchises's carvings, animal or human, you knew you could speak openly, that you could ask for help in any matter, no matter how critical. When the Greeks were massacring all the Amazons, we hid Myrine and a number of her sisters in huts whose anteroom contained a small wooden calf, goat, or pig made by Anchises. Wordlessly the women would draw them over to the fire, throw a piece of clothing over them, blacken their cheeks, press a spindle or a spoon into their hands which knew nothing of women's work, even take the youngest child from the bed and place it in the lap of the harried foreign woman. Not once were we disappointed by a family to whom Anchises gave a carved figure. He knew people. And his hut under the fig tree outside the Dardanian Gate was visited only by people who suited him. Otherwise he would talk with everyone, he did not turn away anyone who wanted to visit him. He welcomed even Andron, the young officer who worked for Eumelos and who had us searched after we had delivered Briseis. That went against my grain very much: for what if Hecuba should run into this man here, where she often came in order to spare Anchises from having to come to her in the palace; what if Oenone, Parthena the nurse, Marpessa, or even Arisbe should meet him! "Why not?" Anchises said, unmoved. "Better here than somewhere else. Go ahead and talk to him. What does it cost you? One shouldn't give up on anyone until he's dead." I felt ashamed without being able to agree with him. As far as I could see, he had no dealings with the gods. But he believed in people. When it came to that, he was younger than all of us. It was at his place, under the changing foliage of the giant fig tree, that we began to live our life of freedom; in the middle of the war, completely unprotected, surrounded by an ever-growing horde of people armed to the teeth. Meanwhile, the internal order of the palace,

which I had taken for eternal, was changing before my un-
believing eyes the way wood chips, straw, and grass floating on a
river are carried along by the stronger current. The stronger
current was the king's party, to which I, his daughter, did not
belong. Instead, it was composed of younger men who went
around in groups, expressed their views loudly when they met,
continually felt they were under attack, believed they had to
defend themselves against reproaches which had never been
voiced, and found officious men—bards, scribes—who supplied
them phrases for their punctilious affectations. "To save face"
was one such phrase. "To show no reaction" was another.
Anchises shook with laughter. "Whatever does that mean!" he
cried. "As if people could *not* save their faces! Or are they telling
us, without realizing it, that the faces they customarily show to
the world are not their own? Simpletons."

Indeed, Anchises made everything easier. For it was not easy
for me to leave the domain of the fig tree, at least that is how
it seemed to me. Part of me—the gay, friendly, unconstrained
part—stayed behind, outside the citadel, with "them." I used to
say "they" when I referred to the people in Anchises's circle,
not "we"; I was not yet allowed to say "we." Vacillating and
fragile and amorphous was the "we" I used, went on using as
long as I possibly could. It included my father, but did it any
longer include me? Yet for me there was no Troy without
King Priam my father. Each evening that part of me which was
loyal to the king, obedient, obsessed with conformity, returned
to the fortress with a heavy heart. The "we" that I clung to
grew transparent, feeble, more and more unprepossessing, and
consequently I was more and more out of touch with my "I."
Yet other people knew perfectly well who I was, they had
established my identity, to them it was clear: I was a prophetess
and interpreter of dreams. An authority figure. When their
future prospects looked bleak, when their own helplessness
afflicted them, they came to me. My dear sister Polyxena had
been the first; she was followed by her women friends and by

her friends' friends. All Troy was dreaming and referring its dreams to me.

Yes. Yes. Yes. Now I will have a talk with myself about Polyxena. About the guilt which cannot be extinguished, not if Clytemnestra were to murder me twenty times over. Polyxena was the last name spoken between Aeneas and me, the occasion of our last (perhaps our only) misunderstanding. He believed that it was on her account that I could not leave with him, and he tried to convince me that I could not help my dead sister by staying. But I knew that, if I knew anything. We did not have time to finish talking about my refusal to go with him, which had to do not with the past but with the future. Aeneas is alive. He will learn of my death. If he is the same man I love, he will continue to wonder why I chose captivity and death rather than him. Perhaps he will understand even without my help what it was that I had to reject at the cost of my life: submission to a role contrary to my nature.

Evasion, digression, those are always my tactics when her name comes up for discussion: Polyxena. She was the other woman. She was the woman I could not be. She had everything I lacked. Of course I know they called me "beautiful," even "the most beautiful," but their faces remained solemn when they said it. When she passed by they all smiled, the highest-ranking priest as well as the humblest slave, the most dim-witted kitchen maid. I search for a word to describe her; I cannot help that; my belief that a successful phrase—words, that is—can capture or even produce every phenomenon and every event, will outlive me. But where she is concerned I fail. She was composed of many elements, of charm and melt-ingness; and of firmness, even hardness. There was a contradiction in her nature that was both maddening and attractive. You wanted to seize it, protect it, or rip it out of her even if you had to destroy her in order to do it. She had many friends whom she did not hold at arm's length, from social strata I did not mix with at that time; she used to sing with them, songs she made up herself. She was kind and at the same time had the evil eye, with which she could see inside me but not inside herself. Yes. It took self-denial for me to accept her, she did not meet me halfway. Since I became priestess, since the year she did not speak to me, we dealt with each other as the custom of the palace required of sisters. But we both knew that we could not avoid a clash, and each of us knew that the other knew.

So I was shocked when she, Polyxena of all people, came to tell me her dreams. And what dreams! Insoluble tangles. And I, I of all people, was supposed to tell her what they meant. She could only hate me after that, and in fact this is what she seemed to want. She delivered herself into my hands with an unbridled, inquiring, and dreaming gaze. She dreamed that she was in a garbage pit and stretched out her arms toward a radiant figure for whom she was consumed with passion. Who was the lucky man, I asked, trying to joke. Did he have a name? Polyxena said dryly, "Yes. It's Andron."

Andron. Eumelos's officer. Words failed me. My accursed office. "Yes," I said. "The things people dream, you know. You dream of the last person you saw that day. It doesn't mean anything, Polyxena." I did not say anything about the garbage pit. Neither did she. She went away disappointed. Came again. In her dream she had coupled in the most degrading way with Andron, Eumelos's officer, whom she hated while she was awake. So she said. So what was wrong with her? "Hey, Sister," I said as hoydenishly as I could, "I believe you need a man." "I have one," she said. "He gives me nothing." She was agonized. Hatefully, as if she was able to take revenge on me at last, she demanded that I tell her what she could not tell herself: That something alien inside her was forcing her to burn with passion for this puffed-up young cub. For this nonentity of a man who had no other way of getting people to talk about him than by entering the dishonorable service of Eumelos. She abhorred him, she said. I cannot say that I was any help to her in the beginning. Instead of loosening the knot that constricted her, I pulled it tighter by my incomprehension. I did not want to know why my sister Polyxena could feel the deepest gratification only by getting down in the dirt and submitting to the unworthiest of men. I could not help the contempt I felt at Polyxena's dreams; of course she sensed this and could not stand it. She began a relationship with Andron in secret. That was unheard-of. Never had any of us sisters had to conceal her amorous inclinations. Incredulous and deeply uneasy, I watched the underside of life in the palace reveal itself, as if it were being turned to disclose a lewd grimace. I watched how its balance overturned as its center shifted. Polyxena was one of the victims the palace buried beneath it.

What I did not understand then, and did not want to understand, was that many were prepared to be victims, not only from the outside, but through something in themselves. Everything in me revolted against that. Why?

Now all of a sudden it is truly still. I am infinitely grateful for the stillness before death. For this moment that fills me completely so that I do not have to think anything. For this bird who flies soundlessly and far away across the sky, transforming it almost imperceptibly. But my eye, which knows the look of all the skies, cannot be deceived. Evening is coming on.

Time is running out. What else do I have to know?

I could not help despising Polyxena because I did not want to despise myself. That cannot be, but I know that is how it is. Why do I go on living if not to learn the things one learns before death? I believe Polyxena perished in a way that was fearful beyond measure, because not she but I was the king's favorite daughter. She perished because I based my life on that tenet for far too long. Because I insisted on its truth. Refused to let it be impugned. To whom else did she confide her secret besides me, her sister; me, the seeress? What use to her, what use to me, to repeat now the phrase I came up with at the time, in my infirmity: "I am only human, too." What is that supposed to mean, "too"? I was overtaxed, that is true. She, Polyxena, expected too much of me, because too much had been expected of her. In short, while she was sleeping with Andron she began to dream about King Priam. Seldom at first but always the same thing; then more often, in the end every night. It was more than she could bear. In her distress she came back to me again, after all. Her father violated her in her dream, she said. She was weeping. No one can answer for his dreams, but one can keep them to oneself. That is what I gave my sister to understand. I believe I was trembling with indignation. Polyxena broke down. I took care of her and made sure that she kept silent. At this time I could not receive Aeneas and he did not come on his own, either. I stopped visiting Anchises. In my entrails sat an animal that gnawed at me and preyed on my mind. Later I learned its name: panic. I found rest only in the temple precincts.

I immersed myself in the ceremonial with seeming fervor, perfected my techniques as a priestess, taught the young priestesses the difficult skill of speaking in chorus, enjoyed the solemn atmosphere on the high feast days, the detachment of the priests from the mass of the faithful, my guiding role in the great pageant; the pious awe and admiration in the looks of the common people; the superiority my office conferred on me. I needed to be present and at the same time unaffected. For by that time I had stopped believing in the gods.

No one noticed that except Panthous, who used to observe me. I could not say for how long I had been an unbeliever. If I had had some shock, an experience resembling conversion, I could remember. But faith ebbed away from me gradually, the way illnesses sometimes ebb away, and one day you tell yourself that you are well. The illness no longer finds any foothold in you. That is how it was with my faith. What foothold could it still have found in me? Two occur to me: first hope, then fear. Hope had left me. I still knew fear, but fear alone does not know the gods; they are very vain, they want to be loved too, and hopeless people do not love them. At that time my aspect began to change. Aeneas was not there, he had been sent away as usual. I felt there was no point in telling anyone anything that was happening inside me. We had to win this war, and I, the king's daughter, believed in it less and less. I was in a fix. Whom could I talk to about that?

On top of this, the progress of the war seemed not to bear me out. Troy was holding its ground. This phrase was a bit too grand, because for some time it was not under threat. The Greeks were plundering the islands and the coastal cities some distance away. They left nothing behind their strong wooden fortifications but a couple of ships, tents, and a small guard troop—too strong for us to destroy them, too weak to attack us. What deprived me of hope was the very way we had gotten used to this state of affairs. How could a Trojan laugh when the enemy lurked outside his gates? And the sunshine. Always sunshine. Phoebus Apollo, darkly radiant, overpowering. The always identical places between which my life elapsed. The shrine. The temple grove, dry that year: the Scamander, which used to irrigate our garden, had dried up. My clay hut, my bed, chair, and table—the quarters I used at times when service to the temple forbade me to leave its precincts. The path to the fortress, sloping gently upward, always accompanied by two guards who were supposed to follow two steps behind me and did not speak with me because I did not permit it. The gate in the wall. The cry of the guards, always a different silly password to which the sentries above gave a silly reply. "Down with the enemy!" "Send them to blazes!" That kind of thing. Then the scrutiny of the officer of the watch. The sign for the gate to be opened. Always the same tedious route to the palace, always the same faces outside the craftsmen's houses. And when I had entered the palace, the always identical corridors leading to the always identical rooms. Only the people I met seemed to me more and more alien. To this day I do not know how I managed not to notice that I was a captive. That I was working under compulsion the way prisoners work. That my limbs no longer moved of their own free will, that I had lost all desire to walk, breathe, sing. Everything required a long-drawn-out act of decision. "Get up!" I ordered myself. "Now walk!" And what an effort everything was. The unloved duty inside me ate up all my joy. Troy was impregnable to the enemy; it became so for me as well.

Figures move through this unmoving picture. Many have no names. That was the time when I forgot names quickly and had trouble learning new ones. All of a sudden there were many old people, old men. I used to run into them in the corridors of the palace, which at other times were totally deserted: half-crippled mummies, laboriously pushed along by slaves. They were going to the council. Then I also used to see my brothers, who otherwise spent their time with the troops: Hector-Dim-Cloud, who always spoke to me, wanted to hear how I was, how the women were; who entrusted Andromache, whom he loved deeply, to our protection. And Paris, crushed, smiling a crooked smile, only the shell of his former self, but more sharp-edged than ever. I was told he would stop at nothing—not where Greeks were concerned but Trojans; a dangerous man. He had one disgrace after another to make up for, all his life. He was not one you could count on. (Yes. It was then that I began—I could not seem to help myself—to divide the people I met into two groups in view of an unknown future emergency. You can count on him, but not on him. What was I doing it for? I did not want to know. Later it turned out that I had rarely been wrong.)

And King Priam, my father. He was a special case, and special to me. He crumbled. That was the word. King Priam crumbled as increasingly he was forced to flaunt his rank as king. He sat stiffly at the great celebrations in the hall court, in a seat which recently had been elevated beside and above Hecuba, and listened to the hymns in his praise. In his praise and in praise of the heroic deeds of the Trojans. New minstrels had sprung up; or the old ones, if they were still tolerated, changed their text. The new texts were glory-gabbing, showy, and sycophantic. Impossible that I was the only one who noticed that. I looked around me: the lusterless faces. They had themselves under tight rein. Did we have to behave this way? "Yes," said Panthous, with whom I had begun to talk again sometimes, because I had no one else. He told me the gist of the directive which had just been issued to the high priests of all the temples: The emphasis in all ceremonies was to be shifted from the dead heroes to the living ones. I was dismayed. Our faith, our self-confidence was founded on the veneration of dead heroes. It was they whom we invoked when we said "eternal" and "infinite." Their greatness, which we regarded as unattainable, made us, the living, modest. That was just the point. "Do you believe," Panthous said, "that modest heroes who can hope to achieve glory only after death are the right opponents for the immodest Greeks? Don't you think it more prudent to sing of the living heroes rather than the dead ones, and thus avoid revealing how many have already been killed?" "But don't you see how much more dangerous it is to agitate the foundations of our unity carelessly!" I said. "That you of all people should say that, Cassandra," said Panthous. "You yourself believe in nothing. Just like Eumelos and his men, who are at the bottom of everything. How are you any different from them?"

Coolly I set him straight. Would this Greek man reprimand a Trojan woman? How could I prove to him, or to myself, that he was wrong? At night I did not sleep. The headache began. What did I believe in, anyway?

If you can hear me, listen now, Aeneas. We never got this matter clear. I still have to explain it to you. No, I did not feel a twinge at your behavior; I understood why you were withdrawn even when you were with me, even when you lay with me; I understood that you could no longer bear to listen to my foolish, never-ending protest: "I want the same thing they do!" The only thing is, Why did you not contradict me? Why did you not spare me forgetting myself so far as to say the same thing to Eumelos himself, when he and I had our first truly open, bitter confrontation?

It was after Achilles the brute had captured our poor brother Lycaon and sold him to the odious king of Lemnos in exchange for a precious bronze vessel—an insult that made Priam groan aloud. There seemed to be only one person in the citadel who knew how to answer the infamous presumption of the enemy: that man was Eumelos. He tightened the screws. He cast his security net (which hitherto had strangled the royal household and the civil service) across all of Troy; now it applied to everyone. The citadel was locked after darkness fell. Strict personal searches whenever Eumelos deemed necessary. Special authorizations for the security personnel.

"Eumelos," I said, "that is impossible." (Naturally I knew that it was possible.) "And why?" he asked with icy politeness. "Because by doing that we'll be hurting ourselves more than the Greeks." "I'd like to hear you say that again," he said. Fear gripped me then. "Eumelos," I cried imploringly—I am still ashamed of that—"Please believe me! I want the same thing you people do."

He pursed his lips tightly. I could not win him over. He said formally: "Excellent. Then you will support our measures." He left me standing there like a dumb clod. He was nearing the height of his power.

Why was I so downcast? So downcast that I got involved in an interior dialogue with Eumelos—with Eumelos!—that went on for days and nights? Things had come to a sorry pass. I wanted to convince Eumelos. But of what! That is what you asked me, Aeneas; I was mute. Today I would say I wanted to convince him that we could not become like Achilles, just to save ourselves. To convince him that it was not yet proved that, just to save ourselves, we had to become like the Greeks. And even if it were proved, wasn't it more important to live in our own way, by our own law, than just to live? But who was I trying to fool? For was it true, what I said? Wasn't it more important to survive? Wasn't that the most important thing of all? The only thing that mattered? Does that mean that Eumelos was the man of the hour?

But what if for a long time we had been facing a different question altogether: Whether to take on the enemy's face knowing that we would be destroyed anyhow?

Listen, Aeneas. Please understand me. I could not go through that again. Many days I lay on my bed, drank a little goat's milk, had the windows draped, closed my eyes, and remained motionless, simply not to remind the animal who was tearing at my brain of my existence. Marpessa walked very softly up and down; she fetched Oenone, who gently stroked my forehead and neck as only she knew how. Her hands were always cold now. Was winter coming already?

Yes, winter was coming. The great autumn market had been held outside the gates, the ghost of a market. The vendors were Eumelos's men in disguise; the real vendors stood among them, frozen. The customers were Eumelos's men in disguise; we, the customers, stood among them fumbling with terror. Who was acting whose part? In tight formations, insecure, impudent, the Greeks. By chance I was wedged in next to Agamemnon while he bought a very expensive, beautiful necklace from a goldsmith without haggling over the price. And then he bought a second, identical necklace and held it out to me: "Isn't it beautiful?" A deathly silence stretching from horizon to horizon surrounded us. I said quietly, almost amiably: "Yes. It's very beautiful, Agamemnon." "You know me," said Agamemnon. "How should I not?" He looked at me strangely for a long time; I could not interpret his gaze. Then he said softly, so that only I could understand him: "For the life of me I'd like to give this to my daughter. She is no more. Somehow she resembled you. You take it." Then he gave me the necklace and left hurriedly.

None of my family ever mentioned this necklace. I wore it sometimes, I am wearing it still. A little while ago I saw its mate around Clytemnestra's neck; she saw the mate of hers around mine. We reached up to touch our necklaces with an identical gesture, looked at each other, agreed as only women agree.

I asked Panthous in passing: "Which daughter was that?" "Iphigenia," he said. "And it's true what they say about her?" "Yes. He sacrificed her. Your Calchas ordered him to."

They act in haste and foolishly. Believe the incredible. Do what they do not want to do, and mourn their victims with self-pity.

The fear is back again.

New troops from outlying provinces had arrived in the citadel, you often saw black and brown faces in the streets now, troops of warriors squatted everywhere around campfires; all of a sudden it was no longer advisable for us women to be out alone. If you saw it properly—only no one ventured to do that —the men of both sides seemed to have joined forces against our women. Demoralized, they withdrew into the winter caves of their houses, to the glowing fires and the children. In the temple they prayed with a fervor that displeased me because they wanted our god Apollo to serve as substitute for their stolen life. I could not stand it any longer. Protected by my priestess's robes, I went to see Anchises again. Whenever I came to see him after a long interval away, I felt as if my visits to him had never been interrupted. Admittedly, two young women whom I did not know got up and left, in a natural way, without embarrassment; but it hurt nonetheless. Anchises had just begun to weave those tall baskets. Everyone took it as a whim, but now that you are on the road, Aeneas, where could you have stowed your supplies, where could you have carried your father, light as he has become now, if not in a basket of this kind?

So he did not stop preparing the reeds while we talked. We

always began by talking about remote subjects. He always served me that wine from Mount Ida that got into my blood, and flat barley cakes he had baked himself. I told him word for word the conversation I had had with Eumelos.

Then he jumped up, threw his bald head back, and roared with laughter. "Yes! I can well believe it! That's just like the scalawag!"

Whenever he laughed I used to laugh with him. Already everything was easier, but the most important part was still to come; Anchises instructed me. When he instructed me he used to call me "girl." "So, girl, pay attention now. Eumelos needs Achilles the way one old shoe needs the other. But there is a primitive trick behind it, a flaw in his reasoning which he has passed on to you in all his diabolical innocence. And this trick can work only so long as you do not come on its weak point. Namely: He is presupposing what he had still to create: war. Once he has gotten that far, he can take this war as the normal state and presuppose that there is only one way out: victory. In this case, of course, the enemy dictates the courses open to you. Then you are caught in a vise and you have to choose between two evils, Achilles and Eumelos. Don't you see, girl, how Achilles has come along at just the right time for Eumelos? How he could not wish for a better adversary than that fiend?"

Yes, yes, I saw. I was grateful to Anchises, drew the conclusions he left me to draw. So we ought to have arrested the evil before its name became "war." We ought not to have let Eumelos become established. We—who then? The king, Priam, my father. The conflict for me remained. It had been shifted from Eumelos to King Priam. And in the conflict lay the fear.

I was afraid, Aeneas. That was the thing you were never willing to believe. You did not know what that kind of fear was. I have a fear-memory. A feeling-memory. How often you laughed, when you returned from one of your many journeys, because I could not give you the kind of report of events you expected. Who had killed whom by what methods, who was rising or falling in the hierarchy, who had fallen in love with whom, who had stolen whose wife: you had to ask other people to find out these things. I knew it all of course, that was not the point. It is those who are not involved in events who learn most about them. But although I did not wish it, my memory simply did not take these facts seriously enough. As if they were not real. Not real enough. As if they were shadow-deeds. How can I explain to you? I will give you an example. Polyxena.

Oh, Aeneas. I can see her every feature as if she were standing before me, her face in which misfortune was inscribed: how was it that I could see that? And how was it that I could hear that undertone to her voice which inspired my melting fear that my sister would come to a bad end? How often I felt like grabbing her hands and shrieking aloud what I saw. Why did I hold back? Why did I brace all my muscles against this fear-based certainty? No one need tell me why the birth of the twins was so difficult. My muscles have turned hard. I had the feeling that I was screening with my body the place through which, unbeknown to everyone but me, other realities were seeping into our solid-bodied world, realities which our five agreed-upon senses do not grasp: for which reason we must deny them.

Words. Everything I tried to convey about that experience was, and is, paraphrase. We have no name for what spoke out of me. I was its mouth, and not of my own free will. It had to subdue me before I would breathe a word it suggested. It was the enemy who spread the tale that I spoke "the truth" and that you all would not listen to me. They did not spread it out of malice, that was just how they understood it. For the Greeks there is no alternative but either truth or lies, right or wrong, victory or defeat, friend or enemy, life or death. They think differently than we do. What cannot be seen, smelled, heard, touched, does not exist. It is the other alternative that they crush between their clear-cut distinctions, the third alternative, which in their view does not exist, the smiling vital force that is able to generate itself from itself over and over: the undivided, spirit in life, life in spirit. Anchises once said that the gift of empathy could be more important for the Greeks than the accursed invention of iron. If only they could embrace someone besides themselves within the iron concepts of good and evil. Us, for example.

Their singers will pass on none of all this.

And what if they—or we—did pass it on? What would be the result? Nothing. Unfortunately or fortunately, nothing. Not song, only commands do more than stir the air. That is not my tenet, it is Penthesilea's. She despised what she called my "affectations." "Your dreams against their javelins!" she said. She had an awkward, miserable way of laughing. I would have been only too happy to prove my point to her. She turned out to be right, you might say, if there is any right on the side of the javelins. I understood too late (once again too late!) that she offered herself, her life, her body, to carry the wrong too far in the sight of us all. The abyss of hopelessness in which she lived.

One day Hecuba and Polyxena came into the temple just at the time I was serving there. The strange thing was that they wanted to sacrifice to Apollo and not, as they usually preferred, to our protectress Athena, whose temple was much more conveniently located in the city. They did not tell me the purpose of their sacrifice—fruits of the field. I saw only how at one they were, and my heart contracted. Their appeal to the deity—I learned much, much later—was so unnatural that they could not make it to a goddess but only to a male god: Polyxena feared she was pregnant, and they asked Apollo to take the pregnancy from her. She wanted no child by Andron, to whom she was as much a slave as ever. Why did the conflict she lived with appear on her face in that hour as a fragile, beseeching expression? Why did Achilles the brute have to see that expression? My breath stopped cold when he walked in. He had kept away from Apollo ever since he had killed my brother

Troilus here, even though—regrettably in my opinion—negotiations had determined that this temple was to be a neutral place, open to the Greeks too, for the purposes of worshipping their god. So in he came, Achilles the brute, and saw my sister Polyxena; and I, from the altar where you can see everything, saw that he saw her. How much she resembled our brother Troilus. How Achilles devoured her with his hideous glances, which I knew well. I think I whispered: "Polyxena." Then dropped in a faint. When I woke up, leather-cheeked old Herophile sat beside me. "She is lost, Polyxena is lost," I said. "Get up, Cassandra," said Herophile. "Pull yourself together. Don't let yourself go like that. Now is not the time for visions. What is supposed to happen, happens. We are not here to prevent it. So don't make a fuss."

All of a sudden our temple became a much-sought-after spot. Lower-level negotiators met there, to arrange the crucial rendezvous: The Trojan Hector met the Greek hero Achilles. I stayed in the chamber behind the altar, where you can hear every word. I heard what I already knew: The Greek hero Achilles wanted the Trojan princess Polyxena. Hector, who had learned from Panthous that among the Greeks fathers and elder brothers exercise authority over their daughters and sisters, seemed to go along with Achilles' wishes, as it was agreed he should. Fine, he said, he would hand over his sister if Achilles in turn would reveal to us the layout of the Greek camp. I thought I had heard him wrong. Never before had Troy demanded of an adversary that he betray his own people. Never had it sold one of its daughters to the enemy at such a price. Andron, to whom Polyxena was so attached, stood motionless behind brother Hector. And Achilles the brute, though he had proved that he did not fear the sanctuary, did not go for either of their throats. Could he suspect how closely the first ring of armed men had surrounded the shrine? Hardly. He said he would consider the whole thing; but he would like to be allowed to see Polyxena once more. Strange to say, brother Hector did not want to permit this. Then friend Andron intervened with his sprightly voice. "Why ever not!" I heard him say. Oh, Sister, I thought, if only you could hear him, your pretty good-for-nothing. It was agreed that that evening Polyxena would show herself to her future owner on the wall beside the Scaean Gate.

I begged Polyxena not to show herself. "Why ever not?" she said, just like Andron. So she had no reason not to; but was that enough? What positive reason did she have? "Do you love this brute? Are you capable even of that!" I said before I could stop myself. That is the sentence I cannot forgive myself for. It transported my sister beyond my reach. I saw it at once, by the expression on her face: transported. In panic I grabbed her hands, apologized, kept on at her as if I were out of my senses. In vain. In the evening before sunset she stood on the wall wearing that new, remote smile, and looked down on Achilles. He stared. He was almost drooling. Then my sister Polyxena slowly bared her breast, while at the same time—still with that faraway gaze—she looked at us: her lover, her brother, her sister. I answered her look imploringly. "Hey, Hector!" Achilles the brute roared up at us in a hoarse voice. "Do you hear me? I agree to your terms."

The terms were agreed upon. For months my sister Polyxena was the most admired woman in Troy. She had wanted that—to punish those she loved by ruining herself. The deeds the war gave birth to were abortions. When she offered her breast to the Greek, Polyxena had lost Andron's child in the form of a little clot of blood. Triumphantly, shamelessly, she made it known. She was free, she said, free. Nothing, no one had a hold on her.

That is how it was.

I went to Anchises. The company I used to meet with were still there. My suspicion was correct: Slave women from the Greek camp used to meet here with the women from our city. And why not? It took more than that to surprise me nowadays.

So I thought. Then they surprised me, after all. We learned that Achilles had absolutely refused to go on fighting for the Greeks. Plague had overrun the Greek camp; the seer Calchas claimed it had been sent by the god Apollo. A little slave girl whom the great Agamemnon regarded as his property must (Calchas said) be restored to her father, who also happened to be a seer. Agamemnon had to be indemnified for his loss. No doubt with some assistance from her father Calchas, Briseis, our Briseis, was taken away from Achilles, who for so long had been free to do as he liked with her, and assigned to the great fleet commander, Agamemnon. The slave girls said he kept her in a special tent. That he did not visit her either by day or by night. The only man who visited her, they said, was her father Calchas, who had gone completely gray. When I ventured to ask how she was, the only reply was a long mute look.

I was freezing. I felt cold to the innermost fiber of my body. Anchises seemed to know how I felt. "Aeneas is coming," he said softly. "Did you already know?" Then warm blood pumped into my face. Aeneas came. His ship got through. I was alive. Aeneas was depressed. He had been drawn into the war completely. He had brought hope of reinforcements. Delaying tactics had to be employed against the Greeks. Single combats were held between some of their men and some of ours. Actually they were athletic contests fought by rules acceptable to the Greeks. All Troy stood along the wall watching the duel between our Hector and Ajax the Great—a particular pleasure because we saw that Hector's tenacious training had paid off. As a fighter Hector-Dim-Cloud was a match for anyone. Hecuba went away, white-faced. The two heroes exchanged their arms, and the fools along the walls applauded. Arms of woe. Achilles the brute used Ajax's sword-belt to tie Hector to his chariot when he dragged him around the citadel. And Ajax the Great used Hector's sword to commit suicide when he was preyed on by madness.

Objects slipped out of our hands and turned against us, so

then we attributed exaggerated significance to them. What expense went into the manufacture of Hector's shield, sword, javelin, and armor! He was entitled (it was said) not only to the best weapons but to the most beautiful. Once I ran into him—early spring was already in the air—outside the armorers' door. He joined me notwithstanding our accompaniment by Eumelos's guards. Sometimes a single conversation is enough. It turned out that he had been observing me. "You seem to be drifting away from me, Sister," he said, without reproach in his voice. "But do you know where you're going?" No question had touched me so much for a long time. Hector. Dear one. He knew that he only had a short time to live. I knew that he knew. What could I have said to him? I told him that Troy was no longer Troy. That I did not know how to deal with that. That I felt like an injured animal in a trap, seeing no way out. Whenever I think of Hector I feel the edge of the wall down my back as I pressed up against it, and smell horse dung mixed with earth. He put his arm around my shoulder, drew me to him. "Little sister. Always so exacting. Always such grand aims. Maybe you have to be that way, we have to put up with you. Too bad you're not a man. You could go and fight. Believe me, sometimes that's better." Better than what? We smiled.

Otherwise only our eyes spoke. Said that we loved each other. That we had to say goodbye to each other. Never again, Hector, dear one, did I want to be a man. I often thanked those powers which answer for our sex that I was allowed to be a woman. That I did not have to be present on the day we both knew you would fall; that I could avoid the battlefield where Achilles was up to his old mischief after our men killed his dearest friend, Patroclus. Achilles' slave girl came to Anchises, her features distorted. In order to appease her obstinate master, Agamemnon had brought Briseis, our Briseis, back to him personally. In what a state! The girl was weeping. No, she would never go back. Let us do what we liked with her. Arisbe made a sign to the charming Oenone. This young slave girl, who asked us to hide her, marked the beginning of the free and easy life in the caves. Next summer I saw her again; she was a changed person. I, too, was ready to become that changed person who had been stirring inside me for so long already, underneath the despair, pain, and grief. The first stirring I allowed was the stab of envy when the slave girl of Achilles went off I knew not where, clasping Oenone tightly. "What about me? Save me too!" I almost cried. But I had still to experience what lay in store for me: the day when I lay on my wickerwork bed in a cold sweat knowing that Hector was entering the battlefield, and knowing that he was being killed.

I do not know how it happened; no one was ever allowed to tell me about it, not even Aeneas, who was present, although I felt no concern for his safety. In the deepest depths, in the innermost core of me, where body and soul are not yet divided and where not a single word or a single thought can penetrate, I experienced the whole of Hector's fight, his wounding, his tenacious resistance, and his death. It is not too much to say that I *was* Hector: because it would not be nearly enough to say I was joined with him. Achilles the brute stabbed him to death, stabbed me to death; mutilated him, fastened him on to his chariot by Ajax's sword-belt, dragged him many times around the fortress. I was, living, what Hector became dead: a chunk of raw meat. Insensible. My mother's shrieks, my father's howls: far away. Should he entreat Achilles to give him back the corpse, the king wanted to know. Why ever not? The way my father walked the floor at night. If I had still been I, it would have moved me infinitely. It moved me a little that when he came across Achilles sleeping, he could not bring himself to assault him treacherously. Then I was standing unmoved on the wall once more, at the familiar spot beside the Scaean Gate. Below were the scales. On one side of the scales was a mass of raw meat that had once been our brother Hector; and on the other all the gold we had, for Hector's murderer.

This was the low point or the high point of the war. The coldness inside me. Andromache lying inanimate on the ground. And Polyxena's face, which suited this occasion, the voluptuousness of self-destruction. The contemptuous way she threw her bracelets and chains onto the mountain of gold, which still fell a little short of the weight of Hector's corpse. We were learning new things at a dazzling rate. Until now we did not know that dead people were worth their weight in gold. Then we learned another new thing: You could exchange a living woman for a dead man. Achilles shouted up to Priam: "Hey, King! Give me your beautiful daughter Polyxena and keep your gold."

Polyxena's laughter. And the king's reply, quickly agreed upon with Eumelos and Andron: "Persuade Menelaus to give up Helen, and you can have my daughter Polyxena."

From that day on I stopped dreaming, a bad sign. That day and the following night, that part of me from which dreams come, even bad dreams, was destroyed. Achilles the brute occupied every inch of space outside and inside us. That night, when he cremated the body of his darling Patroclus, Achilles the brute butchered twelve captives as a sacrifice, the noblest born, among them two sons of Hecuba and Priam. That night the gods abandoned us. Twelve times the cry, that of an animal. Each time my mother's fingernails dug deeper into my flesh. Then thirteen funeral pyres—one enormous and twelve smaller ones—sent their crackling, dreadful red flames against the black sky. There was a smell of charred flesh; the wind was coming from the sea. Twelve times the red-hot iron burned out of us that place from which pain, love, life, dreams can come. The nameless softness that makes human beings human. When Hecuba dropped behind me, she was an old woman, hollow-cheeked, white-haired. Andromache a whimpering bundle in the corner. Polyxena sharp and resolute like a sword. Priam, devoid of all royalty, a sick old man.

Troy lay dark, deathly still. A troop of our warriors, led by my brother Paris, stormed into the cellar rooms of the citadel where the Greek captives crouched shaking with fear. One of the palace maidservants came and fetched me. I went into the cellar, which stank of decay, sweat, and excrement. The Trojans and the Greek captives stood facing each other in trembling silence, separated by an abyss one step wide; above the abyss the bright blades of the Trojans. Then I walked, without my priestly garments, along the narrow interval, grazed by the hot breath of the Greeks, the cold blades of the Trojans; step by step, from one wall to the other. Everything still. Behind me the Trojan blades lowered. The Greeks wept. How I loved my countrymen.

Paris blocked my way at the exit. So, Priestess, you do not permit my men to repay deeds in kind. I said: No.

That was almost the only word left for me to say.

Panthous drew my attention to the fact that words have physical effects. "No" had a contracting, "yes" a relaxing, effect. However did it happen, why did I let it happen, why did Aeneas stay away so long? Panthous approached me again. Even though we could no longer stand each other. I got angry for no reason when I merely looked at him—narrow, shrunken, wearing the women's garments of the priest, and the big head on top. Always the cynical grin. I did not like people on whom you could smell the fear. He could not bear compassion that had contempt in it. Without my noticing, spring had come again. We were standing under the olive trees in the grove of Apollo, at evening. It had struck me that I never saw Panthous anymore except in the vicinity of the temple. "Yes," he said. "Beyond this fence begins the wilderness. The danger." I took a long, thorough look at him. Which animal did he resemble now? A threatened polecat. Drawing his lips back from his teeth in fear, in seeming disgust, and baring his eyeteeth. Attacking because he is afraid. I felt sick. An image came over me, I could not stave it off. People with clubs were driving a polecat out of his den, through the temple precincts, chasing him out of the reserve and killing him; he died with a whistling, hissing sound.

He saw the dismay in my eyes and threw himself on me, buried me underneath him, stammered my name into my ear, begged for help. I gave in to him. Responded to him. He failed. In his rage and disappointment he hissed like the animal.

It came out that I had saved his life that night along with the others: he had been in the cellar among the captive Greeks. He could not forgive me for not having been afraid of the sword blades. "You people won't get me," he hissed. "The Greeks won't get me, either." He showed me the capsule with the powder. He was right. We did not get him, nor did the Greeks—the Amazons got him.

Penthesilea's women. Aeneas (it now appeared) had led them here by a safe route. He, with his white hands, walked along beside dark Penthesilea with her wild black hair that stood out from her head in all directions. Was I deceived, or did Aeneas's gaze cling to her? Then came Myrine, little pony, out of breath at the end of a long race that had no further destination. What did that woman want in Troy? People told me, Aeneas told me: "She is looking for battle." So had we reached the point that anyone who was looking for a battle, man or woman, was welcome here? Aeneas said, "Yes, we have reached that point." He expressed very guarded views of the small, tightly knit band of women. Guardedly we lay side by side, talking about Penthesilea. It was crazy. I could not say a word about the night when the Greeks killed the captives. Aeneas did not ask. His body glowed white, white in the darkness. He touched me. Nothing stirred. I wept. Aeneas wept. They had finished us. Desolately we parted. Dear one. When we really parted later on, there were no tears, no comfort either. Something like anger on your side, resolution on mine; each of us understood the other. We were not yet through with each other. To separate that way is harder, easier.

These words have no meaning for us. Harder, easier. How can you draw such fine distinctions when everything has become unbearable?

What does that mean? What is going on? What do these

people want? My chariot driver is leading old women and men to me (apparently secretly), old people from Mycenae who seem to approach me with reverence. "Marpessa, do you see that?" "I see it, Cassandra." "Can you guess what they want?" "As well as you do." "I don't want to." "Tell them, but it won't help." Our chariot driver is acting as their spokesman. They want me to tell them the fate of their city.

Poor people.

How they resemble my Trojans.

Do you see, Aeneas, that is what I meant: the same thing all over again.

If I tell them I know nothing, they will not believe me. If I tell them what I see coming, which anyone else could do as well, they will kill me. That would not be such a bad thing, but their own queen would punish them for it. Or does no one have me under surveillance here as they did in Troy? What if in captivity I am free to express myself? Dear enemies. Who am I to see you as nothing but the victors, instead of as the ones who will live? The ones who must live so that what we call life will continue. These poor victors must live on for all the people they have killed.

I tell them: "If you can stop being victorious, this your city will endure."

"Permit me a question, Seeress" (the chariot driver). "Ask." "You do not believe that, do you?" "Believe what?" "That we can stop being victorious." "I do not know of any victor who could stop." "So if victory after victory means destruction in the end, then destruction is planted in our nature?"

The question of questions. What a shrewd man.

"Come closer, Chariot Driver. Listen. I believe that we do not know our nature. That I do not know anything. So in the future there may be people who know how to turn their victory into life."

"In the future, Seeress. I am asking about Mycenae. About myself and my children. About our royal house."

I am silent. I see the corpse of his king, drained of blood like a head of livestock at the butcher's. I tremble. The chariot driver, suddenly pale, steps back. I must say nothing more to him.

It will not be long now.

Who was Penthesilea? Clearly I did not give her enough credit, and she did not give enough credit to me. Sharp-eyed and sharp-tongued, she was a shade too strident for my taste. Her every appearance, her every sentence, was a challenge to someone. She was not looking for allies among us. She was not merely fighting the Greeks; she was fighting all men. I saw that Priam was afraid of her, and Eumelos surrounded her with a thick security cordon. But the dread the common people felt at her unqualified attitudes surrounded her more impenetrably than any screening service. We suspected, but mostly did not want to know, what things lay behind her that still lay ahead of us. "Better to die fighting than to be made slaves," her women said. She had them all in the palm of her hand and would incite or pacify them however she chose, by moving her little finger. She ruled as only kings rule. The worthy Trojans whispered in horror that these women had killed their own menfolk. They were monsters with only one breast (it was said), who had burned out the other at a tender age in order to use their bows more efficiently. Thereupon they appeared bare-trunked in the temple of Athena, showing their beautiful naked breasts and carrying their weapons. "Artemis," they said—that is what they called Pallas Athena—"carries a spear herself; she would not want us to come to her unarmed." The priests sent all the Trojans out of the temple and let the warrior women have it for their wild rituals. "They kill whomever they love, love in order to kill," said Panthous. Strange to say, I ran into Penthesilea and Myrine at Anchises's place. Normally they could not stand to have men anywhere near them. They put up with Anchises, who looked at them with a wily and unprejudiced gaze. All the women I knew were there. They said they wanted to get to know each other.

It turned out that in many ways they were at one. I say

"they," for I held back at first. That part of the inhabited world which we knew had turned against us ever more cruelly, ever more swiftly. "Against us women," said Penthesilea. "Against us people," Arisbe replied.

Penthesilea: The men are getting what they paid for.

Arisbe: You call it getting what they paid for when they are reduced to the level of butchers?

Penthesilea: They are butchers. So they are doing what they enjoy.

Arisbe: And what about us? What if we became butchers, too?

Penthesilea: Then we are doing what we have to do. But we don't enjoy it.

Arisbe: We should do what they do in order to show that we are different?

Penthesilea: Yes.

Oenone: But one can't live that way.

Penthesilea: Not live? You can die all right.

Hecuba: Child, you want everything to come to a stop.

Penthesilea: That is what I want. Because I don't know any other way to make the men stop.

Then the young slave woman from the Greek camp came over to her, knelt down before her, and laid Penthesilea's hands against her face. She said: "Penthesilea. Come join us." "Join you? What does that mean?" "Come to the mountains. The forest. The caves along the Scamander. Between killing and dying there is a third alternative: living."

The young slave woman's remark cut me to the quick. So they were living. Without me. They knew each other. The girl I called the "young slave woman" was called Killa. It seemed that Oenone (whom I never saw in Paris's vicinity anymore) was her friend, they suited each other. Marpessa, my servant, seemed to enjoy great respect in that world. Oh, to be part of it! The same bright longing in Myrine's eyes. It was the first open look we afforded each other.

Penthesilea: "No." The spark in Myrine's eyes went out at once. Violently I reproached Penthesilea: "You want to die, and you are forcing the others to accompany you."

That is the second sentence I regret.

"What!" shrieked Penthesilea. "You speak to me like that! You of all people: neither fish nor fowl!"

It would not have taken much for us to fly at each other's throat.

I had forgotten all that until now. Because I did not want to admit that a woman could crave death. And because her death made ash of everything we had known of her before. We had believed that the terror could not increase, but now we had to recognize that there are no limits to the atrocities people can inflict on one another; that we are capable of rummaging through someone else's entrails and of cracking his skull, trying to find out what causes the most pain. I say "we," and of all the "we's" I eventually said, this is still the one that challenges me most. It is so much easier to say "Achilles the brute" than to say this "we."

Why am I moaning? Marpessa was there—you were there, Marpessa, when Myrine, a bloody heap, scratched at the door of the hut where we had taken refuge. It was black as death, no fires burned that night to light it up, the dead were not gathered until morning. There was not a single spot on Myrine's body where we could touch her without her moaning with pain. I can still see the face of the farm woman in whose hut we found shelter, while Myrine lay before us and we dabbed her wounds with an herbal juice. We—you and I, Marpessa—had no tears. I was hoping it would be over quickly. When we heard the Greeks entering these huts for the first time in their search for Amazon stragglers, we threw a mountain of unspun wool over Myrine in the corner: her little scrap of breath did not stir the mountain. We squatted around the fire in filthy, torn clothing. I remember that I was sharpening a knife to cut up vegetables, and that when a Greek burst in, his gaze fell on the knife at the same moment mine did. Then we looked at each other. He had understood me. He did not touch me. To save face he took away with him the goat that Anchises had carved, which had stood in a wall niche. Weeks later, when Myrine became aware of what had happened, she could not forgive herself for having been saved. She would not say a word but Penthesilea's name. Yes, I am moaning again the way we moaned then whenever we thought or heard that name. Myrine did not leave her side during the battle. When Achilles was taking Penthesilea to task, five men held Myrine; I saw the hemorrhages under her skin. Other women told us about it, not Myrine. Achilles was beside himself with amazement when he ran across Penthesilea during the battle. He began to play with her, she thrust at him. They say that Achilles shook himself; he must have believed he was out of his mind. A woman—greeting him with a sword! The fact that she forced him to take her seriously was her last triumph. They fought for a long time; all the Amazons had been thrust away from Penthesilea. He threw her down, wanted to take her captive; she scratched him with her dagger and forced him to kill her. The gods be praised for that if for nothing else.

I can see what happened next as if I had been present. Achilles the Greek hero desecrates the dead woman. The man, incapable of loving the living woman, hurls himself on the dead victim so that he can go on killing her. And I moan. Why? She did not feel it. We felt it, all of us women. What will become of us if that spreads? The men, weak, whipped up into victors, need us as victims in order not to stop feeling altogether. Where is that leading? Even the Greeks felt that Achilles had gone too far. So they went further in order to punish him: Had horses drag the dead woman across the field—he wept for her now—and threw her into the river. Flay the woman in order to strike at the man.

Yes. Yes. Yes. A monster was on the loose and raged through the camps. White-eyed, its features distorted, it raged in the van of the formation that carried Penthesilea's corpse, and kept growing larger on the way from the river where they had pulled her out. Amazons, Trojan women, nothing but women. A procession leading nowhere on earth: leading to madness. Not one Greek was to be seen. When they reached the temple, where I was doing the service, they were no longer recognizable. The companions of the corpse came to resemble human beings as little as she did. Not to speak of the howling. They were at the end of their tether and they knew it; but knowledge had wiped out the zone in which one knows. Their knowledge was in their flesh, which hurt unbearably—the howling!—in their hair, teeth, fingernails, in the marrow of their bones. They suffered beyond all measure, and suffering like that has its own law. "Everything it gives rise to falls on the heads of those who caused it": that is what I said later to the council. At the time, facing the women, facing the corpse, I was torn by an anguish that never left me afterward, no matter what happened. I learned to laugh again—unbelievable miracle—but the anguish remained. This is the end of us.

They laid Penthesilea under a willow tree. They wanted me to begin the dirge. I did so, softly, in a broken voice. The women, standing in a circle, chimed in shrilly. Began to sway. Sang louder, twitched. One threw back her head, the others followed. Their bodies convulsed. One woman staggered inside the circle, began to dance beside the corpse, stamping her feet, throwing out her arms and shaking. The screeches grew deafening. The woman inside the circle lost control of herself. Her mouth was wide open and foaming. Two, three, four other women lost control of their limbs, reached the point where the pinnacle of pain is indistinguishable from the pinnacle of pleasure. I felt the rhythm transfer itself to me. As the dance began inside me, I felt a strong temptation to abandon myself now, when things were beyond help, and exit from time. The rhythm told me that my feet preferred to exit from time, and I was about to surrender to it completely. Let the wilderness engulf us again. Let the undivided, the unmanifested, the primal cause, devour us. Dance, Cassandra, move! Yes, I am coming. Everything in me urged its way toward them.

But then the wretched Panthous appeared. "Go away!" I screamed, and at the same time a Trojan woman screamed: "A Greek!" The rhythm broke down. Keen, dead sober, plans to save him sped through me. Divert the women, hide the man. Too late. Eumelos! Not there. Why not. The gift of prophecy! Apollo, do not let down your priestess now, let her save your priest. I raised my arms, closed my eyes, shrieked as loudly as I could: "Apollo! Apollo!"

Panthous had already turned to run away. If only he had stood still! Maybe the women would have followed me, not him. For several seconds there was a deathly stillness. Then this shriek, a shriek of murder and despair. They ran me down. I lay there for dead beside dead Penthesilea. Sister, I envy you the fact that you cannot hear. I heard. The drumming steps of the pursuers. The moment they stopped. The hiss, the hiss of the polecat. The sound of wood striking flesh. The cracking of a skull. And then the stillness. "Penthesilea, let's exchange places. Hey, my dear. Nothing is sweeter than death. Come, my friend, and give me your aid. I cannot go on."

I was very light to carry, Aeneas said later. No, he did not mind having to carry me so far. What hurt him was the way I called him "friend" with someone quite different in mind. He swore not to leave me alone anymore. He kept the vow when he could. In the end I released him from it.

So I came to the women in the caves, carried in Aeneas's arms. "Someone had to carry you to get you here," they used to tease me later. "Otherwise you would not come."

Would I have stayed away otherwise? Out of arrogance? I do not know. It seemed, did it not, that everything was repeating itself, everything from that long-ago time when I was mad? My bed. The dark walls. Instead of the window a bright glow coming from the entrance. Arisbe present from time to time. Oenone almost continually. No one else in the world has hands like hers. No, I was not mad. Solace was what I needed. Peace that was not the peace of the grave. Living peace. Love's peace.

They did not stop me from disappearing inside myself completely. I did not speak. Hardly ate. Barely moved. Did not sleep, to begin with. Gave myself up to the pictures that had eaten their way into my head. "Time must pass," I heard Arisbe say. How could time help me? The pictures grew paler. For hours on end, I believe, Oenone's light hand stroked my forehead. At the same time I heard her murmurs, which I did not understand, did not need to understand. I fell asleep. Aeneas was sitting beside me, a fire was burning, the soup Marpessa brought me was fit for the gods. No one tried to spare me. No one behaved with constraint on my account. Anchises, who seemed to be living here too, spoke as loudly as ever and made the cave boom with his laughter. Only his body grew fragile, not his spirit. He needed adversaries, sought out Arisbe, began to fight with her but meant me. Arisbe, with her trumpeting voice, her stiff horse's hair, her red-veined face, gave him a piece of her mind. The fire flickered up the walls; what kind of stones were those? "What kind of stones are those?" I said, astonished at how natural my voice sounded. Then there was a silence into which my voice fitted; now it had found exactly the space intended for it.

What kind of stones were those? Had I never seen them before today, then? they asked. They threw dry logs onto the fire to give me light. "Figures? Yes." Carved out of the stone longer ago than anyone could remember. Women, if I was not mistaken. Yes. A goddess in the center; others making offerings to her. I recognized her now. Flowers lay before the stone, wine, ears of barley. Killa said reverently: "Cybele." I saw Arisbe smile.

That evening she sat with me while the others slept. We talked unreservedly, amiably, and matter-of-factly. "Killa," said Arisbe, "needs to attach a name to the stone. Most women need to," she said. "Artemis, Cybele, Athena, some other name."

Well, they should do as they liked. Perhaps gradually, without even noticing it, they might come to take the names as a likeness. "You mean the stones stand for something else." "Of course. Do you pray to the wooden Apollo?" "I haven't for a long time now. But what do the images stand for?" "That's the question. They stand for the things in us that we do not dare to recognize, that is how it seems to me. There are very few people with whom I discuss my thoughts about that. Why hurt other people? Or disturb them? If we had time . . ."

All of a sudden I noticed that my heart was in great pain. Tomorrow I would get up again with a reanimated heart that was no longer beyond the reach of pain.

"You think that man cannot see himself, Arisbe?" "That's right. He cannot stand it. He needs the alien image." "And will that never change? Will the same thing always come again? Self-estrangement, idols, hatred?" "I don't know. This much I do know: There are gaps in time. This is one of them, here and now. We cannot let it pass without taking advantage of it."

There at last I had my "we."

I dreamed that night, after so many desolate nights without dreams. I saw colors, red and black, life and death. They interpenetrated, they did not fight each other as I would have expected even in a dream. They changed form continually, they continually produced new patterns, which could be unbelievably beautiful. They were like waters, like a sea. In the middle of the sea I saw a bright island which I was approaching rapidly in my dream—for I was flying; yes, I was flying! What was there on the island? What kind of creature? A human being? An animal? It glowed the way only Aeneas glows at night. What joy. Then headlong fall, breeze, darkness, awakening. Hecuba, my mother. "Mother," I said. "I'm dreaming again." "Get up. Come with me. You are needed. They won't listen to me."

So I was not to be allowed to stay? To stay here, where I felt at ease? Did that mean I was all well? Killa clung to me, begged: "Come on, stay!" I looked at Arisbe, Anchises. Yes, I had to go.

Hecuba led me straight to the council. No. Wrong. To the hall where the council used to be held. Where conspirators crouched together now, led by King Priam. They refused to let us in. Hecuba declared that they—the king above all— would be responsible for the consequences if we were not admitted now. The messenger came back. We were to come in. But only for a short while. They had no time. For as long as I can remember the council had no time for matters of importance.

At first I could not hear because I was seeing my father. A ruin of a man. Did he know who I was? Was he drowsing?

The matter concerned Polyxena. No, it concerned Troy. No, it concerned Achilles the brute. It concerned the plan that Polyxena was supposed to lure Achilles into our temple. Into the temple of the Thymbraian Apollo. Under the pretext of wanting to marry him. One suspicion after another raced through my head. "Marry? But—" "Nothing to worry about," I was told. Just pretend. In reality—

I could not believe my ears. In reality our brother Paris would sally forth ("sally forth"! Paris himself used that term!) from behind the image of the god, where he would be hidden, and he would strike Achilles in his vulnerable spot: the heel. Why there specifically? He had confided his vulnerable spot to our sister Polyxena. And Polyxena? Was playing along. Naturally. "How does she feel about it?" Paris asked insolently. "She's looking forward to it."

"That means you're using Polyxena as a decoy for Achilles."

Broad grin. "You've got it. That's it. Achilles will come into the temple without shoes: she insisted he fulfill that condition."

Laughter all around.

"Alone?"

"Well, what do you think? Of course alone. And he will not leave the temple alive."

"And Polyxena? Will she wait for him there alone?"

"Except for Paris," said Eumelos. "And except for us, of course. But we'll stand outside."

"And so Achilles will embrace Polyxena there?"

"Make-believe. When his attention is sufficiently distracted" —laughter—"Paris's arrow will strike him."

Laughter.

"And Polyxena has agreed to this?"

"Agreed? She's eager for it. A real Trojan woman."

"But why isn't she here?"

"We're only settling the details here. Which don't concern her. We're doing the cool planning. Being a woman, she would only get that in a muddle."

I closed my eyes, and I saw the scene. In all its details. Heard Polyxena's laughter. Saw the murder in the temple—Achilles as a corpse, oh! who would not yearn to see that sight!—still clinging to Polyxena.

"You are using her."

"Using whom?"

"Polyxena."

"But aren't you capable of getting the point? It's not she we're concerned with. We're concerned with Achilles."

"That's exactly what I'm saying."

Until then my father had been silent. Now he spoke: "Be silent, Cassandra!" Furiously, angrily. I said: "Father—" "Don't try that on me anymore," he said. " 'Father.' I indulged you for far too long." "All right," I said, "she's sensitive. All right, she does not see the world as it is. She's a bit up in the clouds. Takes herself seriously, women like to do that. She's spoiled, she can't fit in. High-strung. Stuck up." "About what, Daughter? Can you tell me that? With your nose always up in the air? And shooting off your mouth? And despising those who fight for Troy? After all, you know our situation. And if you don't endorse this plan of ours for killing Achilles, the worst of our enemies, right now—do you know what I'd call that? Lending aid and comfort to the enemy!"

Such stillness around me, inside me. Like now. Like here.

My father went on to say that not only should I immediately endorse the plans which were up for deliberation; I should also undertake to keep silent about them and, once they were carried out, to expressly defend them against all comers.

So this, though unexpected, was the moment I had feared. I was not unprepared, why was it so hard? Rapidly, with uncanny rapidity I considered the possibility that they might be right. What does that mean, "right"? Considered the possibility that the question of rights—Polyxena's right, my right—did not even arise because a duty, the duty to kill our worst enemy, ate up the right. And Polyxena? She was headed for ruin, no doubt about that. She was already a hopeless case.

"Now, Cassandra. You're going to be sensible, aren't you?"

I said: "No."

"You don't agree to the plan?"

"No."

"But you will keep silent?"

"No," I said. My mother Hecuba grasped my arm fearfully. She knew what was coming now; so did I. The king said: "Seize her!"

Once again the hands grabbing me, not too hard, just enough to lead me away. Men's hands. No release through faints or visions. As we left I turned around; my look fell on my brother Paris. He did not want the blame, but what could he do? Did they not have him in their power forever because of his blunder with Helen? Weak, Brother, weak. A weakling. Hungry to conform. Just look at yourself in the mirror. With this final look I saw through him completely, and he saw through himself too, but he could not take it. More rashly than anyone he pressed on with that act of madness that was now inevitable. They say that afterward he let them display him, riding astraddle, to the people and the troops, as the conqueror of Achilles. "Paris, our hero!" That could not diminish his self-contempt, which was incurable.

In profoundest darkness and uttermost stillness they led me to a place which I had always regarded as uncanny and menacing: the grave of the heroes. That is what we used to call it, and we children used it for our tests of courage. It lay apart, in a protruding and abandoned section of the fortress that gave directly onto the wall. Often (my hearing had grown unbelievably acute) I could hear the sentries on patrol. They did not know that I was down there below them. No one knew except the two confidants of Eumelos who had taken me there (yes, Andron was with them, handsome Andron), and the two dissolute women who used to bring me food. I had never seen the like of those two in Troy before. Someone must have dug them up especially for me from the lowest depths, from the place people sink to when they have given up on themselves. They are intended to harshen my punishment, I thought at first; and I even caught myself thinking nonsensically, If only my father knew about that. Until the voice of reason asked me ironically: "What if he did? Would they let me out of here? Would they bring me different women? Better food?"

No.

From the first hour on, I worked away incessantly at the wickerwork that lined the round cavity, where I could just barely stand up at the center. I found a thin, loose strand of wicker (just as I found one now) and pulled it out of the weave —oh, it took hours, maybe days. I set out to release it completely, the whole length, as far as it went. For more than an hour now I have tried to do the same thing, but the willow basket where I am sitting is newer, its weave is not so rotted and filthy. I was seized, am seized, with zeal for the task, as if my life depended on it. At first—when to my good fortune I still felt numb and insensible and told myself they could not do this to me, not to me, not my father—I believed that they had buried me alive. For I did not know where I was, and I had heard them carefully wall up the hole after they put me in through it. The stench that assailed me. Such things did not exist. Where was I? How long does it take a person to starve to death? I crept around in the dust—what do I mean, dust, it was loathsome rot. Was my container round? Yes, round and lined with wicker, which did not admit a single ray of light even when a day and a night and another day had presumably gone by; so very likely it was thickly plastered with mud on the outside. That is what I thought, and I was right. Finally I found bones and realized where I was. Someone was moaning, "Mustn't lose my mind, not now"—my voice.

I did not lose my mind.

Then after a long time the scraping sound. The trapdoor that opened close to the ground, I did not see anything! but with difficulty I found it out. The bowl was shoved in and I tipped it over when I reached for it—tipped over the water! Then the flat barley cake. And for the first time the lewd screeching of one of the women.

That was the underworld. But I had not been buried. I was not to die of hunger. Was I disappointed?

I could always refuse the food.

It would have been easy. It may be that that is what they expected. After two or three days, I believe, I began to eat. And during the long intervals—I hardly slept at all—I pulled, tugged, twisted, and tore at the wicker. Something that was stronger than everything else was tearing at me. Many days I thought of only one thing: One day it must be over.

What must be over?

I remember that suddenly I paused, sat for a long time without moving, struck by the lightning realization: This is pain.

It was pain, which I had thought I knew. Now I saw that until then it had barely grazed me. You do not distinguish the boulder that buries you beneath it, but only the force of the impact; so my pain at the loss of everything I had called "father" was threatening to crush me with its weight. The fact that I was able to give a name to the pain, the fact that it answered to its name, gave me a breath of air. One day it must be over.

Nothing lasts forever. This was the second breath of relief, although relief is too strong a word for it. There is a kind of pain that stops hurting because it is everything. Air. Earth. Water. Each bite of food. Each breath you draw, every movement. No, it is indescribable. I never spoke about it. No one asked me about it.

The wicker wand. Now I have gotten it free. Now I have it in my hand. Now it will not be much longer. I am hiding it. No one will find it. The tree it was cut from grew on the Scamander River. When the pain let me go, I began to talk. With the mice, whom I fed. With a snake, who lived in a cavity and twisted herself around my neck when I was sleeping. Then with the ray of light that penetrated the opening where the wicker wand had been removed. The dot of light gave me back the day. Then I talked to the women, something they had never experienced before. They were the scum of Troy; whereas I, immeasurably privileged, had wandered in the palace above them. Their vulgar glee at my plight was understandable. I noticed that they could not succeed in insulting me. They noticed it, too. Oh, the words they taught me. They spat at me from the shaft through which they crawled on their bellies to poke my food in through the trapdoor; the longer I was kept prisoner, the more greedily I waited for it. I did not know whether they understood what I said. I asked them their names. Shrill laughter. I told them mine. Contemptuous screeches. One of them (the younger judging by her voice) used to spit into my water bowl. I was forced to learn that not everyone can retrace his steps once he has been degraded to the level of an animal. The women turned more threatening. I began to be afraid of them.

One day the trapdoor scraped open when it was not mealtime. I waited in vain to hear a screech. A cultivated male voice—so such a thing did exist!—spoke to me. Andron. The handsome Andron. "Here, Cassandra." As if we were meeting at supper in the palace. "Come here. Take this." What was he giving me? Something hard, sharp. I felt it with trembling fingers. Did I recognize it? Oh, that beautiful voice, swollen with triumph. Yes—it was the sword-belt of Achilles. Which, as I must surely be able to imagine (he said), could have been obtained only by killing its wearer. Yes, everything had gone according to plan. Yes, the Greek hero Achilles was dead.

"And Polyxena? Please! Polyxena?"

Curtly, far too curtly: "She's alive."

The trapdoor fell, I was left alone. Now came the hardest part.

Achilles the brute was dead. The plot had been successful. If things had gone according to my wishes, the brute would still be alive. They had proved right. When you are successful, it proves you are right. But hadn't I known from the outset that I was not in the right? So. So had I gotten myself locked up because I was too proud to give in to them?

Well, I had time. I could reexamine the case, word by word, step by step, thought by thought. Ten times, a hundred times I stood before Priam, a hundred times I tried to agree with him, to answer yes at his command. A hundred times I said no again. My life, my voice, my body would produce no other answer. "You don't agree?" No. "But you will keep silent?" No. No. No. No.

They were right, and it was my portion to say no.

At last, at last the voices grew silent. One day I wept with happiness inside my basket. The younger of the two women pushed something in to me on top of the flat barley cake. My fingers recognized it at once even before my head could form the name: Anchises! Wood! One of his animals. A sheep? A lamb? Once I was outside I saw: it was a pony. Myrine sent it. She persuaded the younger of the warder women, I do not know how. Moreover, the woman stopped barking at me after that. Oh, I was so moved by that little piece of wood that I forgot to eat. They knew where I was. They had not forgotten me. I would live and be with them. We would not lose each other again until the inevitable happened, the fall of Troy.

And in fact that is how it happened. When I got out I

lived for a long time with my hands held in front of my eyes because I could not tolerate any light; and preferably inside the caves. Myrine, who did not leave my side, forced me little by little to look into the light. We did not talk about Penthesilea, or about her own wounds, until the last time we were together. I saw her naked. She was covered with scars. My skin was smooth until the end, until now. I hope they know their handiwork; then one cut will be enough. At that time only a woman could touch me. Aeneas came, he sat beside me, he stroked the air above my head. I loved him more than my life. He did not live with us like many young men whom the war had damaged in body or soul. They arrived like shadows; our blazing life restored their color, blood, zest. When I close my eyes I see the picture. Mount Ida in the shifting light. The slopes with their caves. The Scamander, its banks. That was our world, no landscape could be more beautiful. The seasons. The scent of the trees. And our free existence, a new joy for each new day. The citadel did not reach as far as here. They could not fight the enemy and us at the same time. They left us alone, took from us the fruits we harvested, the cloth we wove. We ourselves lived in poverty. I remember that we sang a lot. Talked a lot, evenings by the fire in Arisbe's cave, where the figure of the goddess on the wall seemed to be alive. Killa and other women used to pray to her and place offerings. No one tried to stop them. We knew we were lost, but we did not force that knowledge on those who needed a firm hope. Our good cheer was not forced, though it never lost its dark undercoat. We did not stop learning. Each shared his own special knowledge with the other. I learned to make pots, clay vessels. I invented a pattern to paint on them, black and red. We used to tell each other our dreams; many of us were amazed at how much they revealed about us. But more than anything else we talked about those who would come after us. What they would be like. Whether they would still know who we were. Whether they would repair our omissions, rectify our mistakes. We racked our brains trying to think of a way we could leave them a mes-

sage, but did not know any script to write in. We etched
animals, people, ourselves inside the rock caves, which we sealed
off before the Greeks came. We pressed our hands side by side
into the soft clay. We called that immortalizing our memory,
and laughed. This turned into a touch-fest, where we spon-
taneously touched each other and got acquainted. We were
fragile. Our time was limited and so we could not waste it on
matters of minor importance. So we concentrated on what
mattered most: ourselves—playfully, as if we had all the time
in the world. Two summers and two winters.

In the first winter Hecuba (who sometimes came and sat with
us quietly) sent Polyxena to us. She had lost her mind. She
had gone crazy with fear. We found out that she could only
bear to have soft things around her, gentle touches, dim light,
muted sounds. We learned that as Achilles was dying in the
temple, he had made Odysseus promise to sacrifice Polyxena,
who had betrayed him, on his grave after the Greek victory.
Her face was ravaged, but when she heard a flute playing far
away, she was able to smile.

In the first spring Priam sent for me. I arrived and saw that
no one recognized me in the streets of Troy. That was fine with
me. My father, who did not say a word about anything that
had happened, informed me dryly that we had a potential new
ally, what was his name? Eurypylos. With fresh troops, not
something to be sneezed at. But he wanted me for his wife if
he was to fight on our side.

We were silent for a while; then the king wanted to know
my reply. I said: "Why ever not?" My father wept feebly. I
would have preferred him to be angry. Eurypylos arrived; there
were worse men than he. He was killed the day after his first
night with me, in one of the makeshift fights waged by the
Greeks because they were unable to take the city. I went back
to the Scamander again; no one mentioned my brief time away.
During the last year of the war there was hardly one pregnant
woman in Troy. Many looked enviously, compassionately, sadly
at my belly. When the twins were born—it was hard, I lay in

Arisbe's cave, once I cried out to the goddess: "Cybele, help!"—they had many mothers. And Aeneas was their father.

I have experienced everything a person must experience.

Marpessa is laying both her hands against my back. Yes, I know. They will be coming soon. I would like to see that light once more. The light I used to watch together with Aeneas whenever we could. The light of the hour before the sun goes down. When every object begins to glow with its own light and gives off its own particular color. Aeneas said: "It wants to make a stand once more before the night." I said: "It wants to let the rest of its light and warmth stream out and then to let in the darkness and cold." We could not help laughing when we realized that we were speaking in metaphors. That was how we lived in the hour before dark. The war, a wounded dragon incapable of further movement, lay heavy and faint over our city. The next move it made was bound to dash us to pieces. Abruptly, from one moment to the next, our sun could set. Lovingly and exactingly we followed its course on each of our days, for they were numbered. It amazed me to see that different though we all were, the women by the Scamander felt without exception that we were testing something, and that it was not a question of how much time we had. Nor of whether we could convince the majority of Trojans, who of course remained in the dismal city. We did not see ourselves as an example. We were grateful that we were the ones granted the highest privilege there is: to slip a narrow strip of future into the grim present, which occupies all of time. Anchises, who never tired of maintaining that it was always possible to do this; who was growing visibly weaker, was no longer able to go on weaving his baskets, and often had to lie down, but went on teaching that the spirit is higher than the body; who continued to fight with Arisbe (he used to call her the Great Mother, she had grown even bulkier, was lame in the hip, bridged with her trumpet of a voice distances she could no longer walk): Anchises, I believe, loved our life in the caves wholeheartedly, loved it without reservation, sadness, and scruple. He was fulfilling a dream of his and was teaching us younger ones how to dream with both feet on the ground.

Then it was over. One noon I woke up under the cypress tree where I often spent the hot hours of the day, and thought: "Desolate. How desolate everything is." The word came back again and again, each time ripping open the pit inside me.

Then a messenger came to Oenone: Paris was wounded. He was asking for her. Wanted her to save him. We watched her preparing the basket of herbs, bandages, and tinctures. Bending over: her beautiful white neck, which could hardly support the weight of the head anymore. Paris had gotten rid of her at the time he needed the many girls. Grief for the man had eaten its way inside her, grief not on her account but on his. She could not get over the way he had changed. Like nature she remained identical in change. When she returned she was a stranger. Paris was dead. The temple physicians had summoned her too late. He had died in agony, of gangrene. Another woman hit with that same frozen look, I thought. As Paris's sister, I was supposed to attend his funeral. I did so. I wanted to see Troy again and found a grave. The inhabitants were all grave-diggers who lived on only to bury themselves with somber pomp in each of the dead. The rules of interment, which the priests continually elaborated and which had to be scrupulously observed, consumed the working day. Ghosts were carrying a ghost to the grave. I had never seen anything more unreal. And most ghastly of all was the figure of the king at the head of the procession, his decayed body draped in purple, being carried by four strong young men.

It was over. That evening on the wall I had the conversation with Aeneas after which we parted. Myrine never left my side again. Surely it was an illusion that the light over Troy seemed pale in the last days. Pale the faces. Vague the words we said.

We were waiting.

The collapse came swiftly. The end of the war was worthy of its beginning, an infamous deception. And my Trojan people believed what they saw, not what they knew. Believed that the Greeks would withdraw! And that they had left standing outside the wall this monster, which all the priests of Athena (to whom the thing was supposedly dedicated) rashly dared to call a "horse." So the thing was a "horse." Why so enormous? Who knows? As enormous as the reverence of our beaten foes for Pallas Athena, protectress of our city.

"Fetch the horse inside!"

That was going too far; I could not believe my ears. First I tried a matter-of-fact approach: "Don't you see the horse is far too big for any of our gates?"

"Then we'll enlarge the wall."

Now we paid the penalty for the fact that they hardly knew who I was anymore. The shudder that had once attached to my name had already faded. The Greeks restored it to me. The Trojans laughed at my screeches. "She's crazy, that one. Come on, break open the wall! Now bring in the horse!" Their anxiety to install this token of victory in their midst surpassed every other urge in intensity. Never were there victors like these, who in a mad frenzy transported the idol into the city. I feared the worst, not because I could see through the Greeks' plan move by move, but because I saw the baseless arrogance of the Trojans. I shrieked, pleaded, adjured, and spoke in tongues. I did not get to see my father, who, I was told, was unwell.

Eumelos. I was standing before him once again. I saw the face which you forget from time to time and which for that reason is permanent. Expressionless. Pitiless. Unteachable. Even if he believed me, he would not oppose the Trojans, and maybe get himself killed. He, for one, intended to survive (he said). And the Greeks would be able to use him. Wherever we came, he would be there first. And would pass us off with a shrug.

Now I understood what the god had ordained: "You will speak the truth, but no one will believe you." Here stood the No One who had to believe me; but he could not because he believed nothing. A No One incapable of belief.

I cursed the god Apollo.

The Greeks will tell their own version of what happened that night. Myrine was the first. Then blow after blow and cut after cut and thrust after thrust. Blood flowed through our streets, and the wail Troy uttered dug into my ears; since then I have heard it night and day. Now I will be freed from it. Later, fearing the images of the gods, they asked me if it was true that Ajax the Lesser had raped me by the statue of Athena. I said nothing. It was not beside the goddess. It was in the grave of the heroes, where we were trying to hide Polyxena while she screamed and sang. Hecuba and I stopped up her mouth with tow. The Greeks were searching for her in the name of their greatest hero, Achilles the brute. And they found her because her boyfriend, handsome Andron, betrayed her. Against his will (he bellowed), but what was he supposed to do, after all, they were threatening to kill him? Ajax the Lesser ran him through, laughing loudly. All of a sudden Polyxena was completely in her right mind. "Kill me, Sister," she begged softly. Oh, wretched woman that I was. I had arrogantly thrown away the dagger Aeneas had forced me to take at the end. I needed it not for myself but for my sister. When they dragged her away, Ajax the Lesser was on top of me. And Hecuba, as they held her fast, uttered curses whose like I had never heard before. "A bitch," Ajax the Lesser yelled when he was through with me. "The Queen of the Trojans is a howling bitch."

Yes. That is how it was.

And now the light is coming.

When I stood on the wall with Aeneas to watch the light for the last time, we quarreled. Until now I have avoided thinking about it. Aeneas, who never badgered me, always let me be, did not want to twist or change anything about me, insisted that I go with him. He tried to order me. It was senseless to throw oneself into inevitable destruction, he said. I should take our children—he said that: *our* children!—and leave the city. A band of Trojans were prepared to do so, and they were not the worst people, either. They had taken on provisions and armed themselves, and were determined to fight their way through. To found a new Troy somewhere else. Begin again from the beginning. I deserved credit for my devotion. But enough was enough.

"You misunderstand me," I said hesitantly. "It's not for Troy's sake that I must stay, Troy does not need me. But for our sake. For your sake and mine."

Aeneas. Dear one. You understood long before you would admit it. It was obvious: The new masters would dictate their law to all the survivors. The earth was not large enough to escape them. You, Aeneas, had no choice: You had to snatch a couple of hundred people from death. You were their leader. "Soon, very soon, you will have to become a hero."

"Yes!" you cried. "And so?" I saw by your eyes that you had understood me. I cannot love a hero. I do not want to see you being transformed into a statue.

Dear one. You did not say that it would not happen to you. Or that I could protect you from it. You knew as well as I did that we have no chance against a time that needs heroes. You threw the snake ring into the sea. You would have to go far, far away, and you would not know what lies ahead.

I am staying behind.

The pain will remind us of each other. When we meet later, if there is a later, we will recognize each other by it.

The light went out. Is going out.

They are coming.

Here is the place. These stone lions looked at her.
They seem to move in the shifting light.

CONDITIONS OF A
NARRATIVE ❦ CASSANDRA

This dark race is beyond help;
for the most part you had to remain
silent so as not to be considered
mad like Cassandra, when you prophesied
what already lies outside the gate.

—GOETHE, 1794

Ladies and gentlemen:
This enterprise bears the title "Lectures on Poetics," but I will tell you at once, I cannot offer you a poetics. One glance at the *Classical Antiquity Lexicon* was enough to confirm my suspicion that I myself have none. "Poetics" (the definition reads): theory of the art of poetry, which at an advanced stage —Aristotle, Horace—takes on a systematic form, and whose norms have been accorded "wide validity" in numerous countries since the age of humanism. New aesthetic positions are reached (the book says) via confrontation with these norms (in parentheses, Brecht). I do not deride, and, it goes without saying, I do not deny the influence of prevailing aesthetic norms on every writer—as well as on every reader, who attributes to personal taste what are really internalized norms. Yet I have never felt the raging desire for confrontation with the poetics, or the model, of a great writer (in parentheses, Brecht). This has only struck me in the last couple of years, and so it may be that, incidentally, these essays will also treat a question that I have not been asked: the question of why I do *not* have a poetics.

But mainly I want to ask you to follow me on a journey, in a literal as well as a metaphorical sense. For the past two years I have been tracking a key word: "Cassandra," and having felt the recurrent urge to trace a rough outline of the roads where this word led me, I intend to do so on this occasion. Many or most, maybe the most important things will go unsaid; indeed, probably they are unknown to me as well. I want to set a fabric before you. It is an aesthetic structure, and as such it would lie at the center of my poetics *if* I had one. But this fabric which I want to display to you now did not turn out completely tidy, is not surveyable at one glance. Many of its motifs are not followed up, many of its threads are tangled. There are wefts which stand out like foreign bodies, repetitions, material that has not been worked out to its conclusion. This is not always intentional; I myself had first to work to master the material, and I make you witness of this work process. I also make you witness to a process which has changed my lens on the world. But this process of change has only just begun, and I feel keenly the tension between the artistic forms within which we have agreed to abide and the living material, borne to me by my senses, my psychic apparatus, and my thought, which has resisted these forms. If I may formulate a poetological problem so soon, let it be this: There is and there can be no poetics which prevents the living experience of countless perceiving subjects from being killed and buried in art objects. So, does this mean that art objects ("works") are products of the alienation of our culture, whose other finished products are produced for self-annihilation?

Thus, I have taken a personal approach in these lectures. I employ various subjective forms of expression, looking at them in terms of the work that they can achieve, that I can achieve in them. The first and second essays—a two-part *record of a trip to Greece*—attest to how the figure of Cassandra takes possession of me and takes on her first, provisional incarnation. The third essay has the form of a *work diary* that tries to trace the vise grip between life and subject matter. In the fourth essay, a *letter*, I ask questions about the historical reality of the Cassandra figure and conditions for the woman writer past and present. My overall concern is the sinister effects of alienation, in aesthetics, in art, as well as elsewhere.

1 ❧ TRAVEL REPORT, ABOUT THE ACCIDENTAL SURFACING AND GRADUAL FABRICATION OF A LITERARY PERSONAGE

You can move cities but not wells.

—A CHINESE BOOK OF WISDOM

So I wanted to go to Greece, unaware what I was looking for, and merely because it would have been criminal to miss this opportunity. I filled out the forms, listing "tourism" as my reason for travel; informed no one, including myself, that I was looking forward without emotion to the prospect of their return and their transformation, by an unfathomable process, into a valid visa; simulated rather than felt a pleasurable anticipation; kept an altogether ironic attitude ("Ah, so my soul is seeking out the land of the Greeks!"); equipped myself with little information beforehand, under the pretext that I wanted to take in impressions directly; and was hardly at all surprised that I burst out laughing when, through a fault of the airline, we missed the plane intended to take us to Athens.

From now on things had a chance to turn interesting. Gaily we* tripped back down the airport staircase. Not law but chance would govern our journey, a more autocratic ruler, in-

---

* "We" refers to Christa Wolf and her husband, Gerhard Wolf, who throughout the essays is referred to as "G."—Trans.

calculable, enigmatic, hard to outwit, impossible to command. Chance—fugitive stuff which no story with a view to seem "natural" can do without; but how difficult it is to get it into custody. A taxi. The vise of the ineluctable loosened. For once, the premises that produce a foreordained result for every second of our lives did not mesh but locked on empty air. Moira, Fate, sought us in vain inside the plane that was just landing in Athens, on which we had been scheduled passengers. Meanwhile, we, untraceable, unregistered shadow figures without luggage, drove through the streets of Berlin, capital of the East German Democratic Republic. Alien, strangely moved, unrecognizable, we walked through an unrecognizable city, ate East Asian food in the Palace Hotel with the sum stipulated on our customs and visa declaration; got some opera tickets, and, along the lively Friedrichstrasse, told each other the tale of the donated day. We observed precautionary measures as we crept into our own empty apartment; slept; in the evening watched *The Abduction from the Seraglio* with dismay, laboriously remembering the pacts one must abide by if the magic is to work. We could not dream that for four or five weeks we would be unable to get out of our heads the text and melody of the opera's concluding lines: "He who values not this grace / Merits nought bu-u-t disgra-a-ce."

The following morning, in the empty apartment where no more telephone calls, no more letters strayed by mistake, I began to read Aeschylus's *Oresteia*. I witnessed how a panic rapture spread through me, how it mounted and reached its pinnacle when a voice began to speak:

> *Aiee! Aieeeee!*
> *Apollo! Apollo!*

Cassandra. I saw her at once. She, the captive, took me captive; herself made an object by others, she took possession of me. Later I would ask when, where, and by whom the pacts were joined that made this magic. It worked at once. I believed every word she said; so there was still such a thing as unqualified trust. Three thousand years—melted away. So the gift of prophecy, conferred on her by the god, stood the test of time. Only his verdict that no one would believe her had passed away. I found her believable in another sense: It seemed to me that she was the only person in the play who knew herself.

Dropping my reserve and not asking the cause of my emotion, I also refrained from asking what Aeschylus might or could have intended with this character. Before Cassandra opens her mouth we have learned: The war against Troy is over. King Agamemnon, who led the Achaeans and before whose fortress of Mycenae we are standing, is expected home after a ten-year absence; his wife, Clytemnestra, and the old men who had to stay behind are waiting for him. He arrives. Beside him on the triumphal chariot sits Cassandra, the Trojan woman, daughter of the Trojan king, Priam, who is dead along with her brothers and most of her sisters. Troy has been destroyed, and she had prophesied it all, but her countrymen did not believe her. Now she ventures to prophesy to the foreign strangers standing around her that their own king—who a moment ago, at his wife's urging, trod the purple carpet of victory to enter his fortress—will be murdered by this same wife. She smelled at once the curse that lay on the House of Atreus. The chorus of old Argive men are surprised. She does not comply with Clytemnestra's generous invitation to take part in the sacrifice which is being made ready inside. They wonder: Does she even understand Greek?

> CHORUS: *Come, Cassandra! Go inside.*
> *Descend from your chariot, submit to the yoke!*
> CASSANDRA: *Apollo! Apollo!*
> *Leader of the ways, you!*
> *To all the others*
> *you give protection!*

> Me you annihilate,
> Apollo,
> for the second time!*

Again the chorus marvels: Does the god speak through the mouth of a slave? How can this slave woman complain to Apollo, of all people, in violation of decency, rule, and custom? A fleeting question pops into my mind: Is the Apollo invoked by the Trojan woman from Asia Minor a different Apollo from the one venerated by the Greeks on the mainland? Then she begins to shriek again, heaps one impropriety on top of another, calls the house of Agamemnon, on which she is dependent, a "human slaughterhouse." Whereupon the old men, who at first compared her with a "wild creature, newly captured" and assured her of their sympathy, now begin to grow suspicious, reserved.

> Resourceful as the bloodhound on the scent
> is the foreign woman.
> Already she smells what she was after:
> murder.

They are quite modern in their thinking, these old men who lived more than two thousand years ago—it is not a human being but a dog who is digging up what they all know about the past of their royal house: infanticide and cannibalism. It is going too far for the foreign captive to shriek it out in the public square.

---

* All quotations from Aeschylus's *Oresteia* have been translated directly from the four German versions used by Christa Wolf in her research, because it was from these (which differ slightly from comparable English versions) that she derived her impressions of Aeschylus's Cassandra. However, the reader will find it relatively easy to locate the equivalent passages in any English translation, and so no attempt has been made to give page or line references to any particular English-language edition.—Trans.

> *Behold! The witnesses! Red with blood!*
> *Screaming children! Infants!*
> *The feast of slaughter!*
> *There! The roasted flesh.*
> *Which the father . . . eats!*

Unquestionably the chorus could supply the overwhelmed seeress the names that go with her nightmare visions: Atreus, the father of Agamemnon, who slaughters the children of his brother Thyestes and serves their flesh to their father. This kind of thing does not seem to be customary in Asia Minor even in disputes over the throne. But no: the patriotic old men forbid the unauthorized foreign woman to speak.

> *Be silent!*
> *We know that you understand the art of prophecy.*
> *But we need no prophecy,*
> *not here!*

Whose side is Aeschylus on, really? Or is he trying to pull off the feat of giving everyone his due? By now at least three hundred years have elapsed since the time of Homer, who passed on the tidings of the Trojan War. The concluding notes inform me that Aeschylus won first prize for the *Oresteia* in the tragedy competition at Athens in 458 B.C. The events he refers to, like his characters themselves, are by now receding into the twilight of myth. In these circumstances I think the tragedian may not have found it too difficult to show justice to all.

The date is March 20, 1980. Chance, Tyche, has me spellbound under a gaze. Some being of sky or earth (I do not know who) must be gloating at the fact that I have been sitting for hours locked inside the passenger boarding area of Berlin-Schönefeld airport, with Aeschylus in my lap, dismissed by passport, registration, and customs officials, prevented from leaving through any door, dependent on a Syrian Airlines plane which is reported to have not yet taken off from Copenhagen; surrounded by young women and couples from West Berlin who want to take advantage of cheap pre-Easter flights from Schönefeld to Athens and whose children have transformed the boarding zone into a playground and sports center. The lines of Aeschylus dangle before my eyes like a coarse netting through whose wide meshes I see a figure stir. It moves in a way that is hard to describe. Well informed, I could say. I see her removing the insignia of her rank.

> *Away with the prophet's staff! Laughter and mockery!*
> *Away with the priestly fillet around my head!*
> *Away! Away! I live still and I break this rod in twain.*
> *Down with the wreath, may it bring happiness to another!*
> *Do you all see? Apollo removes my priestly garb.*
> *I wore it very long, and full of patience.*

Now I feel in her a relief for which her words alone are perhaps insufficient evidence. Free at last of an oppressive vocation, she owes nothing further to the god ("Now the seer is leading his seeress to the ax"), nothing to her countrymen ("They destroyed Ilium, I saw it, saw how it happened"); she is without a calling even if not free of the compulsion to "see." She still owes something to herself—but what? Self-knowledge, detachment, coolheadedness: That is what (struck to the quick) I think I can detect in her voice. Is there something resembling triumph? Is she superior now to those—"friend and foe" —who used to laugh at her and call her fool, beggarwoman, deceitful witch, mad, miserable, a poor wretch? Is she accusing them? Certainly not. Her tone is not vengeful. I seem to know more about her than I can prove. She seems to look at me, to affect me, more keenly than I would wish.

The smaller children, four or five boys the same age, have exhibited their toy weapons to each other, then broken up into minigroups which fight and tear about, emitting bursts of gun-

fire, along the corridors to the customs gates. We needed coins
for the telephone and had to reveal that we are the only East
German citizens among the passengers. Meanwhile, a twelve-
year-old girl has found out that the other telephone will work
without coins, and now it is surrounded by adolescents recklessly telephoning their boyfriends or girlfriends in New York,
Athens, or Stockholm. If our plane takes off around 10:20 P.M.,
as we have been told is likely, we would be in Athens at around
2:00 A.M. C.'s voice over the first telephone sounds very faraway and discouraged: "Are you really coming? The table was
laid a long time ago."

The tired waitress at the drinks buffet takes orders for the
last time, naturally she accepts foreign currency; then she too
closes down, turns off the light over the counter. We are left
to ourselves and to our doubts. Does anything else still exist
outside the palely lit boarding lounge—an airport, the city it
belongs to, a country, other countries, the continent? A spectral
voice tells us that our airplane has been held up in a city called
Copenhagen by a strike of the underpaid flight personnel and
is now struggling through the night to reach us—us, this handful of stranded people brought together by chance, whom we
two were not meant to have joined but for the intervention of
the uncanny. But does any such plane really exist? And what
about the telephone that "works without money"—isn't it in
on the plot, too? Isn't it perhaps using complicated tape-
recording devices (after all, nowadays anything is possible,
don't you think?) that play voices to the people who use it,
voices that simulate an outside world, whereas in reality—

Cassandra outside the gates of Mycenae (I cannot visualize
it: the Lion Gate? The gates of the palace inside the fortified
wall?):

> *Hail to you, gates of death.*
> *I ask only one thing more, one single thing:*
> *That death's stroke does not miss its aim*
> *so that I can die quickly, and without quivering.*

I look at the young women around me. Don't we all wish this? For ourselves and our children? Eventually the gates to the airfield, with their threefold security locks, will have to open. What if they lead into a wasteland? Wasn't that the sound of a plane landing?

> CHORUS: *How can you go to the bloody altarstone as calmly*
> *as a beast driven by the god?*
> CASSANDRA: *The time is ripe, my friends, and death is near.*
> CHORUS: *Even the last hour counts.*
> CASSANDRA: *Already it is here, and flight is meaningless.*
> CHORUS: *Your misery makes you brave.*
> CASSANDRA: *Perhaps. Good fortune requires no courage.*

Exactly how did she experience the collapse of all her alternatives? How is it that she has only this one way left open to her, and walks along it voluntarily rather than making them drag her? "Leave me! I must go in now! Farewell." And then a "mistake" on Aeschylus's part. Never would she have said this: "Indoors as well as outdoors I can/Mourn Agamemnon's fate." Agamemnon—the last in the series of men who have done her violence (the first was Apollo, the god). Mourn for him? Not if I knew her as well as I thought.

The children are romping about like mad. One has separated from the others, a super-cunning, plumpish little tattletale who runs around to the mothers and tells them: "They keep calling me 'tart.'" When the mothers do not react—how progressive they all are!—he persecutes the littler ones until one of them falls down and gives himself a bad bump on the head, and is picked up and comforted by his mother. The little tattletale, unmoved (my God, one day this boy is going to grow into a man!), says: "I frightened him off, he kept calling me 'tart.'" The laughter we share puts us on familiar terms. Sigrid. One evening later on she will sit beside us in an Athens taverna eating roast mutton chops. *Her* Greek friend, a writer and the translator of a new version of Aeschylus, spent the whole night with *our* Greek friend in Athens, waiting for the same plane. She exchanged telephone numbers with us, her friend exchanged the identical numbers with our friend. Tyche, chance, luck.

We have almost given up hope when a narrow door opens onto the airfield. By the time I am seated inside the plane, I feel a lucid, overstimulated wakefulness instead of the longed-for tiredness. A Boeing jet. Two stewards; two stewardesses, who carry out the instructions of their male colleagues. The implacably serried ranks of the group of Syrian travelers who do not dream of vacating even one of their seats so that a West Berlin couple can sit together with their adopted Vietnamese child, "Thomas." The faded Syrian women, dressed all in black, obey unconditionally the signals from their menfolk. Cassandra could have looked like one of them, one of the younger ones. But today, so many centuries later, not one of them could speak like her (what has been done to them in the meantime?).

> *Life is past: O my friends.*
> *But I will not lament*
> *like the bird in the thicket,*
> *the bird who is out of his senses with fear.*
> *After my death you shall bear witness*
> *that I was brave . . .*

One of the Syrian men is opening and shutting all the compartments running above the rows of seats, with no consideration for the people sitting below; opening and shutting. I cannot think of any way to show him my anger when he comes alongside us, stretches up, opens, shuts, does not find what he is looking for. There are also Danes in the plane, blond, pale, and reserved. The children from the boarding lounge are storming in the center aisle. An ark.

> *Now the seer leads me, the seeress, here,*
> *that I may atone for my guilt—this way to doom!*

What guilt? What does the Greek poet mean? Or what is he letting slip out without really meaning to? Is he merely alluding to the guilt she incurred early on when she deceived the god, who, as we now see, craves revenge? She has confessed what she did, to the chorus of old men, who now, after all, do prove capable of a staunch empathy.

CASSANDRA: *Apollo the seer bestowed this office on me.*
CHORUS: *Apollo, you say? Then . . . did the god love you?*
CASSANDRA: *A wrestler who groans during the match:*
Blind with desire Apollo wooed me.
CHORUS: *You . . . united with him?*
CASSANDRA: *No, I promised him I would. But—I lied.*
CHORUS: *And were already a seeress?*
CASSANDRA: *Yes, already I had promised my people every grief.*
CHORUS: *And how did the god punish you?*
CASSANDRA: *No matter what I said, no one believed me.*
CHORUS: *We believe you: To us your words rang all too true.*
CASSANDRA: *O woe. O woe, woe!*
The torment of seeing sweeps me away again.

It is improbable that Cassandra could, in "reality," have been referring to this guilt. I imagine her as free of religious awe. But another "guilt" may have given her trouble: She was able to position herself outside her own people to such an extent that she could "see" their disastrous fate. Those who are unconditionally involved in the struggle see nothing. But the "seeing" imposed on her seems to come upon her like a seizure.

I get unnecessarily angry when the steward expressionlessly serves me a fast-frozen steak. It is one o'clock in the morning, humor seems to be missing from the passenger list. Seldom, I think, have I been with a group where everyone cares so little about everyone else. Beside me sits a young female teacher from Hesse who knows all about Greece. In a flash she has looked up every desired air, bus, and rail connection for a fellow (woman) traveler, and then she begins to converse with the Danish painter who has the place by the window. I hear him say that he spends three months a year on a small Aegean island. Everything in its primitive state, he says; he would not have it any other way. The young teacher replies that she can understand that, really. After that, they never stop talking, and I wonder what actually stops me from screaming out loud. Screaming for them to be quiet. For the steward to take away my lukewarm steak again. For the children to sit down. For the Syrian women to stop going to the toilet in tightly massed groups.

Naturally Cassandra loved this god, or whatever he was; for that very reason she had to reject him when he grew obtrusive. Western female logic? More like male logic, witness Aeschylus. But why did she choose a man's profession when she trained to be a seeress? Why did she want to become like men? Why was it in fact a man's profession to be a seer? Had it always been so? If not, since when? And are those generally the sorts of questions that are able to free Cassandra from myth and literature?

The educational system is an unparalleled disaster, says the woman teacher. It deprives the children of every prospect of self-realization. But she finds it terribly interesting that the painter has been able to awaken the creative drive even in ten-year-olds. Because— (I hear, but then I miss the bridge made of fluent linguistic components that leads to the sensational words "atomic energy.") The eternal, wearisome gurgling of our civilization, leading nowhere. Coffee in plastic cups. A glass of water. The airplane marks the beginning of a zone where one is grateful to accept a glass of water.

What kind of man was Priam, Cassandra's father? And how did her mother, Hecuba, so superabundantly blessed with sons, treat her few daughters? And what kind of life did this king's daughter lead in Troy, her father's city? Already I notice that I cannot get rid of her, she is like a spell that has been put on me. Is there no protest against this decree? Why, actually, does she, the barbarian woman, submit to the Greek god? Who was it—wasn't it Marx—who called Greek antiquity the "childhood" of Western man? Are children entangled in such multilayered problems of conscience that we, the older-than-old, are able to understand them straightaway?

Fasten your seat belts, please. No smoking. The last troop of Syrian women crowds onto the seats without their menfolk lending them the slightest assistance. The schoolteacher is going to visit the painter on his lonely island. Ships travel back and forth very seldom, he says. Cassandra climbs down from Agamemnon's chariot full of loot and goes toward the "gate of Hades." No female contemporary of Aeschylus could have spoken her last words, because of course no woman even had a seat or a voice in the theater, not to mention in any other public institution. What she says is unsuitable for a woman.

> Oh, man's fate, when happy, bears comparison
> to a shadow; when unfortunate—
> a damp sponge sweeps across and blots it out!
> And more than the shadow's fate, this extinction pains me.

What does she want, then: to be immortal? A woman? What dim memories are stirring in the Greek man, to create women like this?

We land at two in the morning. The first Greek man we meet is waiting for us beside our friend; his name is Dionysus. Half dazed with exhaustion, we climb for the first time, in the darkness, into the vehicle which will become our second home in Greece, and which it would be unfair of me now, provisionally, to call a "minibus" simply in order to call it something. In my memory the road from the airport to the center of Athens is studded with a dozen lamp stores, bizarre islands of light in the pale morning twilight. Then, without transition, the single bright lamp over the round table in the room of our friends,

N. and C. A table thickly laid with food which we can only sample because of our exhaustion. The Greek banquet. The first swallow of retsina on Greek soil. Transferred in the darkness from one table to another, we know nothing of the cellar taverna at the corner where the dark, lean waiter draws off this wine from huge barrels set into the wall; nothing of the maze of narrow streets surrounding the house; nothing of the little crammed shops where C. buys flour for the pita bread, vegetables for the filling, goat cheese for the salad; we have seen nothing of the orange and olive trees whose fruits we are eating. Welcome to Athens.

How many different bloodlines have gone into the makeup of this group who sit around the table, under the spell of hospitality? Greek, Turkish, Rumanian, German, Polish forebears all have their share in us. I cannot help thinking how the banquet came into being in the dawn of time, under much the same circumstances as these, the first time one clan shared a modest surplus with another clan, not without expecting to receive a gift in return. That is why the ancient Greeks had no choice but to go to war when Helen was abducted by the Trojan youth Paris: because Paris carried off the wife of his host, Menelaus. Did Homer and the others who handed down the cycle of legends about Troy suspect that in following the myth they were helping to conceal the actual facts? Did they suspect that the Achaeans' struggle against the Trojans—whoever they were—was about sea trade routes, about access to the Bosporus which Troy controlled? So Western literature begins with the glorification of a war of piracy. But who could wish that Homer had not existed, or would want him changed into a historiographer who stuck to the facts?

What race does Cassandra belong to? Aeschylus's chorus, and Clytemnestra too, suspect that she does not know Greek. But she herself leaves no doubt about that. When the chorus leader pretends not to hear her grisly prophecy that Agamemnon is doomed to die at his wife's hands, she urges him:

Do you fail so completely to understand what I
have prophesied?
And yet I understand your Greek speech well.

What is her mother tongue?

I did not know what to make of the city we first caught sight of late the next morning, because I did not have anything to look for there. Details of pictures filtered through, excerpts from the unrolling film of everyday life: cats prowling through the roof landscape of the crumbling house across the way. The fruit seller on the ground floor of the house next door whose displays I looked down on from above. Light-blue venetian blinds which I viewed from our tiny balcony—now tightly shut, now half open, then with wide-open lids. Finally, on the third day, a black-haired, pale-skinned woman shaking out a brilliant-colored blanket. The mute, hard-bitten caretaker who rode up and down with us in the elevator cubicle. In the shop on the left, the two sisters' patient, moonlike faces, always the same, shining out of the darkness behind the displays of nuts, bakery goods, bread. The huge exit road that divided our quarter of narrow streets and little shops from the national park where the Seville oranges glow in the dark foliage. One night, bypassing fragrant shrubbery, we reached the foot of the Acropolis, which I had seen all day floating in the deep-blue sky like an airship, smaller than expected, high above the houses where people have their home, surprising the way it abutted a row of streets. Why not say what people expect to hear? Beautiful! Who would want to be the monster left indifferent by the Acropolis of Athens?

Surrounded by tourists I walked across Syntagma Square and for a long time watched the two marionette soldiers in front of the government buildings strutting toward and then away from each other in ridiculous slow motion, wearing grotesque berets, rifles stiffly at their shoulders, clapping their wooden shoes. I felt a compulsion to list the cities I had already walked through this way. The words and melody of the opera still stuck in my brain: "He who values not this grace / Merits nought bu-u-t disgra-a-ce." Then finally I was able to transfer them to Mario, Dionysus's little son, who did not understand a word of German but demanded to hear the verse every time I saw him: "Sing the German song again!"

The spirit of place held back. Sightseeing made me feel numb, I might have known it would. On Friday, on the trip to Piraeus—what were we doing in that packed, speeding bus?— I saw nothing but stills from Spanish color films which I galvanically impressed upon my mind. These two young men in their olive-green and cobalt-blue outfits in the dark-green garden, behind the white wall broken by a lattice gate. The gate gave a clear view of the delicate little garden table where the two men sat down and—if the films and stills were right— carried on cynical, meaningless conversations while they drank their garishly colored drinks out of odd-looking glasses. It was the same with the vast coastal arc where the harbor lay. Although I deliberately conjured up its name more than once— Piraeus Piraeus—I heard no echo. What multitudes of ships and nations have approached this bay over the centuries. Now we are sitting here under the awnings in front of plates of the choicest fish. Expensive, expensive. N. is right, we do not yet know the value of money here. The stiffly shy Englishman behind us, who cannot defend himself against the gypsy women with their huge, artfully embroidered coverlets.

How old was Cassandra when she died? Thirty-five? Did she come to feel she had survived a lot, too much? New to me was the question of whether indifference might not be the price of survival. Indifference, the least welcome thing of all, the alien element where we are most sure to founder, even more surely than in impotence and guilt. No, I told the young gypsy woman, I do not want my hand read. That's true, isn't it? said C.— one doesn't want to know the bad things that are to come. But that noon under the bright Greek sun on the foreign coast, there was nothing I feared more than the verdict that *nothing* was to come. How hyperalert I was the first time I crossed over the border, how greedy to hear the first words in a foreign language; how captivated by my first foreign city. Captivated by love, small wonder (I heard the ironical echo say inside me, the echo which I am used to by now). You cannot expect love from this city. The miracle of self-renewal—that can no longer be expected from any city. To be destined to walk on lifeless stone, between mutely erect stone walls, under mute and meaningless skies—that oracle seemed to me inescapable and unacceptable. After all, you can come to Greece too late.

Not only victors but victims, too, climbed up to the Acropolis. Man and beast, they took turns on the altars of the temples which stand superimposed or side by side. The lamb took over from the young man, the chicken from the captive woman. It was the same with the gods: the earlier god, the earlier goddess were always sacrificed to the later. At the very bottom, at the foot of the Athena Nike temple, is the shrine of the earth goddess Gaea, filled with rubble, covered, built over, invisible to us later-born. In exchange we have the reproduction of the renowned Phidias's colossal statue of Pallas Athena, ivory and gold and armed with helmet, shield, spear, and breastplate; with the miniature statuette of Nike, goddess of victory, in her left hand; powerful and cold. Motherless. An evil thought emerging with shield and spear from the head of her father, Zeus. Never, I think, has she been more godforsaken and more remote from her nature than in Phidias's costly idol. The desolate and mostly clueless, antlike obtrusiveness of the tourists, who, like me, are resting on chunks of marble, glistening sharp-cornered stone, smooth to the touch. Objects ought to be speaking to me, but that fact does not loosen their tongues. The color snapshots N. is taking will not stir my imagination when I get them home, any more than they do here. Of course, we were at the Acropolis, too (I will say). And so? A vast heap of rubble. Splendid views of a city destroyed by building. And a blinding glare of reflected light, I had never experienced the like of it; yes, really, even though it was only April.

And then we went to see the *korai* ("maidens") from the Erechtheum, which have been placed in the museum on the Acropolis to safeguard them from total destruction. They stand in a semicircle, gaze down at us spectators, and weep. The stone is weeping, and I do not mean metaphorically. Tears have streamed over the faces of the stone maidens and eaten them away. Something more powerful than grief has engraved itself in these beautiful cheeks: acid rain, polluted air. Once these faces may have been blank and expressionless; our century has forced its own expression on them, that of mourning, which finds an echo in me as if I had been kicked from inside. All the emotions that mourning brings with it begin to stir—anger, fear, dread, guilt, shame. I have arrived. I understand this mountain of stone and bones. I understand the overcrowded, hurrying, homicidal, money-chasing city that pumps out smoke and exhaust fumes, trying to catch up in a few years with what some of its Western sisters took more than a century to achieve. I understand: You, the need of the present-day city, were not compatible with the need of the stone maidens with their serene, proud bearing, who supported, for more than two thousand years, the canopy over the grave of the snake-king Cecrops, founder of Athens. The *korai*, the maidens, once the fertility goddess Persephone and her daughter, later reduced to supporting beams, now infertile, placed out of bounds. Shall I try to prevent them from appearing to my inner eye over and over in the guise of symbols, not only while I am in Greece, but afterward, too? Shall I try to name the "meaning" they stand for, which is really a non-meaning? The barbarism of the modern age. The question that disturbs me: Was there, is there, an alternative to this barbarism?

Am I already broaching the theme?

The self-devouring city. A force has come over me. Have the sightless eyes of the *korai* opened up to me? Now I roved through the city with these ancient burning eyes, and I saw today's people, my contemporaries, as descendants. That young woman leaning in the door of the shop where she sells Turkish honey and Oriental spices: a descendant of those Achaean women who had waited away ten years of their lives by the time the heroes returned from Troy, and who—small consolation —may have modeled for the *korai*. Those men in the unique fish hall saturated with the pungent odors of the sea who toss the twitching fish onto the wooden tables with a swift sharp motion and kill it with little hatchets, cut it up with sharp knives: great-great-grandsons of the early Greek seafarers. Furrowed brown peasant faces in the meat halls, where the drawn and quartered sacrificial beasts hang in rows on meathooks, drained of blood. Who were their ancestors? Thessalians? Macedonians from the supply lines of Alexander the Great? Smoking his pipe behind a steaming roast of aromatic chestnuts: a Turk. The slender dark girls who run out from a dim school gate into the blindingly bright street are familiar to me from pictures of the Minoan Cretans, and the street vendor with his mobile glass showcase of gold jewelry is, in his gestures and the cut of his face, an Italian descended from Venetian merchants and soldiers who colonized the Mediterranean region. They all pressed toward me from the crowd hurrying away from Omonia Square, while we were struggling to reach it. I was not able to catch their eyes. Apart from a few bold, naked looks from men, which a woman learns to fend off here simply by straightening up, no attempt was made to look at each other. City-monads, I thought; who fired them off, what nucleus do they orbit, what holds them together? "The hunt for the drachma," says N. "Self-interest. Each needs the other in order to sell him something, cheat him, tap him, suck him dry. And Omonia Square is their hunting ground," he said, "both above and below ground." And the heart of the preserve, where it was still as the heart of a whirlwind, was the taverna where we were sitting. Cool grotto light, as in all the Greek tavernas, emanating from the blue-green painted walls, a light which immediately seems to cool off and calm down those who enter in a fever. Their deep-dyed impatience is met by the waiters' brisk service; broad slices of fresh white bread already stand waiting; tomatoes, green cucumbers, olives, oil and vinegar are already on the table; there is a quarter liter of retsina for everyone; the aroma spreads; behind the counter, fish and meat are frying in open pans; and the innkeeper, small, massive, solemn, greets his guests with a dignified nod. The feast is ready. Show yourself worthy of it. The dignity of eating, in countries where you cannot take it for granted that everyone will be able to eat his fill every day; where avarice has not yet been able completely to suppress the gesture of hospitality, which, even if it has a price, meets with a ready welcome. We foreigners are all the more dependent on it because here we have no command of words, are incapable of deciphering even the signs outside the shops, must rely on pictures, smells.

But isn't the word the very thing that has taken over control of our inner life? The fact that I lack words here: doesn't this mean that I am losing myself? How quickly does lack of speech turn into lack of identity? A curious notion: If a Cassandra were to appear now—and from the look of things she must exist among the women here—I would not recognize her, because I would not understand her speech. Supposing that she fell into a frenzy like the first Cassandra—I would not be able to judge whether one of these smartly dressed, white-gloved police officers was entitled, up to a point, to seize her upper arm soothingly but also admonishingly, rebukingly; to draw her out of the circle of curious onlookers, who, because of the excitement they show here, seem more involved than people in cities to the north; and to deliver her to the ambulance which is already waiting in one of the side streets. A superstitious awe prevents me from thinking with her head and saying what she would say, but in my own language. For her message would apply to more than one city. That is why she was able to prophesy the doom that would befall the House of Atreus after the death of Agamemnon, after her own death—the doom that would come through Orestes, the son who was believed dead.

> But our death shall not go unatoned,
> another will come to avenge us:
> The mother-murderer who makes the criminals atone,
> a fugitive and a beggar, homeless he returns home,
> to cap with the final stone the blasphemous wall reared
> by his race.

The faith in prophets (I think then) is, to a large extent, faith in the power of the word. As if in response to a challenge, I catch myself feeling confident that the alien chaos, to which I feel more vulnerable here than I do at home, could take on an orderly structure surrounding words, like iron filings around a magnet. The centering around the Logos, the word as fetish —perhaps the deepest superstition of the West, or at least the one of which I am a fervent devotee. Hence, the mere fact that I do not know the language gives me an inkling of the possible terrors of exile. When did it begin, this unfortunate habit of trying out foreign cities to see how it would feel to live there? The question is, When did the feeling of having a homeland disappear? (This moment in Cassandra's life must have come when she realized that her warnings were senseless, because the Troy she wanted to save did not exist. That was her hard luck. What could Troy do about it?)

The threads which connect us to our obligations must have torn at some point when we were flying across the Balkans in our ark. When? Where? No way to tell. N. looked around him in the taverna with an expression that witnessed his sensitivity to the most delicate vibrations of this interior world. I saw him pick up the scent. To what extent had the foreign land already become home, home a foreign land? Had it accepted him? Did it smell his strange scent and shut him out? Hadn't emigration taken away his ability to stay afloat in these waters? Was I mistaken, or did his heart go out to the old woman, tattered, wasted, who was going from table to table with little nosegays? Lilies of the valley, oh, lilies of the valley. A wave of longing

for a shady, damp spot under a rhododendron bush in a front
garden in Mecklenburg. What is the woman saying? "Her husband is sick," N. says indignantly, as if his indignation could
make the husband healthy. The woman touched him. Exile,
I thought again; that is to be saved, and unrelated to anything.
One of the circles of Hell, but which? Whereas those three
gypsy women in their long, bright-colored skirts, their vivid,
gleaming blouses, their fringed kerchiefs, who are sitting down
at a table by the door—they carried a circle of relatedness around
with them, which goes to show that it need not consist of a
house, a yard, property, a place, a country, and a certain brand
of sky, as it does for us more stationary types. But that man
with a hat and briefcase who just came in—he came every noon
at the same time, N. informed us—there was someone with
fixed and permanent roots for you. No longer as young as he
once was, but still on the job; a man who would stick it out
until the end (I saw that his rather stiff pride, whether innate
or freely chosen, was the man's shelter and his cage). He posted
himself at a table close to the bar, greeted the innkeeper se-
dately, received a respectful greeting in return while the waiter
was already setting down a glass of ouzo on his table; he drained
it to the last drop at once, but with dignity; then he put a coin
on the table, saluted the innkeeper with two fingers raised to
his hat; the innkeeper thanked him with a bow, and he left.
"Two minutes," said G., "but every day." There you have it.

And there is not a trace of irony in the large or small gestures of these people. Once we are out on the street again, we
lose the power of speech, forced to join in the afternoon rush,
when the struggle for survival shifts from the offices and fac-
tories onto the street. I meet the glance of a stone Medusa, a
frightful Gorgon's head, but in the middle of this crowd I have
no time to turn to stone. The old curses seem to have lost their
effect; almost suffocating in the tainted air of the overcrowded
buses, fatigued, dripping with sweat, we are incapable of wish-
ing for anything but that it be over. By turning to stone? And

what if we did? Did we notice, N. asks, how the exhaust fumes weigh on one's chest? So that's what is weighing on my chest, the exhaust fumes; comforting to know that. I could almost have taken it for a nightmare. Yet it, too, must be made of the wishes of human beings; only, somewhere between the wish and its fulfillment their malicious gods twisted and jinxed it into something exorbitant, dreadful, grimacing. "What is your word for happiness?" "*Eutichía*," said N., "the good chance." "Very nice," I say. A saying like "In the long run you make your own luck" could not develop among these people. That is why, ever since the times of Homer, of Aeschylus, they have not been able to describe misfortune as guilt. How generous of the Greek tragedian to allow the captive barbarian woman to pronounce the prophecy of doom over an early Greek royal house.

What prophecy could still surprise us; could lure from us cries of woe like those uttered by the chorus of old Argive men when they hear it proclaimed that their king is at that moment being slaughtered by their queen? Aren't we beyond all proclamations and prophecies, and so beyond tragedy?

C.'s heated, frenzied whispers in the tiny kitchen back at N.'s house. Skillful, nimble, working offhandedly, she slices vegetables, herbs over the sink; washes tomatoes, cucumbers, leeks, parsley, spinach, onions, garlic; slits open the tentacles of the squid, washes them, puts them in boiling oil; the kitchen begins to smoke and smell fragrant; the gauze-screened window to the air shaft is pushed open; spinach and curds are mixed to make the filling for the pita; the dough is flexed and rolled out with the poker-thin rolling pin, clapped together, rolled out again, thinner, thinner still, until the light shines through the thinnest spots. "I hope you don't mind that we're not having any meat." C. reaches for pots and pans with trembling fingers, I place my hands on hers: "Please, calm down." But she cannot be calm. As if someone were standing behind her. No, it is not me, it is Madam who stands behind her. "You don't know what she's like," she says; but she dearly wants someone to know it, to know her daily routine under Madam's thumb; the exclusive quarter of town; the incredibly expensive detached villas, the huge rooms, the vast quantities of dirty laundry, the insolent children, the meal that must be ready on the dot when the boss lady leaves her shop—handicrafts and wrought goldwork, "the most expensive there is, believe me, she thinks of nothing but money. She doesn't care in the least what her husband does, really. Or what the children do. I have to look after them, too; they like my German apple cake. And the grandmother, too. Do you know what she says to me? 'My daughter is a wicked woman.' Seriously. And twice a week I have to scrub the big marble balcony that runs around the entire house" (she makes her do it with a caustic lye that turns her fingertips raw) "and I almost go blind from the glittering light on the balcony. Can you imagine that?" Shall I say: Yes, ever since I was on the Acropolis? "Why don't you leave?" I say. "What do you want with a tradeswoman who exploits you?" "Do you think so?" says C. "I don't know." Gradually she succeeds in infecting me. When I think of "Madam," I picture a woman who is a cross between a monster and a goddess, a feminine vamp who cannot be resisted, a female subspecies hitherto unknown to me.

The squid is done, the pita bread ready in the oven. I am mixing the salad at the moment when Antonis rings the bell. So there is a man named Antonis to go with the voice on the telephone, who thinks of everything for us, arranges everything, takes care of everything. Who knows everyone here and spends his days telephoning a dozen people on our behalf. The four of us sit at the round table which completely fills the so-called main room of the tiny apartment. Instead of the brown table-cloth, C. has put out a white one; there is just enough table-ware for four. The two-liter bottle of retsina which N. has fetched from the corner taverna is cold. We talk.

Penetrating deeper with words, questions, confessions than the eye can, but stop short of the questions that sympathy suggests: Antonis, what's the matter with you? His eyes, opened wide, as if petrified in perpetual terror; the mobility of his face marked with wrinkles and furrows; the incessant restlessness of his hands. What has he seen? What is he trying to hold on to? What is slipping away from him? Is he what he seems: an envoy of the gods who govern this city, and at the same time their victim? His strained, hunted face—why should the Erinyes pursue him, a man like him? What is gnawing at him? Did we see him on television, he asks, when he criticized the government for its social legislation? How they simply faded him out—in the middle of a live transmission! when he became too critical. "What do you call that in German?" "Fade to blank," we say, and N. translates. "Very good," says Antonis. "It must be a pleasure to write in German." Do people in our country read his books? he asks. Are there reviews? We must send them to him without fail. Two of his books have been read the world over. What does he need reviews for? The word "crushed" comes into my mind. A man on whom too heavy a burden has fallen.

At night all four of us lie awake. The heat. The fear. Very early in the morning I hear C. get up, get ready softly, go. Madam has to issue orders to C. before leaving for work herself. Madam boasts to her friends that she has a German woman working for her. Usually Greeks work for Germans.

Mrs. Tharsos, who wants to show us "something special," is German, but she has been living in Greece for four decades, married to a professor who is Greek. She drives us north, through forests, forests. At some point the road branches off toward Marathon; our destination is Oropos. She always brings friends from Germany here; but younger people—didn't we agree?—have no feeling for sights unless they jump out at you. Actually, her Greek son-in-law (she says) has forbidden her to associate with her grandchildren . . . And her daughter? I ask at last. "Ah, my daughter. Do you know what that's like, being married to a Greek man? Who sacrifices everything to what he calls his honor?" Silence. Her daughter decided in favor of her husband, just as she herself had done long ago, she says. Silence. "And your husband, Mrs. Tharsos?" "Oh, my husband. I can't say another word to him about my daughter and her husband. He simply leaves the room. I can't talk with him about his work, either. Or about politics." Silence. "What do you talk to your husband about?" "About the other children. Our son, our daughter, who are studying in Germany. You can't talk much about people with a Greek man, you know. For him a person is 'good' or 'bad,' and that's all there is to it. I read a lot, you know. And give a few German lessons. No, even now I can't speak Greek without an accent."

Mrs. Tharsos supposes we know what an Amphiareion is, but we do not. She gives an obol to the old man who is sitting in a shack at the entrance and who knows her, and exchanges a few sentences with him. No, he does not have to come with us. Yes, she knows her way around. Smoking his pipe, the old man sits down on his wooden bench again. I have often thought about him. Before and after the tourist season he sits here for weeks without seeing a single person, we are told. What is he guarding? A tract of antique ruins, overgrown with greenery, surrounded by a wire fence and almost all far too heavy to be stolen. He is not allowed to question the purpose of his solitary vigil here, and he does not question it. The office which he punctiliously discharges—it cannot really be called an occupation—is meaning-free, not meaningless. He does not seem to know what boredom is. Nature changes slowly with the seasons. There are not always clouds in the sky for him to look at. Does he become a part of nature? Does he ruminate? But what about? Mrs. Tharsos says he is a friendly, contented man. So the authorities hit on just the right watchman for this shrine. Maybe the spirit of place has molded him. How could a man suffering inner strife, a man plagued by unrest, admit patients to the Amphiareion who are seeking not only assurance about the future but also rest? "Yes," Mrs. Tharsos says, "the Greeks already had sanatoriums."

But above all they knew the relationship between emotional

and physical ailments, and that between a man's well-being and his prospects for the future. And who is more eager to know his future than a man who is off balance? He will make a pilgrimage here, to this famous place which is sought out by better spirits. He will hand over his drachma and be pleasantly impressed by the first person he meets here, the amiable, dispassionate, and calm watchman who takes his drachma and hands him his spa ticket made of lead or bronze. Happy to be exempt at last from all personal decision, he will gladly submit to the ceremonies, take part in the sacrifices, visit the theater and the arena, stroll beneath the stone pines and young oak trees inhaling their pungent aroma, drink the potions administered by the priests and their assistants (female assistants, too? Hygeia, the goddess of health, is a woman!); will lie down, swathed in cloths, on one of the couches on whose marble bases we are seated, inhale the fragrant air . . . will sleep and—dream. For that is what he is here for. And the priests, who may be able to recognize the most vehement phases of the dream by the rapidity of eye movements under the closed lids, exactly as our encephalograms do today—the priests will awaken him and ask what he has dreamed. And he—perhaps still lying on the couch —will tell them, as well and honestly as he can. Will they also get him to free-associate about his dream? In any case, they will "interpret" his future, for his dream, or a quantity of his dreams, will have told them what kind of person he is and where his inclinations lie. They will not admit the slightest doubt that it is fate and the gods who determine the destinies of men. But if they do guard an occult knowledge, it is the knowledge that the behavior of man can influence fate and the gods, and that they themselves can help determine this behavior by whether they strengthen or weaken their patients. One day a priestess—Cassandra, or whatever her name may be —must arrive at this same knowledge, too. After all, they say that she was one of those seers who did not foresee the future by inspecting the entrails of sacrificed beasts or the flight of birds, but read it out of people's dreams. How did she manage that process? Even if the word "manipulation" had not yet been invented . . .

Absolute stillness, nothing but bird cries. The colors: green and white and blue. The quantities of Greek spring flowers. G. finds thyme, which we rub between our fingers so we can smell the scent. Lavender. In the past, Mrs. Tharsos says, they used to put bouquets of lavender between the linens. She talks a little about the old days. I have a distinct feeling that we are sitting inside a circle where we are accessible to view from the very remote past, just as, by the same token, we are in a position to experience what happened here ages ago. I feel an inner eye open, feel a touch, very soft, casual, unemotional, almost mocking. Our talk trickles away, it grows still. How could it not be healthful to sleep here? She will come back soon, Mrs. Tharsos tells the attendant. He'll be here, he replies.

We take the road along the sea, find an isolated taverna where they are just doing the spring cleaning with floods of water. Nevertheless, ten minutes later a huge plate of little baked fish is standing before us, along with salad, leeks. We eat outside, with only the road separating us from the flat, pale-brown sea. At the table next to us, four civil servants from Athens in black suits, stiff and sweating. On the other side, the innkeeper's big family is loudly and cheerfully eating the same meal as the guests. The wind from the sea sweeps under the tablecloths, which are made of paper like all tablecloths in Greek tavernas. "Maybe it's true," says Mrs. Tharsos. "To blame other people for your own life makes you unnecessarily lonely. Self-manipulation—there's always that, isn't there?"

Antonis telephoned. We have to register as aliens with the police. It will cost us a morning. We go to the police station in the morning. I cannot explain it, but the moment the three of us set foot in the old office building, we turn into a gang. N., versed in the language and, to a degree, in certain customs of bureaucracy, precedes us as gangleader; he is followed by G.,

as a male gang member, and I, as the female accomplice, bring
up the rear of the procession. Three staircases. Everywhere you
go, the bosses live upstairs, but it is not everywhere that they
live in an ancient, angled house impregnated with the cold
sweat of generations. The police chief receives us personally,
having been forewarned by Antonis; he looks the way a police
chief ought to look, and even wears the appropriate narrow
mustache. In a dignified manner he expresses his joy at our
visit to his city, a distinction that makes us feel oppressed
rather than honored. But thanks to Antonis, he has not remained ignorant of our profession, and so it occurs to him to
ask what we are really looking to find here. This question is
directed with inscrutable friendliness, and man to man, to G.,
who with a likewise inscrutable expression tells him the truth:
tourism. "Aha. Special interests?" Little by little the eyes of
the three men come to rest on me. "The classical period," I
assert. "I am interested in the Greek classical age. But in the
Minoans, too." The chief of police for alien registration looks
at me as if an interest of this kind, and in this place, were
tantamount to a perversion. "And what about writing?" he asks
amiably. Didn't we want to write about Greece? "Certainly
not," says G., far too vaguely, then N. again takes charge of
the proceedings and declares in a tone so firm as to be almost
impolite: "No. They do not by any means want to write." As
if we did not even know how to write. And turning to us, he
says emphatically in German: "You don't want to write a single
line about Greece, understand." G. is silent, but I, convinced
of the truth of this assertion, say: "Of course not."

Well, in that case.

Then the comedy of the situation strikes me all at once. I
can see G. concentrating unwaveringly on the police chief's
hammered-silver desk set; then I begin to scrutinize the indoor
palm tree. N., in true gangleader style, is telling the receptive
man behind the desk God knows what about the past and
future plans of these slightly suspect tourists from a virtually

unknown country, and I inform no one but the indoor palm tree that I can imagine a whole series of nasty situations in which I would play a delinquent role. Inside official bureaus, the borderline between the lands of the innocent and the suspect grows thin, very thin, and you never know whether you are wholly inside the one and have not already got one foot in the other. But fortunately, in this case we seem to find ourselves (as so often happens) inside a film, where, although we have no hope of ever meeting the director who assigned us our unfamiliar roles, we have already rehearsed this particular scene a hundred times. But wherever can they have hidden the camera this time—in that rectangular waste duct in the wall above the door? In the buttonhole of the chief of police for alien registration, who is just rising to his feet so that he can turn us over to a junior branch chief, summoned by the press of a bell, for further processing? (The latter, too, has imposing features, by the way, but never would they suffice to make him a genuine chief.) Then the film director, who never prearranges things with the actors in films of this kind, sends in another branch chief, who apparently holds a privileged position in the hierarchy, since he can appear in his chief's presence unsummoned, and for the sole purpose of saying goodbye to him. He is leaving for his village tomorrow, he says.

The atmosphere is transformed like lightning; several brimming barrelfuls of cordiality rain down. "This fortunate man," cries the Athens chief of police for alien registration, "is going to his village tomorrow!" Whereas he himself must stick here at his post like a galley slave, until the last day before Easter. Consequently our parting turns tender as soon as N. has revealed his intention to go "to his village" for Easter, too, in Thessaly—"ah, Thessaly!"—and to take us along. Tourists who accompany a Greek to his village for Easter are to be treated as guests.

Two words muttered by N. between his teeth as we leave transform us back into a gang for the benefit of cameras and microphones: "It's working!" Whereupon we are referred by our department chief to a kind of clerk—a clerk who has read Kafka, to be sure—and are each permitted to receive and fill out several king-sized questionnaires, which, however, remain worthless paper unless accompanied by passport photos and duty stamps. Photos? We groan aloud. The gods cannot have intended such a fate. But N. briefly consults an ancient Cerberus sitting in a shiny chair at the head of the staircase, who apparently has no strictly defined professional duties, and finds out what is to be done. Mutely we march down three flights of stairs, keeping to our tried-and-true three-rank formation, to a simple wooden shed where an ingenious photographer has set up shop—praise be to free enterprise! Having demanded a price which N., speaking between his teeth again, calls "unscrupulous," he takes our photographs in a twinkling, and only minutes later hands to each of us, through a crack in the curtain, a little bag of passport photos which would indeed do credit to any criminal file.

This time not I but G. seems to have second thoughts as we start to climb the stairs again. "They won't do," he says. "Why not?" says N. "Everything will do fine. Or do you want to look handsome for the alien-registration police!" More duty to pay; transformed into stamps, they are dampened at the water fountain in the vestibule, glued to our questionnaires, and stamped at the desk of the Kafkaesque clerk, whereupon he, acting apparently under the instigation of our questionnaires, fills out with violet ink and a scratchy pen a record card which, he soothingly assures us, incorporates us forever into the archives of the Athens alien-registration police.

As we arrive back at N.'s tiny apartment, the telephone rings. Antonis. Surely we had not been to see the alien-registration police already? he asks. He had spent the whole morning making telephone calls and had learned that it was not necessary for us to report there. Now, I thought, the best we can hope for is that the photographer will hold on to an enlarged close-up of N.'s face.

We have suffered enough humiliation; all we want now is to forget it all, to wash down the insecurity and exasperation with the cool retsina kept in massive barrels, set in the wall of that corner taverna which is already famed among us although we have not yet made its acquaintance. N. invites us. We have to climb down a few steps into the grotto light, into the coolness of the cellar. Salad, wine, green-bean soup. Now, we are told, we are going to hear about the HOUSE, whose spirit, or evil spirit, possesses N. N. turns out to be right: The taverna is just the place to tell us about the house of his fathers.

I imagine that this taverna in the Athens House, with its thick cellar walls, is very old. I imagine that generations of Greek men have sat here to eat thick green-bean soup and tell about the "house of their fathers," for that has been their theme from time immemorial. Homer's *Iliad*, a song of the fates of the great Greek families, may have formed out of the infinitely many trickles of tales told in the ports, the market-places, and the tavernas over centuries, which then swelled into a narrative river: "Sing, O Goddess, the wrath of the Peliad Achilles . . ."* (Achilles, son of Peleus). Storytelling is humane and achieves humane effects, memory, sympathy, understand-ing—even when the story is in part a lament for the destruction of one's fathers' home, for the loss of memory, the breakdown of sympathy, the lack of understanding.

The house of his fathers (N. says), in that Thessalian village which we have yet to see, is actually the house of his grand-father, where he grew up. And the house of his grandmother, whom we know. I can see her before me, the ancient, small, withered, nimble, alert, suspicious woman, her fleshless tiny little bird's head, her sparse hair, her black skirts. Who only a year or two ago was running with the agility of a weasel over the fields of Mecklenburg, against the wind and with her arms spread wide as if she wanted to lift off the ground. She knew how to fly when she was young. She could push off, tuck up her

* The opening lines of the *Iliad*.—Trans.

legs, and fly along close above the ground; she had lost this power with old age, so the story went. Had we known, asked N., that this grandmother was not his real grandmother but his grandfather's second wife, who had taken him away from his mother so as to enjoy in her village the respect accorded to a woman who raises a male heir? So, his grandmother. The one who always used to stroke my cheek. N.'s family history becomes yet another degree more obscure, turns into a tangle of threads from which he extricates a tracer thread for us that afternoon in his taverna: the thread of his flight with his grandparents, still young at the time, who went to join the partisans in the mountains in 1947 and took him, their twelve-year-old grandson, along. You remember, when the English, in league with the Greek government they had put into power, violently suppressed the movement for national liberation. "Do you remember?" That seems to be N.'s refrain, for what meaning would there be in the victims, in the thousands of the homeless, the gnawing pain of exile that went on for decades, for a people without a memory? Storytelling is the assignment of meaning, and if telling the story is not enough—if, like another Odysseus, you return almost thirty years later and see that people were *not* waiting for you, that your paternal home is falling into ruin, your family is hard up, the neighbors are sending their goats onto your land—then you go there and you simply rebuild the house, do you understand that? We believe we understand. N. cannot allow a symbol, a dream, to fall into ruin. We know that the pain your own people inflict on you cannot be quieted unless you make strangers of them or yourself; and not the despised, the forgotten man is miserable. ("Those dearest to us, I know, are our bitter enemies . . ." Orestes says in Aeschylus.) Cassandra is most at risk, not when the wrath of the Trojans threatens her life, but when all the threads that link her with them, including the threads of anger, have snapped and a new net has not yet been knotted by her own guilt.

Did suicides occur among the most ancient races?

At last we have telephoned Valtinos, whose number Sigrid gave us long ago in the airport boarding lounge, and who regales us with coffee and wine that night on the roof of his skyscraper. Valtinos, who is just now doing a new translation of Aeschylus's *Oresteia* into modern Greek, finds no textual reference to suicide. Ancient man was firmly tied to family, clan, tribe, so that expulsion, as we know, meant certain death. Death through fear, remorse, dread, probably indeed through the dissolution of that inner framework of values without which we, like they, are incapable of living; whose disintegration exposes us, like them, to the longing for death. Not to mention those cases where we have no choice but to dismantle this framework ourselves, thus placing ourselves in a situation which, because it offers us no acceptable alternative, is called "tragic," and which is so favorable to literature. Why is it—we wonder on this exceptionally mild night while the stars, how else can we put it? "draw up"—why has so little notice been taken of the fact that in social terms Cassandra belongs to the ruling class, the daughter of the king? And that, as Aeschylus tells us, not everyone was allowed to say what he "saw"? Listen to the chorus of the old men of Argos, who are seized by a dark premonition when Clytemnestra escorts Agamemnon into the fortress:

> *If a barrier had not been set*
> *between men,*
> *the mighty and the menial:*
> *if the lowly man were not compelled*
> *to keep silence:*
> *I would say everything!*
> *I would scream,*
> *and it would overflow*
> *from my heart!*

But Cassandra, of aristocratic birth, has the privilege of speaking, of being heard and spoken of by name; even her death is not nameless. I ask Valtinos if he does not believe that, given the choice, she would have done the same thing all over again. "That is a contemporary way of looking at it," he says, "because the ancients did not recognize the existence of this moment of choice." All right, granting that these were contemporary criteria, didn't he agree that Cassandra was the first professional working woman in literature? What else could a woman have become besides a seeress? "In that case," Valtinos says, "Clytemnestra was the first feminist." She ruled Mycenae alone for ten years; she had to witness and endure it when her husband, the "most resolute" Agamemnon, sacrificed her dearest child, her daughter Iphigenia, to the goddess, expecting in exchange to be given a favorable wind for his war fleet as they set out on their journey to Troy. She took a man who pleased her, Aegisthus. Was she to renounce her rights on her husband's return? Go cringing back to the hearth and the distaff?

We drank. It is getting on to midnight, the air is turning cooler. Yes, it exists, this velvet sky, the glitter of southern stars exists. A ruddy yellow Turkish sickle moon hangs low and slanted over the city; the wineglasses are standing on the concrete terrace beside our chairs. Sigrid brings strong coffee in tall cups; her little boy, the one who fell down in the boarding lounge, has to go to bed now. Are we dreaming? Do I have only to pronounce a certain name, so that everything will come together, small miracles will happen, and I will be drawn deeper and deeper into an enchantment? The stars sing, it is a high whirring sound; I will not try to convince anyone, but we heard it that night.

"It's harder than you think," Valtinos says, "to translate the ancient texts into modern Greek, because of the ambiguity of the ancient Greek." He gives an example: Clytemnestra, after she has greeted her husband, Agamemnon, effusively, orders the maidservants to strew red cloths in his path so that the king's feet will not touch the ground as he returns home victorious. (This seems to be the origin of the highly double-edged custom, still practiced today, of spreading a red carpet to honor foreign chiefs of state.) In Droysen's German translation Clytemnestra says:

> *Let his path to the house be swiftly covered in purple,*
> *for the man unhoped for, so that Dike may guide his steps.*

In Walter Jens's German translation I find:

> *Let the path be of purple that brings him, the*
> *   scarcely expected,*
> *back into the house.*

And Peter Stein, in his German production of the *Oresteia,* has Clytemnestra say:

> *Spread the garments on the path*
> *as I have ordered,*
> *cover the ground,*
> *let the purple way be made quickly.*
> *And may Dike, justice,*
> *escort, lead him into the house,*
> *as he no doubt did not expect.*

For the most part, Valtinos says, the translations do not turn to account the ambiguity of these lines: Dike, the goddess of justice, is being invoked as protectress of a murder. The death the woman plans for the man is just in her eyes. Thus, the "purple way" could also be translated as the "path of justice." Moreover (he says), the more deeply he immerses himself in the text, the more examples of oscillating meanings crowd in on him. And on top of that, the various generations of translators have translated these differently, depending on their own moral views and interpretations; that is, depending on whether, unconsciously or not, they have sided with the man or the woman. Even in our language it is hard to get hold of these meanings (he says), for our double standard of morality is different from that of our forefathers. And even this concept of the "double standard"—I cannot help thinking—would not be too easy to translate: it would translate differently depending on whether it was used in a disparaging or a neutral sense.

To be sure (we ponder), the double standard of the ancients is not as omnipresent, all-powerful, and all-pervasive as the double code of Western Christian civilization, which must perform a prodigious mental feat of increasingly subtle and ingenious demagoguery in order to acknowledge the commandment *Thou shalt not kill* as the ethical foundation of its life and, without suffering a moral breakdown, simultaneously rescind it for its practical action. So a blind spot grew up at the center of Western culture which conceals from it the all-important fact of its murderous double life. A deficit which unfortunately—so we say on our roof terrace when it is already after midnight—unfortunately and inevitably makes the processes that are leading to self-destruction invisible to the prime movers of our civilization. It is a feat of witchcraft which we may now see through too late. And literature, by describing this double code, has helped to structure it. As for Aeschylus, he is in all frankness installing a new morality, that of father right—without actually defaming the earlier belief in mother right, Valtinos thinks. All right, so Clytemnestra plays the hypocrite at first, she feigns joy at her husband's return; but not in the service of a double code. (Which is why, later, I did not think it right that Peter Stein, in his stage version, has Clytemnestra speak in the tone of a Goebbels-style demagogue.) She wants to be able to do what she thinks is right. Agamemnon violated the not-so-ancient commandment: "Thou shalt make no human sacrifices" when he killed her daughter and his. When she kills him, she is reestablishing what she feels to be justice.

> *This is Agamemnon, my husband.*
> *Killed by this my hand.*
> *Masterly was the work, and likewise just.*

In my view (I tell the others), Aeschylus reveals his prejudice in the detestation which the two women, Cassandra and Clytemnestra, show for each other.

> CASSANDRA: *... But what animal can lend its name to her?*
> *Dragon, Scylla, monster?*
> CLYTEMNESTRA: *There he lies dead who trampled underfoot my*
> *woman's right ...*
> *And here the slave woman lies beside him to give*
> *warning,*
> *the faithful paramour, who lay around with him*
> *beside the oars and mast; now they have what*
> *they deserve.*

That is how the male poet chooses to see these women: vindictive, jealous, petty toward each other—as women can be when they are driven out of public life, chased back to home and hearth. This is exactly what happened in the decades which Aeschylus sums up in his great drama.

That is a lengthy subject, we say, as we take our leave. In the summer, long after we have left this country, the actors who play Clytemnestra, Cassandra, Agamemnon, and Orestes in Epidaurus will speak the ancient texts in the language of Valtinos. I can understand why he feels overworked. I see his typewriter drowning in paper in his room.

Besides, Cassandra did not really interest Aeschylus (I pontificate on our way home through the nocturnal, deserted city); not the way the murderers interested him. Murderers bore us to tears, we agree. Sometimes, I say, I could kill people possessed by homicidal mania. Much rather kill than describe them. Cassandra, I suspect, defines herself as a non-murderer, as a non-maniac. Where does she get the desire and the strength to contradict?

The book Valtinos gave us is small and light, so we put it into the luggage we are taking to Crete. For no one disputes that we must go to Crete. All of a sudden everyone is talking about the "cradle of the West"; all of a sudden everyone is talking about Minoan culture. Every evening in the port of Piraeus, the ferry known as *Kriti* revives an ancient spectacle: A boat sails. That's right. Traffic throughout the entire port basin is gathering in front of the dark rectangular entrance to the boat. From the upper deck we see the tailbacks of vehicles, which appear increasingly hopeless the nearer we get to departure time. Judging by the gestures, the screams that filter up to us, life-and-death confrontations are taking place between the drivers of the snarled-up motor trucks. Fists flash; one man sits down on the quayside, burying his face in his arms, a broken man. Never will the white berets of the harbor police, which now are mingling among the dark-haired heads, accomplish anything; what are they signaling for? I think; until I realize that the truckful of timber which is arousing everyone's hostility and whose driver seemed determined to stick at nothing is slowly, slowly rolling onto the ferry a millimeter at a time; moreover, the other vehicles are falling into place in accordance with inscrutable patterns, as if the big truck were pulling them along in its wake. And the man who sat weeping on the quayside is not the driver of any vehicle and had no personal interest in the outcome, but only stayed to see the show; now he strolls away whistling, because it is no longer interesting. Now is not the first time I have experienced this scene of departure and farewell in a harbor. No one can experience it for the first time who has ever had to say goodbye, ever had to leave what he called "home." This is not the first time (it seems to me) that a ship on which I am standing has glided away from the port jetty; it is not the first time that this dark gulf has opened between me and the shore. A black figure remains behind on the land, C.; we go on waving to her for a long time; she grows small, then tiny.

Then I looked up and saw the light. It was seven o'clock in the evening. The sun, very low, stood behind us and lit up the harbor of Piraeus; but every single object glowed of itself, in its own color, with a magical light that I took care not to miss any evening from then on. Assuming that it was also evening when the Achaeans set sail from the coast of Troy, the captive Trojan women, crowding at the stern of the ships, may have seen the ruins of their city and the shores of home for the last time, in this same glow. That must have intensified their grief, and at the same time anchored more deeply a love they could cling to when they were in a strange land.

But of the storytellers who have written about them, none was present and none has mentioned this light.

2 ❧ THE TRAVEL REPORT CONTINUES, AND THE TRAIL IS FOLLOWED

> *What does it matter if you do not believe me?*
> *The future will surely come.*
> *Just a little while*
> *and you will see for yourself.*
>
> — CASSANDRA, in Aeschylus, *Oresteia*

The magical light we saw from the boat went out, the neon advertisements sprang out of the dusk in the harbor arc of Piraeus: 7-UP, SHELL, darkness fell rapidly. Theseus, when he had conquered the Minotaur in the Labyrinth and found his way out again with the help of Ariadne's thread, left Crete and came to dock in this port in ancient times; but he forgot to substitute a white sail for the black sail which signified death, so that his father, King Aegeus, threw himself into the sea in his grief for the son he thought dead. But the Athenians' annual sacrifice of young men to the Cretan bull was over. The most various ships bearing the most various tidings plied back and forth between Crete and the mainland for millennia. Today the *Kriti* carries young sun seekers from all over the world, hitchhikers who settle down for the night on the benches of the upper deck; boys and girls in standard uniform—jeans, parkas, soft white tennis shoes, jam-packed light metal carrier racks on their backs, which they lean against the benches. We walked past them; the two groups inspected each other mutely.

Then my name was called, I whirled around: Helen stood before me. Tyche, chance, luck. Helen from Columbus, Ohio, who was sitting across from me in my Berlin apartment the last time I saw her, and next to her Sue, her friend from Los Angeles, California. "Hello," she says. "Hello," I reply. She already knows who we are, she says. As for her, we should know that she does stagework. Fine. Where should we eat together?

It turned out that the second-class dining room was the place meant for people like us, that an Italian spaghetti dish best suited our fund of drachmas, and that Minoan culture was the topic of burning interest to the four of us that evening. Obsessed people cannot feel surprised by their obsession of course, that is one of their symptoms. At least they do not notice it in themselves, but only, with greater or lesser degrees of amusement, in others. So it was inevitable that at some point that evening the moment would come—probably we were already sitting on the beds in our cabin, peeling the fresh, fragrant oranges which N. had given us for the journey—the moment when my spirit, or at least part of it, was released from my body and began to float "above us" (I don't mean on the lower cabin deck: much higher!), detached itself, and felt a mild amusement. What in the world were the American women looking for in our territory, in "our" Minoan culture? What I was looking for was obvious. Among other things (but I was hardly aware of anything else at the time) I was seeking the comparative time scale of the battle for Troy and the destruction of Minoan culture in Crete; both of which events, if the scholarly dating is accurate, took place around the thirteenth century B.C.—Crete having been destroyed before Troy. Helen and Sue were looking for confirmation of their thesis that women called the tune on Crete and that the Minoans were the better for it. Moreover, I was excited by the claims of the American Velikovsky, who—following lines of argument too extensive to set forth here, although I by no means refrained from doing so that evening in the cabin—has put forward a completely new dating system for the history of antiquity. This system brings the fall of Troy, as well as the decline of Minoan culture, three to four centuries closer to our time, namely into the eighth "or late in the ninth century B.C.":

that is, almost into Homer's lifetime. Helen and Sue, whose opinions on contemporary art can differ completely, spoke with a single voice as they quoted several sentences from their travel guide. With deep gratification they told us that they viewed these lines as catastrophic because they showed male archaeologists' total misunderstanding of the basic facts about the female culture they had unearthed on Crete. It was a lively evening in our cabin. My spirit, which continued to hover above us, preserved an image of two blond and two dark heads which took turns shaking as they bent over various books. And for a reason which I will disclose directly, I still remember that I must have quoted the following sentence from Velikovsky: "The tradition about Aeneas who, saved when Troy was captured, went to Carthage (a city built in the ninth century B.C.) and from there to Italy, where he founded Rome (a city first built in the middle of the eighth century B.C.), implies that Troy was destroyed in the eighth or late in the ninth century B.C."*

Quick as a flash Aeneas sprang up before my inner eye, and Cassandra had known him. Merely known him? What was there about him that might have touched her more deeply? Consideration, coupled with strength? So, I was transferring a contemporary ideal to a mythological figure who cannot possibly have been that kind of person? Of course. What else?

My inner voice was silent, not really offended, not bored or impatient, either. It was simply silent and left me, stretched out on the narrow bunk, rocked by the gentle waves of the Aegean, to read Valtinos's book. A bloody history from the partisan period in which the important thing was not the blood but the gradual loss, by an inordinately abused man, of his inner relatedness to his fellow human beings, and in the end to his closest comrades. I did not want to know its inevitable ending, not this

* Quoted from "When Was the *Iliad* Created?," in Immanuel Velikovsky, *Worlds in Collision* (New York: Doubleday, 1950), p. 239.—Trans.

evening. I put the book away, took with me into sleep my fore-knowledge of how rebellion and resistance end in this century. Just at the last I saw the facial expression of this partisan, a young man with dark hair and beard, whose head—such was the archaic language in which my speaking consciousness expressed itself in my sleep—suddenly floated upon the waters; I do not know how else to say it. Somewhere in the last few days I must have come across the singing head of Orpheus. A youthful head, which I knew belonged to a man named Aeneas, was floating on smooth, oily water, surrounded by the petals of water lilies and other verdure. He was looking at me, painfully demanding. And I knew of course, without expressly having to think it, that this Aeneas was also the young partisan whose assuredly ghastly end I had not wanted to know. Knew that these two men, separated by more than three thousand years, had as if casually been imprinted with the same expression, the expression of the losers who do not give up, who know: they will lose again and again, and again and again will not give up, and that is no accident, no mistake or mishap, but it is meant to be that way. The thing that no one ever wants to believe—that head floating on the water believed and knew, and that was the most dreadful shame, the real crying shame, and it was the greatest delight: Aeneas.

So Crete, the island of Minos, approached unbeknown to us, and we took care to be up early as we were bidden, to watch the sun rise out of the sea, and did not miss the view of the Venetian fortifications at the entrance to the harbor. We found ourselves with Helen and Sue once again inside a taxi, and ended up outside a café at the busiest intersection of Herakleion, where the young hitchhikers from the boat were also drinking an espresso.

Antonis's solicitude had preceded us here, so I had to call a certain telephone number and follow the instructions of a female voice that spoke in English. We never got to see the owner of this voice face to face, and so in memory it turned into a spirit voice; all the more so, as it sent us along enigmatic paths whose meaning we could not fathom. It compelled us to travel

westward in a taxi which charged dearly for each of the twenty-
six kilometers of our trip to the (for us) mysterious village of
Chersónissos. (To us it seemed that it was counting each
kilometer two or three times over!) We came to the hotel,
which to be sure lay on the sea and was "modern," as advertised,
but by no means cheap, at least not by our lights. Therefore, no
sooner had we moved into our room, likewise "modern," and
satisfied ourselves that we could walk out its large door directly
onto the beach, than we began to think about when and how
we could get away from here again. For what in heaven's name
were we supposed to do in this former village souped up into a
beach resort, where the restaurants and pensions were mostly
closed now, before the tourist season, and which consisted of a
single long street where you could not even walk in peace because of the traffic? And what in the world were Helen and Sue
supposed to do here, now that they had daringly followed us on
a rented motorcycle, thereby only magnifying the extent of our
problem?

Then we found out what we were supposed to do here: go
walking. Follow the road uphill into the mountain spurs, to the
two enticing white villages which you can see from the road. We
were perhaps supposed to bear witness that in April not only all
of Greece but all of Crete is green and covered with spring
flowers. Altogether untypically; for in Greece and Crete the
typical thing is scorched grass withered to hay, and white-hot
bare rock. For us Greece is the land of a thousand flowers, of
multicolored anemones, the land of the red poppy, whose small
but durable blooms also adorn all the altars. For example, the
altar of the little white village church which a girl—the daughter
of the Orthodox priest or the sacristan?—signals us to enter.
There is nothing to see. Deftly the child has slipped consecrated
candles into our hands, for which she then names the price in a
barely detectible English; deftly she pockets the money. As we
step out onto the street, several pairs of eyes gaze gravely and
steadfastly at us from the darkness of the house where the girl

lives. A farmer with his donkey comes toward us down the steep downslope of the stony road from the mountain; he has been to fetch fodder and looks at us until he disappears with the animal behind one of the white stone walls which fence in the little yards. Six or seven brown-skinned, lean men are sitting outside the taverna in old, worn jackets, wearing caps or black hats on their heads. Silently they let us pass by without taking their eyes off us. The looks of these men turn us into beings from another planet. So, even more, do the looks of the women, dressed in black like their ancestors and wearing headscarves drawn low down onto their foreheads, who carry out their duties in the yards and gardens. Among ourselves we regard each other as different. In the eyes of the Cretan villagers, we melt into a uniform group of curious Western idlers who—we women especially—take liberties which they would tell us to our faces are improper if they were not partly dependent on us for their living.

We ourselves find it not completely proper to sit at the edge of the meadow above the village and to talk about names and titles which no one in any of these villages has ever heard or ever will hear. So, in San Francisco there are theater groups made up of homosexuals and lesbians; but it seems to me that at the same moment that Sue is telling me about them in an animated tone, their existence has already become immaterial to her. Our gaze moves over the village we have just crossed, over Chersónissos, the highway, the strip of land beside the sea. The Aegean, which occupies the greatest part of this vast panorama, lies there deep blue, breathing peacefully, and renders immaterial everything that we go on saying by force of habit. Helen and Sue have jointly translated a play from German, and quarreled in the process; vestiges of the old quarrel are surfacing again, or are they heralds of a new quarrel? As we move on, Helen picks a ripe lemon for G. in one of the lemon plantations. It was a bet, she wins it, and that evening the lemon comes in handy when we squeeze it onto our grilled salmon. The tapes inside us continue to run even when we have changed our location; so we toss each other the names that nowadays are familiar to all Europeans and Americans who have to do with literature; of course we talk about Brechtian theater past and present, and about the role of women in literature. Then (we are already in the neighboring village) we are addressed on the street by what we regard as an "elderly" woman, even though she is surely no older than her mid-fifties. She knows two or three crumbs of English, even a couple of German: *Deutsch gutt*—"German good"—an assertion which we find no more gratifying for its being repeated. By animated persuasion in three languages she gets us to accompany her—café *gutt*, very *gutt*. Then we understand that it is her café, which actually consists of two tiny round tables outside a kind of all-purpose shop in a side street, with four chairs surrounding each little table. "All right?" the woman asks in Greek as we sit down, and we reply: *Kallá!*—"Good." We drink the ouzo she serves us, eat some of the nuts, and order Turkish coffee. The woman sits down with us and fondles my cheek, beaming: *Deutsch gutt*. "Beautiful," she says to us three women as we leave: *schön schön*. To this prematurely aged woman marked by toil, it is the Western way of life that produces beautiful people. Well-nourished bodies, not work-worn; smooth-skinned, with free, uncovered hair, wearing bright-colored blouses, carefree and self-confident: beautiful. But we stand for a long time outside the little shop at the end of the village, looking at the displays of sheep's-wool pullovers and carpets, the famous Cretan bedspreads and scarves, more elegant than the cheap industrial products we are wearing, whose mass production procures us our comparatively easy lives.

The women here, who gaze after us with half-critical, half-yearning glances, never leave their village all their lives, or at most only when they get married. Besides curiosity, our own travels back and forth indicate need as well, but need for what? What is missing? What do we seek, coming here from two such widely separated quarters of the globe, to this third place; remote, in fact an island? What can it mean, the devotion we are ready to give a culture that was submerged two thousand years ago? The tolerance, of which we laid by a store before we even encountered the first material evidences of that culture, while at the same time we stand dismayed before the graves of people who died in this village ten, twenty, or fifty years ago? In the village cemetery, stone slabs cover the dead until their resurrection, which the living perhaps do not believe in or do not desire; and little dungeons have been carved into the marble gravestones where the color photo of the dead person is imprisoned behind glass; a dried bouquet of flowers. A little jug and a small bowl of nuts wait on top as traveling provisions to be consumed by the dead man on his long journey to the kingdom of the dead, just as his ancestors on this same land used to be given gifts to take with them into the grave—food and drink, jewelry, and, depending on their rank, weapons and gold implements—which today give us clues about their everyday lives. Three thousand years from now, will there be anyone left here or anywhere else who still believes that the dead travel somewhere, and they need traveling provisions for their perhaps arduous and dismal journey, provision from the living that they are incapable of supplying themselves? Will anyone still think about making it easier for the dead? Will there still be some empathy, some memory, between living and dead? Remembrance, storytelling, art?

When we try to cast our thoughts forward into the future, they bounce against a wall. We confess this to ourselves beside these graves on Crete. We admit to a tightness in the chest. One way or another, man would be bound to disappear out of a world that was only economics, only this-worldly.

Crete is an island that floats in its own special sea.

The unreal voice on the telephone did not mislead us, but now we want to live in Heraklion, and what's more, to live cheaply. In spite of everything, we end up going to see the police for alien registration, in their low residence, where you walk past a withered grass plot filled with ceramic toadstools and plastic pelicans, straight into the office. Straight up to the wooden barrier behind which the on-duty alien-registration officer, wearing a pencil mustache, listens bored and slightly contemptuous to our requests, and is able to quote from memory the names of three hotels, one of which belongs to the hotel just around the corner. Yes, three hundred drachmas a night, and that is exactly how little we should pay for a hotel room in order to compensate for the expense of the previous night. Blinded by avarice, I am already in the clutches of the Dwarf Woman. The Dwarf Woman comes hobbling toward me down the extremely narrow staircase—or should I say "stile?" She is not only small but also misshapen; she is hauling wet laundry, which she spreads out over the balcony in the mezzanine while she supplies me with information in a medley of several languages: "Yes, a double room. Yes, three hundred. *Gutt gutt.* Bath? Yes, that too, extra special." I, already intimidated by her dwarf shape, by the disparaging way she speaks to me, above all by a picture book of the woman's life which is running through the back of my mind; by her hardness, which is covered by only a thin soft-soap veneer; and seduced by my avarice—I let her show me the room only, not the so-called bath. After all, the room too has a water tap. As I pass the open doors I see beds for the night, of a kind that have existed for hundreds of years; I see that this is a hostel of the most ancient descent; I insist on nothing. The Dwarf Woman drags us off to an office, a tiny unlighted crate where a man of truly dubious appearance makes us fill out registration forms, collects our passports, and, when we demand them back, insists that in exchange we must pay for three nights in advance: your passports or your money. We pay. "Extra special," the Dwarf Woman assures us with the last spasm of friendliness she has left for guests who have already paid, and hobbles ahead of us into our room with the key. All right, so we must be sure not to walk on the floor with bare feet; and even if there had been a wardrobe, we would not have had much to hang inside it; only our question about the toilet yields depressing results. We could still pull out, which would mean losing nine hundred drachmas. The Dwarf Woman spreads wet bedclothes over the railing on the balcony next to our room—which by the way contains two beds and two chairs and is painted with the customary blue-green limewash. She sings while she works; perhaps she ought not to, but that is really her affair.

While descending the stairs we find solace, after all, in the sudden notion that we have happened in on the middle of a Bergman film: no, not Kafka, Bergman. We establish the difference between them and satisfy ourselves that we were right to decide for Bergman. Already we are aiming at detachment. Already the Dwarf Woman and her murky accomplice in the office are receding to a comfortable distance. The patterns which art makes available to us help us over the mountain once again. Who would live without them?

But they do not help for long. At night the sheets, which are simply too short, do not completely cover the rough, dirty covers; our feet cannot help but come in contact with them. It should not bother us, but it does; and my situation is not improved by the fact that, half asleep, I can picture the Dwarf Woman hanging these same sheets over the balcony rails. Besides, for the first time I am feeling queasy. Not because, in an incomprehensible access of delusion, we took our evening meal in the same hotel ("extra-special menu," the Dwarf Woman had said) and it was swimming in even more olive oil than is normal in Greek dishes; but because as the doors swung back and forth behind retreating and emerging waiters, they afforded us glances into the kitchen which did my nerves and my stomach no good. Or because I was still suffering the aftereffects of our evening walk through the streets of the city center of Heraklion. That promenade of male youth, body to body, group to group, a massive stream; provocative gestures, a competitive male display of strength and beauty, the movements designed to show themselves off; flashing eyes, unabashed glances, scuffles, the concentrated charge of aggressive masculinity that would grant no quarter, does grant no quarter if challenged by anyone, man or woman. Every seat in every pub occupied by men, men reading newspapers, drinking, arguing, gesticulating, gambling: men, men. A city of men. Fear, defensiveness, even repugnance sent my body a signal; I began to feel sick (no, it was not just the Dwarf Woman's grimy covers). Our sort would not, do not, have a chance here. The south. The patriarchal south.

The history of archaeology, too, was a male tale until deep into our century: a heroic epic, or at least so its protagonists understood it. When Sir Arthur Evans, after 1900, began to dig on the hill of Kefala south of Heraklion (or got other people to dig), he had already overcome multiple obstacles. And furthermore, he was not even looking for the throne of King Minos but rather for the origins of a Greek script which he believed must be found on Crete. He said he wanted to follow up this trail "like Theseus" into the innermost recesses of the labyrinth. His masculine need for adventure found models and confirmation in very deep, very ancient sources. In any case, Sir Arthur Evans not only discovered that fantastic architectural complex which he was quick to dub "the Palace"; but in the deepest, the Neolithic stratum under the palace, along with weapons and ceramics, he found what he describes as idols of the sort Schliemann had discovered in the deepest layers of Troy. Every mention of the name "Troy" affected me like a bugle call, for inside me the work on Troy, fortress and city, had begun. Should I picture King Priam's fortress as a palace similar to the Palace of Knossos, which I had already inspected exhaustively on an oversize foldout map attached to my travel guide?

If we take the year zero of the Christian era as the axis of time, then the ancient inhabitants of the Palace of Knossos lived at the same distance from this axis as we do, though on the opposite side. I did not know much about the Minoan sites when I took the bus from Heraklion and came to stand at last in the courtyard of the former Palace of Knossos. This was an advantage and a disadvantage at the same time. Nothing stood between me and the effect of the prodigious pairs of horns which bound many of the upper and outer edges of the palace buildings; I did not know how to interpret them. To interpret means: to know the history of a phenomenon, and I did not know the history of the bull in the Mediterranean region and its relation to the cult of the moon. All that occurred to me were associations from mythology: the Minotaur, the bull of King Minos. (Sir Arthur Evans ventured to name the entire culture after him, a culture which, we can readily believe, he unearthed with wonder and enthusiasm: the Minoan.) My *Blue Guide* informed me that this spot, this crumbling soil on which I stood, these stone slabs laid out in the forecourt of the palace—were the very site of the mythical Labyrinth. I used the directions in the guide book as an Ariadne's thread, following a particular path marked black in the confusing ground plan of the palace, which at first glance presents itself as a heap of ruins. It informed me that if I continued on, I would pass the ancient irrigation works; the gigantic receptacles for various types of provisions; up stairs, down stairs, bending once under stone arches, I would get a look into underlying chambers; then again, standing on a platform, enjoy a view of the entire palace grounds; and arrive at those parts of the structure reconstructed by Evans. That concession to public fantasy: the glowing reddish-brown rows of columns which tapered toward the base and were made not of stone but of cedar trunks. And then, finally, the reconstructed frescoes on the walls of certain of the inner chambers.

This encounter induced in me an excitement which has continued until today, virtually unabated by my later reading of commentaries, objections, and rejections of Evans's method of reconstruction, and doubts about its results. And yet all the same this excitement no doubt requires an explanation—especially because it has been and still is shared by so many devotees of Minoan culture. What did I see there? Brightly colored frescoes, fantastic plant and animal shapes. The original site of the famous bull-leaper fresco which we found in the Heraklion museum: It shows a youth making a daring leap over a bull who flashes with power, while a charming, beautiful woman reaches out to catch him and another woman holds the bull by the horns. This scene could be a sacrificial ritual which might end in death and which would explain the Greek *Angst* legend about the wild Minotaur, who devours their young men; it could be a symbolic cult act, a sports event. But no matter— almost no matter—what it depicts, my confrontation with this painting, with the Palace of Knossos and, one day later, the Palace of Phaestos, remains one of the rare cases when follow-up reading has not diminished, but rather enhanced, the luster of the first meeting.

And at last we found the double ax etched into the stone, the *labrys*, which Helen and Sue had particularly recommended to our attention. Some scholars claim that the Labyrinth took its name from the labrys—others firmly dispute it; with good reason, it seems to me. The labrys in turn is said to be a token of the Cretan Zeus, who is known to have been born on the Cretan Mount Ida. Here in Knossos it attends us as a route marker, sometimes barely detectable in the rough uneven stone, then again carved in bunches; also forming a kind of frieze. We will see it again in the simple, extraordinarily animated, even poetic representations of the goddesses cult on the little Minoan seals in the Heraklion museum. Never, we now learn, has the Minoan double ax been found in the hand of a male deity. The ax is a characteristic Minoan symbol, along with the pillar—the stylized sacred tree—and the bull's horns. It is believed to owe its sacred character to the fact that it was originally used to fell trees—in primitive societies a labor performed by women. Then it became identified with the lightning that attracts rain, and the Cretan mother goddess Eileithyia was gradually transferred into the male-dominated Olympian pantheon, with Zeus at the summit beside Hera, his wife. Via this long-drawn-out route marked by struggles, conflicts, and defeats, the double ax came into the hand of Zeus—and when they retraced its route back to its origin, the American feminists took it as a symbol.

By the time we met Sue and Helen again, they had seen without fail every single double ax in Knossos, every single representation of the Mother Goddess in the Heraklion museum, starting with those Neolithic idols with broad buttocks, apt for child-bearing, exulting in fertility. They were early versions of the goddess Demeter, the earth and fertility goddess, whom the Hellenes also adopted. Wherever science dug shafts, cleared away layers of earth, penetrated caves, it always encountered this goddess in the deepest strata. It is worth thinking about, why women today feel they must derive part of their self-esteem and a justification of their claims from the fact that civilization begins with the worship of woman.

How does it help us to know that the ancient Greeks gradually replaced "mother right" with "father right"? What is proved by the fact, authenticated though it seems, that women led the early clans who lived by agriculture; that the children they brought into the world belonged to them; that they continued to determine the inherited succession even in later, highly organized kingdoms; that they were the originators of all cults, of taboo and fetish, dance, song, and many early crafts? Doesn't this harking back to an irretrievable ancient past reveal more clearly than anything else the desperate plight in which women see themselves today? If your first glimpse of the Minoan paintings (of their reconstructions) is a joyful shock, strange to say a shock of recognition: so the Elysian Fields do exist, you knew it all along—nevertheless, they do not lose their enchantment when you learn something more of the circumstances that produced them. Apparently a productive balance was maintained for a certain historical period, but this was not, as one foolishly dared to hope at first, an Isle of the Blessed existing outside the coordinates of its time. Not only the palace painters, but the handed-down myth, and the storytellers, too, have mounted great pictures on the walls of the Cretan palaces (be those palaces shrines or the seat of the king). Indestructible pictures, it seems, and inexhaustible in the reality at their core and in their ambiguity. To learn to read myth is a special kind of adventure. An art that presupposes a gradual, peculiar transformation; a readiness to give oneself to the seemingly frivolous nexus of fantastic facts, of traditions, desires, and hopes, experiences and techniques of magic adapted to the needs of a particular group—in short, to another sense of the concept "reality." For me the structures at Knossos and Phaestos became animated by a throng of people—not at my first visit, but only gradually, in my memory. They were the Minoans. If you look for models of their features in the fresco portraits known as "La Parisienne"—actually she is supposed to be a priestess—and "The Prince of the Lilies"*—similarly thought to be a young male priest—you may still encounter those features today, all of a sudden, in the young woman pressed against you in the bus, in a young man outside a village taverna. Now I could picture Minoan people of the most diverse professions, all delicately fitted into a hierarchically structured community (well, did you expect them to be free of hierarchy?). In this community the priestly office of women, their presence at religious games, even their participation in dangerous exercises like bull-leaping, apparently are no more than relics of more ancient, matriarchal

---

* These are among the fanciful designations of Sir Arthur Evans for the fresco paintings he discovered in Minoan Crete. "La Parisienne" is a detail of the Camp Stool Fresco from Knossos; "The Prince of the Lilies" is also from Knossos. Photographs of these elegant figures and other Minoan wall paintings can be found (for example) in Arthur Cotterell's *The Minoan World* (London: Joseph, 1979); *The Archaeology of Minoan Crete* by Reynold Higgins (London: Bodley Head, 1973); J. W. Graham, *The Palaces of Crete* (Princeton University Press, 1962); S. Marinatos and M. Hirmer, *Crete and Mycenae* (New York: Abrams, 1960); and *Mycenaeans and Minoans* by Leonard R. Palmer (London: Faber and Faber, 2nd ed., 1965). The same volumes offer illustrations of the snake goddess, the terra-cotta Cretan idols, the Phaestos Disc, and other art and artifacts referred to by Christa Wolf.—Trans.

times. Thus, the ardor and enthusiasm of Sue and Helen, when we meet them again in front of the female idols in the Heraklion museum, their almost tender concern for the clay figures of pregnant women and mothers with newborn children at their breasts, seem to have an irrational streak. But I, too, am deeply moved by these little terra-cotta figurines which are not the image of ideals like the art of classical antiquity but bear all the traces of everyday life, the prints of the fingers which formed them. They convey to me far more powerfully than any Apollo of Belvedere the feeling that at bottom these people who prayed to, or thanked, a goddess for children four or five thousand years ago and more were people just like us. They make me feel that it was they—or rather the thousands of generations before them, who sank away into the darkness of prehistory leaving almost no trace—who began to weave the basic network of human relationships, by which we gradually rose above the necessities of instinct and the almost animal tactics of survival. They began as well to weave that net whose warps still determine our thinking pattern today—and, I believe, the direction of our longings besides. For it was not just the sense of reality, what the art historians call "naturalism"; longing, too, must have guided the hand of the Minoan painters when they drew a picture of their lives so sparkling with life and glowing with color. This picture so stirs the imagination of its discoverers and of countless visitors, not only because it was found later than other early cultures, but because here imagination feeds on man's deepest layers. Many interpretations of this culture reflect the unconscious desires of the interpreters, desires whose effects are all the more powerful for being unrecognized; this was especially true so long as scientific explanations were still too vague to set limits to inspiration. Arthur Evans himself—influenced of course by the fin-de-siècle culture in which he lived and had grown up—projects a period view onto his finds which later, less imaginative, less obsessive, more sober scholars find it hard to resist. This is particularly so because the Western public had meanwhile formed an image of that culture from which they would have been glad to derive their own. They saw it as cheerful, productive; as leaving the individual scope for development between freedom and obligation; and, above all, as a *peaceful* culture not imprinted with the code of inevitable self-incurred destruction. Its annihilation, people liked to think, was attributable solely to natural catastrophes. They did not want (if at all possible) to see it exposed to disintegration by social processes, to decay by exhaustion and by the perversion of a formerly productive impulse. The traces of fire in the palaces which we saw in Knossos were attributed without exception to fires following the earthquakes. The fact that until recently not a single human skeleton was found in the abandoned palaces was explained by the alleged departure of all the inhabitants at the first signs of an earthquake. The fact that the palaces were not fortified, not protected by walls, was simply taken to confirm the peaceful character of the Minoans—a people incidentally who did not exist, whom Evans named after their supposed king, and whom the Egyptians, it has since been learned, used to call "Keftiu." Everything that we are unable to achieve was attributed to them: the ability to find meaning in their work; to integrate themselves into a social and religious community without an accompanying need to reduce themselves to an automatic level of functioning; to live without internal and external violence—an island of perfection. So, did this mean that the legend of the man-eating Minotaur, to whom seven Athenian maidens and seven youths had to be offered, i.e., sacrificed, every nine years, was a pure invention on the part of the offended Greeks? And how ought we to understand the myth of the abduction of the Phoenician princess Europa by the Cretan Minos transformed into a bull? Were we not meant to realize that in this mythological version Europe was named after a princess from the Near East who was kidnapped and raped by the Cretans—a name, by the way, that means "the dismal one"?

As I spent two morning hours wandering aimlessly through

the ruins of Knossos, more confused than guided by the guide-book explanations, I became infected with a pathogenic organism which triggered a slight but persistent fever; the fever continued to rise when I got back home to Germany. (You might call it the Crete and Troy syndrome, whose ingredients I would like to analyze, and as I have tried to show, I was prepared for it by my obsession with the name Cassandra, for it was this name that flared up again and again like a signal fire.) Then we set out to travel on to Phaestos, and afterward to the south of the island, where it did not dawn on me until late that we were in the middle of one of the very few adventures that are still possible today, an adventure of the spirit. But at the same time that I wandered through Knossos and we set out south—on that same day, as on the days that came before and after—that excavation may well have been going forward just a few kilometers south of Knossos whose results were reported in a newspaper one year later, in April 1981. The director of the Archaeological Museum of Heraklion (the newspaper said), working with his wife, had discovered the remains of a temple from the Minoan period in the village of Archanes. And among these remains were the remains—for the first time!—of human skeletons, whose arrangement leaves no doubt that one of the skeletons must have been a priest, another a man who had just been sacrificed. The find was a sacrificial ritual which was interrupted by the natural disaster it may have been intended magically to avert. And in the interval, British archaeologists discovered near the Palace of Knossos, among the remains of a house destroyed circa 1450 B.C., the bones of ten young people. The bones bore marks which do not rule out the possibility that the whole site may attest to religious-ritual cannibalism.

The corpse in the cellar, a theme on which Western culture has played variations to the point of satiety. Antonis, who takes us later to the oldest and (he says) best taverna in Athens, located in the Pláka, heard about findings of sacrificial remains before we did. Minoan culture is a riddle, he says, and always will remain so. It seems that the more we know about it, the more it changes from a wonder into a phenomenon, which, albeit still wondrous, grew out of the conditions of time and place. It had a theocratic hierarchy, a stratified feudal class system, exploitation, and slavery. There are no grounds here for the kind of idealization that European classicists applied to classical antiquity—which now appears to us rigid and stiff and misconceived by them. So, in Minoan Crete some people were in all probability revered as gods or as godlike beings. This produced the kind of alienation and narrowness of mental horizons that normally follow from such practices. There was probably slave labor, radical contrasts of wealth and poverty; an increasing trend toward centralization.

But the women. I had to admit that Helen and Sue were right when they showed me the relevant passages in our various guide-books. It *is* remarkable that their authors were all afraid to draw conclusions from the fact that women held such a dominant place in the paintings of Minoan artists. They continued to be afraid even when throughout Western civilization Crete was being turned into the Promised Land of those who looked to the past to satisfy their longings—namely feminists, women committed to the women's movement, who, hard-pressed as they were by the experience of the present and fears about the future, saw in the Minoan kingdoms *the* social bodies to which they could concretely attach their utopian speculations and yearnings. So, once upon a time there really *was* a country where women were free and equal to men. Where women produced the goddesses. (Many male archaeologists and classical scholars find it remarkably difficult to recognize, and then to acknowledge, that all early divinities are female; often, I think, they prefer not to read Engels or Bachofen or Thomson or Robert Graves.) Where women hold the privileged seats at all public presentations, in free and festive makeup. Where they take part in the ritual exercises and even compose the majority of the priesthood. A country where, we have since come to believe, they were the practitioners and instigators of art. Where apparently the effects of matrilinear succession were still being felt, so that a male could succeed to the throne only through the king's daughter.

And so we stroll through the ruins of Knossos and Phaestos, laboring under sweet apprehensions which we do not suspect are most probably misapprehensions—fed us by archaeologists who needed these errors as much as their public. Seeing what we *want* to see. We sit at the southern fringe of the island on the bay of Matala, where at last we see with our own eyes how the blue of the sky becomes indistinguishable from the blue of the sea, and begin to forget the color of northern skies. The caves in the mountain slopes fall off steeply to the sea. It is said that "long ago," whatever that means, people used to bury their dead inside them. Only a few summers ago some "hippies"—the moment it appears the word begins to vanish from memory—still lived lives of suspect freedom there. Now their rearguard, youngsters from almost all the countries of Western Europe, tramp through this fringe of coast, through these caves, carrying shrieking-orange backpacks on carrier frames. They rent little rooms from the poor farmers in the villages for practically nothing, live, like the farmers, on a few pennies' worth of sheep cheese, tomatoes, bread, and olive oil. A few days later they move to another spot on the island, to the next stopping place, on the lookout for something different. Now, when the impulses that this island, that Greece, once gave Europe are dying away, it is as if the old continent felt it could renew its youth from this same source again, through its young people, as they reach back to even more ancient layers of time and culture. As if people—as if we—were free to make a blend of whatever pleased us from all the ages—or whatever pleased us from the *image* we make of the ages. As if we could find a measure (these young people may secretly crave it, too) in the place where measure grew out of the strictest confinement of each human being to his "fate," out of immutable dependencies on pre-existing social factors. As if we could be at the same time completely free and yet measured.

Sue and Helen are not ready to admit that the Minoans used slave labor, male and of course female, too. Here, I think, here in the harbor bay of Matala, is one of the slaves' arrival points. Probably they came in primitive ships whose construction I cannot picture accurately so far. If the palaces of the Minoans (whoever they may have been) were in fact—a strange fact— unfortified, does that really mean, *can* that mean that the in- habitants of Crete were a peace-loving people who managed to last for thousands of years although they traded with heavily armed, warlike neighboring races? Did the coast guard offer sufficient protection? Certainly, the surrounding mountains form ideal lookout posts from which to detect foreign ships, even without a telescope, while they are still far enough out . . . Troy, at any rate, the fortress of Ilium, was not unfortified and unarmed. To be sure, it did not lie on an island but on the Western perimeter of the coast of Asia Minor, an area traversed by the most diverse races in ancient times, with the powerful kingdom of the Hittites among the nations at its rear, and destined, by its location, to secure the entrance to the Dar- danelles. But I cannot change the fact that my notion of the harbor of Troy—my notion of a harbor bay where you can stand on the shores and wait for the ships to come in bearing goods, tradesmen, an abducted bride, then the enemy—my notion of the sea Cassandra looks at, is formed here.

On the beach the wooden stands of the tradesmen are selling sheep's-wool pullovers, bright-colored bags, Cretan carpets and bedspreads. That evening the same railway inspector who had joined us before we got to Phaestos, and accompanied us here, travels back with us on the bus, now carrying a huge bouquet of long-stemmed wildflowers, and once again is very eager to convince us that Crete is the most beautiful country in the world. We find the old men—from whom Aeschylus could perfectly well compile his "Chorus of Argive Graybeards"—still sitting outside the village tavernas. Now they no longer have Turkish coffee but a glass of retsina standing before them. Close by, the impetuous younger men are arguing at the tables; and in the tiny yards we see the women busying themselves with buckets, tools. At the edge of the larger villages are the new buildings, concrete cubes whose lower floor has been completed and is habitable, while the second and often the third story juts up, a concrete skeleton, waiting for the day when the assignor of the building contract is solvent again and can go on building. They have not inherited the sense of beauty their remote ancestors had; or rather, it has been destroyed here, as everywhere else, by the dominion of effectiveness over all other values. For the time being, the women hang their laundry in the upper story, which, although it is open on all sides, has been roofed in.

The bus, which is increasingly crammed with tourists the closer we get to Herakleion, sways through the plain of Mesara past Mount Ida, which we do not see again. It was here, in a cave, that the god Zeus, who later headed the Hellenic pantheon, is said to have been born. This time we are sensible enough not to eat in our hotel, to avoid the smell of rancid olive oil from the kitchen, to try our luck somewhere else "extra special." It does not really bother me too much when the rough, dirty blankets scratch my feet again. I hear a large band of backpackers return home noisily around midnight, when I am half asleep, but it does not disturb me. And next morning I am not put off by it when, looking for a shower worthy of the name, I bump into a sleeper here and there in a corner who has made himself comfortable on a mattress and pulled his parka up over his head. In the museum I gaze hypnotized into the wide-open, staring eyes of the snake-goddess from the Palace of Knossos, and try to catch the look of her predecessors, the large terracotta figures with upraised arms: worshipping? beseeching? lamenting? giving birth?

Sue and Helen despise all male art, all images depicting men.

We stand for a long time in front of the Phaestos Disc,* whose spiral script has so far proved indecipherable—a hymn? a dirge? —and wait for the feelings of awe at sight of the earliest written characters in our culture sphere. Ought we to wish all mysteries to be decoded? So I thought still at that time, feeling slightly gleeful at the discomfiture of my contemporaries who failed to penetrate the code of earlier peoples. Since then my craving has grown to know the secrets of the ancients—who compared to the "ancient Greeks" are the ancient-of-ancients. I long to know what the Disc says. The much-debated question of how the Minoan culture came to fall became a burning issue for me. Was the fall caused by natural catastrophes? By internal strife? By the incursions of the Achaeans, and later of the Dorians, from the Greek mainland?

The destruction of Troy allegedly took place two or three generations after the golden age of the Cretan palaces. The first common source for both the Achaeans' destruction of Troy and the existence of a Cretan king named Minos is Homer; is an epic on the borderline between myth and historical chronicle. Eloquent as stones are, expressive as are dig finds and adequate as they may be for the knowledge of geology and the plant and animal worlds—it is language, it is literature that really tells us about human society. The structures it communicates cannot be conveyed, or can be conveyed only in a limited way, through architecture, vessels, statues, even paintings. The features of the bare-breasted women in the wall paintings of Knossos: Are they noblewomen watching sports events? Priestesses performing a cult act? Wailing women at festival games for the dead? Arthur Evans's "La Parisienne." A single line from a song, perhaps a description in an epic, could decipher her mystery. We do not have that line.

* This is a disc of fired clay 15 mm. in diameter, impressed with picture writing on both sides, which has not yet been positively deciphered but may be in a Luvian dialect.—Trans.

The ambiguity of Minoan culture is part of its magic. For us, no later monument could surpass it. Not the minaret we climbed in Rethymnon, built when Crete was occupied by the Turks; not the Venetian installations and the picturesque old Venetian city of Canea. They satisfied our curiosity, our aesthetic sense, our interest in history, and our need for the exotic. But the Minoans with their "palaces" had aroused our imagination and, at even deeper levels, our buried hope for a "Promised Land." More than a craving for culture began to stir here. Later I found a note stating that King Priam, father of Cassandra and loser of the war for his city, bore rather the traits of a Minoan-Cretan commander and sovereign than those of an Achaean. The historians have gotten used to setting up such contrasts, showing bright and dark colors side by side. As for us, leaving Canea and crossing the crystal-clear Mediterranean dazzling with sunlight, above which lay the blue sky like a solid block, we arrived back at the port of Piraeus on the mainland. The experience of Orthodox-Christian Greece still lay ahead of us before we could travel the Peloponnesus to Argos, the city of Agamemnon; and from there to Mycenae, the fortress of the House of Atreus, Clytemnestra's slaughterhouse. To the place where Cassandra died.

The Easter solemnities began as a burlesque with a touch of thieves' comedy. Many citizens of Athens are first- or second-generation Athenians and still have a village: "my village," they say. N.'s village is located near the Thessalian town of Karditsa, five hundred kilometers north of Athens, and believe it or not, it is hard to get there on Good Friday, when "all Greece" is traveling and "all Athens" besieges the little provincial Athens railway station. We stood on the platform in a wall of people and saw our prospects wane. While we were crossing the station hall, two young men had addressed N. urgently, plying him with suggestions which he rejected and did not translate for us. Now that conditions seemed more favorable to their cause, they returned. N. listened to them, whispered with C.;

then we were told we *could* also travel by bus. This bus, whither we were conveyed by a taxi whose driver was working hand in glove with the young men, was an illegal bus, withdrawn from a regular bus enterprise to make this lucrative tour. It waited until it was filled up by the increasing swell of baggage-laden travelers bearing an increasing swell of horror tales about conditions in the railway station. Judging by their appearance and behavior, the young men running the enterprise might just as well have been a band of kidnappers, the bus to Salonika might just as well have been taking us to Orcus. That was crystal-clear to us, but it did not dampen our spirits. The fare was lower than if we had gone by rail. When we finally got moving, the driver, whose face was not revealed to us until the very end, as is only proper for the brains behind the operation, switched on the car radio. The music, raised to a volume which we could only believe was unintentional, kept the bus shudder-ing for five hours and was an ordeal for our Central European ears. No doubt it represented our share of the atonement for the illicit journey. People had to have their fun, the driver asserted imperturbably in reply to N.'s remonstrances, and not one Greek so much as batted an eyelid. We did not know: Did the vast musical clamor really not disturb them (we had to stuff our ears with cotton because they hurt), or was their silence merely a fresh example of their total indifference toward all grievances which did not directly affect themselves and their families? Even my memories of the landscape where we drove, the colors of sea, sky, trees on the coastal road, are spoiled by the memory of this acoustical torture-by-hit-music which is linked to them like a reflex. But we reached Larissa, we changed buses and arrived at Karditsa, we moved into our narrow hotel room, and we rambled through a northern Greek provincial town getting ready for Easter.

The sacrificed lamb stands at the center of the Greek Easter celebrations, just as three or four thousand years ago it may have stood at the center of the spring festivities of the Demeter and fertility cults, and of the mysteries of Dionysus, celebrated at the various cult places, sanctuaries, and temples of the peoples who lived in this region. Or rather, it may have *lain* there: for the slain lamb—the sacrificial victim whose blood flows in streams and is caught in large bowls by the women—does of course fall to the ground. (Incidentally, it used to be a human being in "days of yore," perhaps a young man who in turn represented the god's son Dionysus; then the lamb took the human being's place, stood in for him as a scapegoat, and only at the onset of Christianity was represented by a man once again, allegedly for the last time.) So, the lamb lies. It lies on the butchers' chopping blocks or on the bare stone in the farmers' yards of Ambeliko, N.'s village. It hangs one hundredfold on the hooks of the butcher shops. A town, a village, a whole country full of piously butchered lambs. And in the churches and the marketplaces the altars are decorated with flowers and dolls representing the saints, whereas among the ancients the place of the saints was held by heroes, whose bones were felt to bring prosperity like saints' bones, whose graves were, like theirs, a sacred zone. I saw here more clearly than anywhere that it is impossible to separate layers of culture, that they interpenetrate, that the earlier cult shines through that of the present, and through that earlier cult shines a cult more ancient still. I saw that there is virtually nothing more enduring than the rituals which it is the storyteller's job to reinterpret as needed. Behind the secularized narrative lies the saint's legend, behind the legend the heroic epic, behind the epic the myth. The experience of the deeps of time, in a place which could hardly be more alien.

As for us, what do we believe in?

Early Saturday morning it is our office to accompany N. to the market hall to fetch the three lambs from his family butcher; to watch how the amiable, rough man impales the animals' drawn cadavers, how he sticks the iron spit through the meat at the hindquarters until it comes out through the mouth in front.

We cart away two lambs, carrying them between us. I go first, holding the front end of a spit in each hand, then come the lambs; G. follows, holding the ends of the spits. We walk in a strange formation through the town, which is churning with activity. We are shown into the little garden behind the house of N.'s brother, where the sacrificial fires will burn tomorrow, providing that it does not rain (inconceivable nightmare!).

Now numbering thirteen, we drive toward the mountain chain in two separate cars, arrive at N.'s village at last. There it lay among the mountain outcroppings; wasn't it beautifully situated? Now we would get to see one of the most beautiful Greek villages in existence. And for some time we had had a white dot in our sights, whose location was indicated to us punctiliously: THE HOUSE. A steep, narrow, stony village street leading upward; then came the fence which N. had had put up, the gate. And then, finally and truly, the house. Never before had I seen and entered a house which symbolized, as this did, everything a house can mean to a human being: home and refuge and shelter and protection and sign of self-affirmation. The house had four strong stone-built walls, hollows for windows, doors, a floor, and a ceiling. There was nothing else. We climbed up to the second floor by ladder. People must have looked out these windows at the plain of Thessaly. "What do you say? Isn't it beautiful?" It was beautiful, and it must have been unforgettable to have been here as a child, to have been driven away and unable to return; something one could never get over.

Tomorrow was Easter.

In the narrow little yards all around us, the lambs who were being slaughtered screamed and bled. From the square in front of the taverna, even higher up the mountain, we saw the huge edifice of the church, almost too large for a village like this, and surrounded by the village houses, mostly small and mostly poor. N., who had lived in the village for weeks as assignor of a building contract, knew the men there; they addressed him, he referred to them as "friends." He had to build his house, no matter who would live there, or when. Our expediency-based logic lost ground and withdrew.

In a village on the plain lived a brother of N.'s mother. Wasn't it a good idea—no, wasn't it fitting and indeed unavoidable to look him up? A detour of no more than an hour. The mother's brother and the other men were in the taverna and were fetched back. They were wearing Sunday-black, thick cloth suits. The women and children were sitting in the parlor in front of the television. The women jumped up at once, smoothed their skirts, asked us to sit down, and bade us welcome by offering us "sweet from the spoon." This custom may have come down from antiquity, when honey was served to the snakes in the sanctuaries, and to the dead as well; for honey was thought suitable for the most excellent beings and consequently for guests, too. Pure honey is no longer served, but rather sugar, a candied substance which like all sweets here is very sweet indeed, along with a glass of clear cool water. We sample both. Then there is wine made from their own grapes, home-processed, accompanied by pastries. A slow conversation about rural and family matters. The way of life in the villages remains stable in face of the political excesses of this century. There are two sides to that: the underside is (among other things) that the working life of women has continued to be restricted. It is far more difficult here than in Central Europe to see the villages as an escape and round-up point for civilization-weary townspeople. The deceptive family peace that arises from the women's total attachment to the fate of the men (or rather to the fate of being a woman), as well as from the indissoluble attachment of the sons to their families, erupts again and again into bursts of barbaric behavior. Or a hint of despair over lifelong, silent endurance and suffering. Those who dream today of turning the clock back to the benefits of agrarian societies have never lived in one.

Back to Karditsa. Easter night awaits us.

Shortly before midnight, we set out from the brother's house. N.'s sister-in-law distributes candles to us all. The only one who does not come with us is the husband of N.'s sister, who, as a member of Jehovah's Witnesses, regards the Greek Orthodox Easter celebration as heretical. We perceive that the charge of heresy can arise only between those of related faiths; not between believers and unbelievers.

It's raining. Hundreds of people are standing outside the church, in the dark, not speaking. The expectation of the crowd communicates itself to me. Twelve strokes of the clock. The church portal opens; the priest psalmodizes loudly: "Christ is risen!" "He is risen indeed!" a few voices call; then the crowd cries it out, deeply moved. In a minute all the candles are lit. The crowd moves out of the church singing. The decorated altar, which we cannot see, is carried along before them through the town, to the marketplace, where it must subsist beside the altar of the other church. The circuitous detour across the fields to make them fertile, which used to take place every spring in honor of the earth goddess Demeter, has lost its meaning in urban culture. An image sticks in my mind of the dark crowd interspersed with flickering dots of light from the candles. It is said that in the culture of the Stone Age and the early Bronze Age, a lover of the female clan elders, later of the female clan chiefs—a young man—used to be sacrificed to the goddess of fertility; later a male child became his substitute; then a human sacrifice was made only every eight or nine years; then animal sacrifices were made instead; finally, bloodless offerings and clay statuettes were offered instead of flesh-and-blood people. In the beginning art was a substitute for sacrifice if it was visual art; magical incantation if it was word art. The husband of the Great Mother was not really killed but only killed via a substitute, as a game, and was allowed to rise from the dead on the night when she made the fields fruitful. The hero, too, was not really dead. A mortal hero cannot found a religion. Christ is risen! The people's needs hardly change over the centuries.

At around one o'clock we—the whole family—sat down to our nocturnal meal, a dish of the cleaned intestines and entrails of the lambs. It was these parts of the animal which, in the past, may have been burned on the altar, while the priests were allowed to eat the choicest cuts of meat, and those who had offered the sacrifices the second-quality portions.

At noon the following day *we* ate the best cuts of the lambs at a banquet. It was raining all over Greece—a challenge to the inventive powers of a people who on Easter Sunday must roast their lamb on a spit outdoors. Our hosts proved lucky in that they lived in one of those houses whose upper stories are still concrete skeletons. They were able to light the fire there on the bare ground and keep it going, and to set up the spits on their mounting. Then the spit-turners could sit down and turn, turn, turn, hour after hour. For the sake of family solidarity, even the Jehovah's Witness brother-in-law took part, against his convictions, in the work done in the service of idolatry. The men poured olive oil and beer over the lamb, and drank wine. The women laid down planks on wooden blocks, spread tablecloths over the planks, mixed the salad, and set the tables. A neighbor arrived and was regaled with the first piece of roast meat. We heard he was a Jew and had to go join his own family. It did not cost him an effort to taste the Christian Easter lamb, and it was served to him without a trace of the ancient Christian hatred against the Jews. From a hundred open stories, from garages, from hastily built board or tarpaulin dugouts issued curls of smoke, which by noon mingled with the aroma of roast meat. At three o'clock we could eat, there was meat enough for three large-scale families like ours. "Enjoy your Easter dinner!" Even the women, who in peasant families often stand at table and go back and forth serving people, sat down. The children, especially the little boys, have carte blanche; they get used to harassing their mothers, their sisters. "Bring me water!" says the littlest tot, and even the oldest granny will get up with a groan and serve the little man. What happens to all the rage that must get bottled up when that happens? Or, almost worse yet, is there nothing left to get bottled up anymore?

On our afternoon walk through the town, which on this day and at this time is emptier than usual, we meet the barber, a sad but enthusiastic man; N. knows him. He invites us into his shop, a little room two meters by three meters, containing two barber's chairs of a kind I know from old films and from fleeting glimpses into men's salons when I was a child. Coffee is made on the little high-pressure furnace; it is served to us hot and sweet, in tiny cups. On the wall are small news photos, mostly cut out of the Communist Party newspaper; among them an ancient little photo of Stalin which the barber points out to us with a smile. The barber knows N.'s family. We see the faces of the two men while they are talking about the days of the civil war; about the time when N.'s grandparents took the boy into the mountains and they fought with the partisans. Unbeknown to them, their faces wear that expression of unappeasable sorrow which I have seen more and more often in recent years on the faces of people with the same experiences, and which stems from disappointment, hurt, hopelessness. The barber clings, with a trace of irony, to Stalin, to the past. He presses our hands for a long time when we say goodbye. My grip on the distant, the primordial past is, I am aware, likewise a remedy against this indissoluble sadness. By now it has almost become a grip on the future again, the flight backward takes the form of a flight forward. An odd self-observation: Knowing that people and circumstances have not gotten very far in three thousand years leads to a feeling of serenity rather than hopelessness.

The little town is dismal and gray on this Easter afternoon. We see its modest workshops and stores; the wandering gypsy women with their children; the once queer, now crumbling town center; the market hall; the young people who hurry in pairs or in groups toward a large pub in a park toward evening. We also see the garish swabs of color which have come to perch on top of the small-town routine in the last few years: bars with screaming neon advertisements, a games parlor, kiosks selling foreign magazines. It is still drizzling. We pass the same points for the third time, unintentionally going in a circle. I try to think of a German word corresponding to the French *cafard* ("the blues"). Gloom, ill humor, tedium; in the hotel we lie down on the beds, which are lined up single file. The next morning they cheat us shamelessly when we settle our bill. N., offended in his honor as a former child of this town, runs back shortly before the bus leaves and straightens things out by means of massive threats. But at the same time he is also slightly irritated by our inability to defend ourselves against cheats. As if certain powers had failed to develop which, though they were never used, still are part of a human being. He remains silent and depressed for a long time as we travel south, this time in a regular bus, regaled with music at a subdued volume.

I try to account to myself for the unyielding resentment people feel when they learn how a city like Aulis is being destroyed by industrial installations, Eleusis destroyed by oil refineries: a different kind of indignation, bordering on anxiety, than is ordinarily felt at the destruction of landscape by industry. Why should the place where her father Agamemnon sacrificed Iphigenia remain inviolate? Why should the Sacred Way from Athens to the Eleusinian mysteries not be desecrated by transport vehicles? Why should a curse lie on the oil transports, but not on the donkey carts which used to carry goods and provisions to the city of Eleusis and the temple of Demeter? Isn't the resistance that we feel a token of retreat and resignation? At least here, we tell ourselves, at least at these places which are so remote from any modern-day religion that they can be sacred to all religions, even to atheists, we should uphold a taboo which everywhere else is disregarded. Yet even as we try to explain our feeling of horror in this way, we are aware that a reverence cordoned off into preserves cannot be reverence but is nothing but calculation, and that it would surely be more "honest"—how words lose their meanings!—if at the end of its days our civilization were to dredge under the shrines of its origin, along with everything else.

On the other hand (accustomed to thinking in antinomies I draw up unsuitable equations)—on the other hand, a group of Greek workers are digging, with the greatest care, in a staked-out block of the ruins of ancient Corinth, under the supervision of some American archaeologists. What was annihilated by the dredger on the one hand is here being salvaged with spades and sieves. Potsherds are placed carefully in boxes and painstakingly recorded by young girls. No matter how often I try, I can never manage to understand how cities, fortresses, landscapes, sanctuaries can lie forgotten for centuries, preserved, if at all, only in writings which no one any longer credits with truth content; until a few fanatics with their Homer in hand begin to scratch in the earth at places designated 2,500 years before . . . But recently I have come to understand the source of the passion that drove Heinrich Schliemann and Arthur Evans, and my understanding is destined to grow until it borders on a passion that will drive me to an immoderate bout of reading and stand in the way of a sensible, rational work plan. The steps of the ancient forum where the apostle Paul may well have preached to the Corinthians, with the pillars of the far more ancient temple of Apollo in the background: This picture affords more insight than books can into the way various strata of belief are linked to various strata of rocks. What kind of faith will the people of the future (assuming there *are* people in the future) read out of our stone, steel, and concrete ruins? How will they account for the hubris of the gigantic metropolises, in which people cannot live without paying the penalty? Of the maze of themes which we, its contemporaries, perceive in our civilization, will only a few remain? Power. Wealth. Delusions of grandeur?

There is a city called Argos, a dusty, unprepossessing city where our bus pauses for a while. Apart from us, no one appreciates the stop but the two men behind us, who have been traveling with us since we left Athens. The elder man, who looks to be in his mid-forties, a slender person of delicate limbs and delicate sensibility, tells his friend, who is almost twenty years younger, the thought which should come to mind when one hears the word "Argos": the House of Atreus. But we had been advised to stay in the picturesque Venetian port city of Nauplia. We followed this advice, and no one could have foreseen that it would be here of all places, precisely between the hours of seven and eight while I was soaking in the glow of the houses around the Nauplia pier; here, at one of the southernmost tips of Europe, that I would be overwhelmed by that sense of forlornness that signals the loss of all the coordinates where we embed ourselves, to which we cling. Forlorn, standing at the farthest outlying point of the pier that extends far into the sea, I watched the early, triumphal sunset behind the fortress of Burdzi and behind the mountain chain that shields the port on the west. Forlorn, I roamed through the queer streets of the Venetian Old Town. A malady which I did not want to call homesickness severed the tie between me and these little streets, this plump round moon, this polished sky. At the hotel reception desk we ran into the two friends from the bus; in the eyes of the elder man I believed I could see a far older, far deeper forlornness.

The next morning we go back to Argos—we, as well as the two friends, with whom we exchanged a knowing smile when we met again. We wait for the bus from Corinth at a godforsaken, drafty intersection, where we are compensated by a signpost pointing east which bears the inscription MYCENAE. The procession of Argive graybeards must have passed this place of old when in Aeschylus's representation, they were alarmed by signal fires proclaiming the end of the war in Troy, and set out from Argos toward the ruling fortress of Mycenae, praising Zeus.

He who leads us the way of thought
to learn through suffering,
subjects us to this law!

Thus even in sleep conscience's anxiety
pounds the heart awake with its sudden beat, and there sprouts
against our will the mind of wisdom.

"To learn through suffering"—this seems to be the law of the new gods, and likewise the way of masculine thought. This way does not seek to love Mother Nature but to fathom her secrets in order to dominate her, and to erect the astounding structure of a world of mind remote from nature, from which women are henceforth excluded. Indeed, women are actually to be feared, perhaps because, unbeknown to the thinking, suffering, sleeping man, they are co-originators of that anxiety of conscience which pounds his heart awake. Wisdom against one's will. The gain of culture by the loss of nature. Progress through pain. The formulae which underlie Western culture, spelled out four hundred years before our era.

Four young Japanese women—is the transition too glaring?—but they really did stand beside us in their variegated, imaginative hats as we waited at the intersection with the two men friends. And they traveled with us to Mycenae, and preceded us, light-footed and lighthearted—that is, untroubled—up the not untroublesome road to the fortress. This is the original fortress—the look of the ruins tells you that—which Cassandra saw at the end, after being deported from a Troy I imagine as looking hardly less grim.

Apollo! O Apollo!
You who lead my ways! O you who are set against me!
Whither have you led me,
ah, into what house! . . .
A human slaughterhouse, its floor spattered with blood.

She alludes to the ghastly meal which Atreus served his brother and rival behind these mighty walls of the Atrides: the cooked flesh of his brother's sons. The woman Cassandra shudders with a shudder that is for human nature, not just for her own fate. Now she stands between the cyclopean walls. From the gate the lions, which now have no heads, stare at her. She must go inside. Walls, walls, even in the inner zone of the fortress. The inhabitants are petrified with fear for their lives, with dread of foreigners—no wonder the stranger-woman experiences a dark premonition. We, on the other hand, climb higher along the sunlit stone paths inside the stream of tourists, surrounded by American college students, ahead of us the four twittering Japanese butterflies. To the right the circle of graves. A glimpse into the graves of those who died in battle in the sixteenth century B.C. This is how the heroes of the Achaeans were buried, not burned on funeral pyres as Homer describes it. The altar; the processional way; the remains of the palace walls.

Here, somewhere around here, Clytemnestra stepped to the portal of the palace and said: Come, Cassandra. Come into the house and step down. Yes, you. She offers the captive permission to take part in the sacrifice, seems not to want to make her slave's lot more difficult.

Cassandra is silent; the chorus voices its suspicion:

It seems to me that the foreign woman needs an interpreter,
for she behaves like a wild creature, newly captured.

To which Clytemnestra replies:

Oh no, not like a wild creature. She is simply out of her senses
and listens to nothing but her own folly.
She can still see her homeland too clearly,
Troy, which we recently conquered. She has not yet learned
to obey the reins. But easy!
Soon she will spit out foam and blood and be obedient!

Now the Japanese women have spread out a cherry-blossom-white cloth on the pinnacle of the former Acropolis of Mycenae, taken all sorts of appetizing tidbits out of their boat-shaped bast bags, and spread them on the cloth. Four big round hats have sat down around it and gaily and daintily begun to eat—a more wholesome meal than the one which took place here so long ago; of course, they are not thinking about that; they may well know almost nothing about it. The American students form groups so that the various cameras can take a series of photos. We rest on blocks of stone.

With my eyes I trace the route the tourist buses take at brief intervals to the car park, where they then wait at the foot of the mountain fortress, parked in a row twenty or thirty deep, until their human cargo clamber up the mountain like ants, obtain some form of gratification, return exhausted, swiftly refresh themselves with ice cream and Coca-Cola, and disappear again, relieved, into their mobile retreat. It was along this same road that the victorious Agamemnon returned home, bringing the captive Cassandra in his train. In those days it may have been narrow and arduous, but it is the natural way of approach to the fortress from the plain. Very likely the king and the slave woman had different feelings as they passed that domed tomb which the excavators have named the "Treasury of Atreus," and which I can see clearly from up here. I must admit that we enter the tomb later without any feeling of sacred awe. Darkness, the spills that burn only a short time. The dome above us: One stone holds the next by weighing it down.

Then we wait at the bus stop for a long time; the Japanese women are with us again, of course. Ten, fifteen times I see the farmer trek back and forth the length of his elongated field with horse and plow, down below the plateau where I am standing; I stop counting the travel buses which arrive and depart; and from my vantage point here below, I imprint on my mind once and for all the picture of the mountain fortress with its ant-paths full of tourists, before we finally admit that the bus we are awaiting is not going to come. Three of the Japanese women have sat down in a row and are reading slender books without showing signs of impatience. The fourth and eldest tells me that she is studying classical philology in England on a scholarship. Today (she tells me) she fulfilled one of her dearest wishes: to see with her own eyes the fortress of Agamemnon and Clytemnestra. "What beautiful hats you all have," I say. She smiles and says "Thank you," in English. But now we must see about getting back to Argos. We take a taxi with two women from Cologne, a mother and daughter, who are suffering grievously from the unreliability of bus connections. Exasperated by the women's pitiless refusal to speak to each other throughout the trip, we arrive at Argos in the afternoon. The two men friends are already sitting in the bus to Nauplia and smile at us as if we had granted them a wish by appearing.

In Nauplia, just at the zenith of the great arc described by the bay, is a taverna where a fresh, multiarmed squid is fixed over the door as a sign. We walk underneath it and into the bar parlor; the proprietor conducts us to the kitchen, where all the dishes are kept lukewarm, if not hot, in open pans. Now experts in Greek cuisine, we assemble our meal simply by pointing our fingers. The light effects have already come and gone, the sun has already set. We did not miss out on either. Tomorrow we still want to travel to Epidaurus.

In a made-up story I would not dare to claim that the two men friends were with us yet again in the same bus. And yet there they are, sitting in the same row of seats on the other side of the aisle; tired this time, or in a bad mood? But I could be mistaken. Have I already mentioned that they are French-speaking? The elder of the two, whose youthful jeans suit strikes me for the first time as not quite suitable, is reading to the younger the same passage from the *Blue Guide* that I have before me in German, the passage about Epidaurus. Epidaurus is the shrine of Aesculapius, the son of Apollo. So the center of the installation we will see is a sleeping and dreaming hall which we have already seen in a smaller edition: the Amphiareion at Oropos. Now the older friend whispers to the younger something that may have to do with dream and sleep cures; but the younger continues to gaze unwaveringly out the window at the continually fresh and admittedly noteworthy views revealed by the road as it climbs, and does not smile. Of course the younger friend has every right (so I persuade myself) to be grave, taciturn, and perhaps even a little sulky.

The ruins of Epidaurus seem to me even more unintelligible than other ruins. The Greek way of life left a very marked imprint here, as the foundation walls for the sleep and dream hall testify. So do the sundry temples for sundry deities, the gymnastics and music hall, and even the hippodrome. Next to all the rectangular layouts is a circular structure, a tholos, "whose significance" (I read) "is still unclear. Probably it was used for secret rites; for it is said to have been erected over the grave of Aesculapius, whose mother was a mortal. Here the priests used to breed the pale-brown serpents sacred to Aesculapius." Aesculapius, the male god descended from Apollo, one of the "new" gods. The fact that his distinctive mark is the serpent indicates that he "took over" the art of healing (to express it neutrally) from women. Moreover, as we have already seen in Mycenae, the heroes were buried in circular graves. It is said that Cassandra's father, Priam, imprisoned her in a "pyramid" inside the citadel after she had prophesied how unhappily the war would end for Troy. Robert Graves suggests that her prison may have been a beehive tomb, from which she uttered her prophecies in the name of the heroes buried there. Cilli Rentmeister surmises that the "bee with her nation of Amazons" must "surely have been regarded as a highly sacred animal symbol in the ancient female societies"; and she cites examples of very ancient circular structures on the island of Malta, temples or houses, whose shapes depicted the body of the Great Goddess: "ample, rounded, voluptuous."

And after all, the theater of Epidaurus is a circular structure too, which, we perceive, is not something that can be taken for granted. And incidentally, it was built, circa 400 B.C., by the same famous masterbuilder as the tholos, Polycletus. The powerful fragrance of the stone pines which grow around the shrine wafts even to this point; the sky is light blue crossed with veils of cloud. We sit on the highest row of seats. Once the Hellene men used to enter the theater just the way the swelling stream of tourists is pouring into it now, far below us. The place where that young man is standing now, at the focal point of the lens formed by the circular theater, is where Aeschylus's Orestes used to stand, the son of Agamemnon and Clytemnestra returned home to avenge the murder of his father by murdering his mother. Whom will he invoke, a god or a goddess? He says:

> *O Hermes in the abyss, god of the dead!*
> *Guardian of the fathers' shadowy throne!*
> *I beseech you: Stand by me and save me! ...*
> *Orestes, who at Apollo's behest came to Argos*
> *to make atonement for Agamemnon ...*
> *O Zeus, let me avenge my father's death,*
> *help me do the deed!*

Three male gods in one monologue. The young man down below us strikes a match. We hear it all the way up here, the public applauds. Someone calls out something to him, the young man whispers: "William Shakespeare"; everyone is able to hear him. Applause. More cries. Next the young man straightens up and says, this time loudly: "To be or not to be, that is the question." Then he leaves the stage. Hundreds of Greek schoolchildren are arriving. Far away from us, in the same row, sit the two men friends. We cannot hear what they are saying. They separate, leaving in different directions. Neither is sitting in the bus on the return trip.

In a few months the great drama will unfold here once again, in Valtinos's new translation. "Blood," the female chorus leader will cry:

> This is the law:
> Blood,
> flowing to the earth,
> demands new blood.

The ancient law of blood revenge, in which Orestes becomes entangled: Never could the son lay violent hands on his mother. Woman was taboo. Aeschylus seems to anticipate that his male public, who have since come to exercise absolute dominance, will still feel disquieted by echoes of the sacred awe of woman. A chorus of women are given the task of branding woman as the greatest evil under the sun: "And then, / worst of all, / the inordinate desire, / the lust of the woman." Ghastly examples are cited as proofs. The process of redrawing once-inviolable woman as a monster already has a long history. The woman must be eliminated! So we hear now without further ado. And when the deed is done, we are told: Keep in mind, all the same, that Orestes is no murderer. This verdict is meant to be hammered into the public; but the Greek playwright foundered in that task, even if not in his aesthetic duty. Despite thousands of years of patriarchal efforts, human consciousness still feels matricide to be a grislier crime than any other. The principle that the son is the son of his father alone could not be sustained. And absolute as Aeschylus's moral concern must be, to soothe the matricide's conscience, his aesthetic concern carries him away just as irresistibly. He is unsurpassed in his description of the murderer's fear when he is placed in a hopeless conflict.

> Quickly! Listen to me! One last time!
> It carries me away!
> I sit in a chariot,
> but I do not drive.

> *It is the horses*
> *who hold the reins.*
> *I have no more power over them,*
> *I . . . can . . . not . . . think.*
> *Think? No! Someone else*
> *is thinking for me!*
> *And deep in the heart sits fear*
> *and sings and begins to dance.*
> *Therefore, so long as I am in my right senses*
> *—am I still in my right senses?—*
> *I will say to you quickly:*
> *It was just that I killed my mother,*
> *the woman abhorred by the god—*
> *a horror hated by the earth!*

Equally powerful are the choruses of the Erinyes (Furies), age-old goddesses who embody the souls of the ancestors and who lament the downfall of the old law, which they regard as the downfall of morality in general. On the other hand, the absolution of Orestes and the taming of the matriarchal Erinyes by the clever-talking Pallas Athena is comparatively insipid, an agitprop epilogue, a finale fit for a tendentious drama. The political intent of Aeschylus the Athenian citizen diminishes the end of his play. Nevertheless, I believe that the fifteen thousand visitors who will see the ancient play in the ancient theater this August of 1980—some Greeks, too, but most of all tourists—will not go home feeling that it had a happy ending. The hairsplitting controversy about whether the unhappy Orestes is the murderer of his mother or the avenger of his father simply shows that antagonism has arisen where there should have been accord and conciliation. This antagonism takes the form of ambivalence in the man, and because it must be incessantly denied, glossed over, reinterpreted, and repressed, it generates fear, hatred, and hostility. And so it has had its grievous consequences down through the millennia, until it reached us, and reached those who will leave the theater of Epidaurus in four months' time as we are doing now.

The Troy I have in mind is not a description of bygone days but a model for a kind of utopia.

3 ❧ A WORK DIARY,

ABOUT THE STUFF LIFE AND

DREAMS ARE MADE OF

> *This autumn the atomic mushrooms became*
> *such a common sight in the newspapers*
> *that aesthetic categories began to form*
> *Whenever you looked at the photographs*
> *the state of the blue planet was foreseeable*
> *The term neutron weapons appeared frequently*
> *Like its brothers, the price of gas and the weather report*
> *it became commonplace as appeals for peace*
>
> *My child has gotten a bad mark*
> *What shall I say it isn't easy*
> *to bear the sight of him the innocence*
> *And we live our improbable*
> *adventurous life improve the bad mark*
> *The child goes to school we plant trees*
> *listen to the test alarm the ABC-weapons warning*
> *know the speeches of the military of every country*
>
> — S A R A H K I R S C H ,* "Year's End"

Meteln, May 16, 1980 The literature of the West (I read) is the white man's reflection on himself. So should it be supplemented by the white woman's reflection on herself? And nothing more?

The supreme commands of NATO and the Warsaw Pact

---

* Contemporary German woman writer, b. 1935, lived first in East Berlin, now writing in West Berlin. (All quotations from authors other than Christa Wolf have been translated from the German by JvH, unless otherwise indicated.)—Trans.

countries are conferring about a fresh arms race, on both sides, to counter the enemy's presumed weapons-technology superiority with something equally effective. The realization that the physical existence of us all depends on shifts in the delusional thinking of very small groups—that is, on chance, to be sure unhinges the classical aesthetic once and for all, slips it from its mountings, which, in the final analysis, are fastened to the laws of reason. Fastened to the faith that such laws exist because they must exist. Literature: a valiant, if groundless, effort to create a shelter at the same time for free-floating reason and for oneself. Because to compose words presupposes conditions which appear to lie outside literature. It also presupposes a measure, for aesthetics is also rooted in the question of what can be ascribed to man.

The Homeridae, through their accounts of heroic deeds of long ago, may have united and structured the masses who listened to them, above and beyond prevailing social structures. The classical Greek dramatist helped create, by aesthetic means, the political-ethical attitude of the free, adult, male citizen of the polis. The hymns, mystery plays, and saints' legends of the Christian medieval poet also served to promote a bond whose two terms, God and man, were both responsive. The courtly epic has a fixed set of characters to whom it relates by praising them. The early middle-class poet addresses his prince in burning protest, and at the same time addresses the prince's subjects, stirring them to rebellion. The proletariat, the socialist movements with their revolutionary class-struggle goals, inspire the literature that accompanies them to concrete partisanship. But in the face of modern-day phenomena, awareness of the incongruousness of words keeps growing. The thing the anonymous nuclear planning staffs have in mind for us is unsayable; the language which would reach them seems not to exist. But we go on writing in the forms we are used to. In other words, we still cannot believe what we see. We cannot express what we already believe.

Meteln, June 2, 1980 But it is not the end of Cassandra's story that interests me most. What interests me is: how she acquired the gift of prophecy. *Dr. Vollmer's Dictionary of Mythology* (1874):

> CASSANDRA, *the most unfortunate of the daughters of Priam and Hecuba. Apollo loved her and promised that if she would give him her love in return, he would teach her to see the future. Cassandra consented but did not keep her word once the god had granted her the gift. In return, he took away people's belief in her utterances and made her a laughingstock. Now Cassandra was regarded as mad, and because she prophesied nothing but misfortune, people soon grew fed up with her disruption of all their enjoyments and confined her in a dungeon. Later she became a priestess of Minerva* [wrong: she became a priestess of Apollo— C.W.], *from whose temple, where she was clinging to the goddess's statue, Ajax . . . dragged her by the hair, and so tore down the statue along with the unfortunate woman.*

The word that appears most frequently in this passage: "unfortunate." Apparently Dr. Vollmer and his collaborators in 1874 found embarrassing and unspeakable the disputed tradition that the Achaean Ajax the Lesser, one of the chief heroes in the conquest of Troy, had raped Cassandra in front of the statue of Athena, at which the helpless goddess could only roll her eyes toward the sky. That was not all. The story also goes that toward the end of the war, Cassandra's father, the Trojan king Priam, married her to a man she had refused, for political reasons—namely, to acquire an ally with an urgently needed contingent of warriors. Probably it was this marriage that produced the twins whom Agamemnon carried off captive with her to Mycenae and who were slaughtered in her wake. Assumption: Cassandra is one of the first women figures handed down to us whose fate prefigures what was to be the fate of women for three thousand years: to be turned into an object.

Questions suggested by the entry in Dr. Vollmer's dictionary: How is it that Apollo, a male, "young" god, can confer the gift of prophecy on a woman? Why did he, why did the transmitters of the tale, hurry to make her gift ineffective again at once? Why did she press for the gift of prophecy? Why do we call someone a Cassandra when he prophesies doom—why did a woman's name bear that stigma, when at the same time and for the same reason Laocoön, the Trojan priest of Apollo, issued warnings and prophesied doom? Laocoön, too, adjured his countrymen not to bring inside their city walls the wooden horse the Achaeans had left behind them. So why don't we call a prophet of doom a Laocoön? Why is it serpents that twine themselves around him and his sons and destroy them?

Meteln, July 8, 1980 Delusion is mathematicized of course. (Just as, paradoxically, mathematics—if you begin to *believe* in it as an independent structure whose laws should be transferred to other structures, there to prove or even generate one of the most life-preventive myths of our time: "scientificness" —just as mathematics, with its indisputable exactitude, peculiarly lends itself to incorporation into a delusion, and to fortifying the delusion so that it is unassailable.) Twice in the past week, the U.S. computer has sounded the alarm: Soviet rockets are flying toward the United States. In such a case, we are told, the President has twenty-five minutes to make a decision. The computer (we hear) has now been switched off. The delusion: to make security dependent on a machine, rather than on an analysis of the historical situation possible only to human beings with an understanding of history that includes understanding of the historical situation of the other side.

The Swedish Peace Research Institute declares in its annual report that the danger of an atomic war in Europe has never been as great as it is today. Sixty thousand atomic explosive devices have been stored throughout the world, the institute says. In the last few years, the time of détente, the two super-powers have vastly escalated armaments in their race to outbid each other.

Meanwhile, we talk about the situation, arrive at the conclusion that it no longer bears thinking about. And yet we cannot help thinking about it. What do I actually mean when I say "delusion"? I mean the absurdity of the claim that the excessive atomic armament of both sides creates a "balance of terror" that reduces the danger of war; that in the long run it even offers a minimum of security. I mean the grotesque calculation based on strategies that were devastating when applied to conventional weaponry, but which are senseless and irrational in relation to atomic weapons. Hence the cynical saying: He who strikes first will die second.

The situation of Europe today is fundamentally different than it was in the thirties before Hitler invaded neighboring countries inadequately armed to defend themselves. Obviously they had no choice but to arm themselves, defend themselves, against the adversary. In this case self-defense made sense. Obviously self-defense against an aggressor made sense in Vietnam; obviously arms are a means of self-defense and liberation in a range of South American countries where freedom movements are fighting. But I am a European woman. Europe cannot be defended against an atomic war. Either it will survive in one piece or be destroyed in one piece. The existence of nuclear weapons has reduced to absurdity all conceivable strategies for defending our little continent.

Do we have a chance? How can I rely on the experts who have led us to this desperate pass? Armed with nothing but the intractable desire to allow my children and grandchildren to live, I conclude that the sensible course may be the one that holds out absolutely no hope: unilateral disarmament. [I hesitate: in spite of the Reagan Administration? Yes, since I see no other way out: in spite of it!] By choosing this course, we place the other side under the moral pressure of the world public; we render superfluous the U.S.S.R.'s extortionary policy of arming itself to death; we renounce the atomic first-strike capability, and we devote all our efforts to the most effective defense measures. Assuming that this involves some risk, how much greater is the risk of further atomic arms, which every day increase the risk of atomic annihilation, by accident if nothing else?

This is wishful thinking, you say? So, is it completely misguided to want to think and to have a say about the life and death of many, perhaps all future generations?

The atomic threat, if it has brought us to the brink of annihilation, must then have brought us to the brink of silence too, to the brink of endurance, to the brink of reserve about our fear and anxiety, and our true opinions.

Meteln, August 10, 1980   Is it possible to conceive of beings endowed with reason who do *not* know how contemporary man is divided into body/soul/mind, who cannot understand this division? Cassandra experiences this divisive operation alive and in the flesh. That is, there are actual forces in her environment which, as the need arises, require of her a denial of part of herself. She learns techniques to deaden emotion. "The first class conflict in history coincides with the development of antagonism between husband and wife in monogamous marriage, and the first class oppression, with the oppression of the female sex by the male" (Friedrich Engels, *The Origin of the Family*). It appears that—since when did this happen exactly?—I can no longer view Cassandra as a tragic figure. I do not think she saw herself that way. Does her contemporaneity lie in the way she learns to deal with pain? So, is pain the point at which I assimilate her, a particular kind of pain, the pain of becoming a knowing subject?

The city of Troy was (they say) built upon the walls of many destroyed cities. (This is Heinrich Schliemann's Troy VII A, which he did not believe was the Troy of the Trojan

War, to be sure, and which has been dated—with surprising and suspicious exactitude, I feel—to the period 1194–1184 B.C.) A city with a palace, citadel, the dwellings of craftsmen, shopkeepers, scribes. With temples, sacred precincts. The whole surrounded by a wall. With rural settlements in the environs, inhabited by an old-established population. A river: the Scamander. A city-state with a ruling house that may well have been regarded as divine; with noblemen (an aristocratic upper class, no doubt frequently related to the royal family); with civil servants, military commanders; craftsmen who perhaps belong to the royal house; with priests and priestesses; probably with large landowners; petty farmers who may be of different descent from the ruling class; with administrative clerks at every level of the hierarchy; with the mass of the working population, about whom little is known because they are mentioned least often in documents. With slaves. This is a rough model drawn from the less than homogeneous descriptions by various researchers into Mycenaean culture (named after the life style at the fortress of Agamemnon, leader of the Achaeans and conqueror of Troy). Troy belonged, in the widest sense, to the Mycenaean culture sphere, which to be sure was modified by features of the culture of Asia Minor (the Hittites) and the no doubt powerful influences of Minoan-Cretan culture, which, as it petered out, passed major influences not only to the Greek mainland but also to the islands and the coast of Asia Minor; "permeated" them. To what extent? What were the specifically "Minoan" traits of Troy? Under King Priam, whose name probably derives from the Orient, was it ruled by a royal house that derived from the Aegean and Asia Minor, who governed a mixed population with Indo-European sympathies? If so, what would that imply about the conflicts which might have confronted Cassandra, particularly with respect to religion and the cults which must have co-existed? To take a utopian rather than a historical view, might she not in the end have freed herself inwardly from *all* faith, including—

indeed primarily!—from her own; for her story would have to be a process of liberation?

Meteln, August 23, 1980   I read Marie-Luise Fleisser's* *Avant-Garde* again, as if for the first time. Sadness at this woman's fate, which seemed to me inhuman, incredible, impossible. Exploited by everyone, abused like an animal. Male society in the raw strikes her unexpectedly, from the Communist poet to the harrowingly petit bourgeois tobacconist and the Nazi janitor. For women, writing is a medium which they place between themselves and the world of men ("Then they will at least admire me . . ."). The inevitable moment when the woman who writes (who "sees" in Cassandra's case) no longer represents anything or anyone except herself; but who is that? Does there exist an ominous right (or duty) to bear witness? Tenacious of life, the supposition that someone must always go on writing. We cannot know whether we are in the darkest center of history or at its end. Europe, if you watch it decline, see it as declining, can at many moments look as beautiful as Atlantis. "Europe," a name that expanded outward from the Greek and Thracian mainland as the Greeks became increasingly aware of the land mass to the north. Europa was the daughter of the Phoenician king whom the god Zeus in bull form abducted from Phoenicia and carried to Crete, where she bore him, among other children, Minos, who was later to be king. An act of violence inflicted on a woman founds, in Greek myth, the history of Europe. My pain for this continent is in part a phantom pain: not only the pain for a lost limb, but for limbs that have not yet been formed, not developed; for unlived feelings, unfulfilled longing. All of this compensated for in literature: for how long? Viewed through a different lens, doesn't even Homer contain a utopian element? Or must he

---

* Contemporary German woman writer, 1901–74. *Avant-Garde* (1963) is a short-story collection; *Tiefseefisch* (1972), from which Christa Wolf quotes later, is a drama.—Trans.

devote all his strength to the task of the moment, to salvage in song whatever tradition had been preserved, over four or five centuries of Dorian incursions, solely by songs and epic poetry? That whole process, the formation of the *Iliad*, is hard to imagine. An event takes place circa 1200 B.C., namely, the Trojan War. A particular city is destroyed (at a time when the destruction of cities was an everyday occurrence) by the united Achaean monarchies, whose wealth, Thomson says, was founded on conquest and plunder. Then they in turn succumb to the Dorian intruders. Flee, taking the wealthy families and their cultural traditions to Asia Minor, where they found new kingdoms described (cf. Thomson) as insignificant states of an agrarian character in which the king is nothing but the chief landowner. In this environment, characterized by the gradual decay of the monarchy and a paucity of events that went on for centuries, the Greek epic is said to have ripened and matured. Highly skilled bards, already schooled by Minoan culture and living in Ionia, took up the themes of the Achaeans, which had been handed down in individual songs and cantos, and now these, freed from their origin, received their final shape over the course of centuries from the artists whom Thomson calls the "Homeridai." In the process (it is claimed) the Homeridae were able to view the predatory events of the Trojan War with detachment, and to penetrate them with their own refined view of the world. A unique process of condensation took place without the aid (or the obstacle?) of a written script. As for the *Iliad*, it was the first known attempt to impose a standard of human emotion on a bare chronology ruled by the law of battle and carnage. That standard: the wrath of Achilles. But the line the narrator pursues is that of male action. Everyday life, the world of women, shines through only in the gaps between the descriptions of battle.

Meteln, September 27, 1980 Why, really, does a person want to live longer? You fool yourself that you still want to see this and that, still want to do this and that—namely, to write. That's true. But what if it doesn't happen? After a long sleep, I find G. in the meadow at the apple harvest. Above—no, in among the harvest—the sky, a clear blue block. I fetch a basket, gather the fallen apples, put the bruised and tainted ones in little piles which we will carry to the compost heap later, sort the good ones into crates, the "give-aways." The miller's bearded friend comes and talks with us about the tiles, which are manufactured in Dahlewitz. Are they of sufficient quality to "raise a gable"? We talk about K., the only thatch-roofer far and wide, who fell off the roof because of a weak grappling iron— on the very day when he was not drinking, everyone says. Double fracture at the base of the skull, a broken lumbar vertebra. He'll never climb another roof, says the man from Dahlewitz. By the way, he's still in the intensive care unit— K., who was part of this landscape.

I see our three figures in the meadow from a long distance off. A feeling of loss of reality—as if someone had made a hole in the plastic bag that has been slipped over us and now the air is escaping along with the sky.

Later, as I sit on the bench outside the house pitting plums, I wonder how many more years I will sit on the bench this way. How many years do I *want* to go on sitting here? A sudden tug of age.

I start some leavened dough, put it on the oven brim to rise. G., assisted by E., who needs work even on Saturdays, carries upstairs through the kitchen the parts of the heavy oak cabinet which we have stripped down to its natural color; it is set up between the beds. All three of us admire it. The men decide that they *will* oil it, after all, so that it will get darker and the oak grain will "stand out better." Meanwhile, I put the dough in the tin, line it with plums and then with streusel, and let it rise again. As I shove the cake into the oven, the T.s arrive from their three-town trip through Schönebeck, Rehna, and Gadebusch; they are brown, refreshed, enthusiastic. While Gerti and I set about turning peppers, cucumbers, and ,tomatoes into a salad, the men, in the bedroom, install the upper part of the writing cabinet on the lower part. We all have to appraise it. How good it looks. How beautiful the bedroom is now. How well the Greek bedspreads suit the red Mecklenburg wood . . . It's true, but I perceive that it makes no difference to me what this or any other room looks like.

When the cake comes out of the oven, G. pushes the big, foil-wrapped fish inside, along with a couple of foil-wrapped potatoes. They'll take three-quarters of an hour to bake. Meanwhile, we set the table—it's getting hot in the kitchen. G. makes a shrimp cocktail, fetches good, cold white wine; slowly we begin to eat. It tastes good, we get jolly. Finally the fish and potatoes are done. An often-repeated event, G. takes them both out of the oven, unwraps them, tests them with a fork, distributes the portions. For me this day is full of events that repeat themselves; good, everyday life. I wonder whether it is "necessary" to experience another hundred or thousand repetitions of these same events. The impulses to live on must come from something new that we can aim at. Otherwise it could happen that, without realizing it, we consent to a verdict.

We switch to a different wine. Conversation turns to the world situation: the war between Iraq and Iran, which has insane features like most things today. To what extent insane? Why aren't all wars insanity, including the Trojan War? Because its aim was "consistent with reality." The Achaeans needed access to the Bosporus, so did that mean that they had to force the Trojans to give up control of access to the Dardanelles? How high does the quota of losses have to be before wars cease to be "realistic"?

Observing how people go about their everyday routine, we wonder—we four around the bright kitchen table, after a good meal, drinking wine—What do they (or we) hope for? Do they hope at all? What are their hopes for their children? For several generations people have always hoped for "something better" for their children than they had themselves; is that impetus used up? Isn't this tiredness to commit oneself a tiredness of hope?

R. knows statistics from the latest official United Nations inquiry into the state of world armaments. According to these figures, there are three European tons of TNT for every person on earth, that is, for each one of us. The Great Powers could annihilate each other more than a dozen times over. And so on. We laugh, slightly embarrassed. "Normal feelings" are numbed by such statistics. Indignation, revolt would be inappropriate. The aesthetic of *resistance* to it all has yet to be developed.

To whom can I say that the *Iliad* bores me?

Meteln, December 7, 1980 Dreams: We are living on a farmstead, smaller, dirtier, poorer than this one where I wake up. We are standing in the yard. From there a netlike, roofed animal run leads into the kitchen; we see a wild animal glide in—a puma! we say, shocked. Horrified, we run inside. The small, smoke-blackened, filthy, and wretched kitchen is divided by a wire grating, behind which I dimly perceive poultry, domestic stock, and now this "puma" as well; but behind it I see a second wild animal with a strange, dreadful, and disgusting shape, for which there simply is not any name. A ghastly depression. "The animals must leave!" I say to H. We all go to eat, sit dejectedly around a round table—then H. calls me into the kitchen. The second of the wild animals behind the wire fence has been shot; it is bleeding from a shoulder wound, looks at us reproachfully, sadly, and at the same time implacably. "Did you shoot at it?" I ask H. "Naturally," he says, "what else could one do?" He has taken a hunting rifle that was hanging on a wall in the kitchen. But he could not shoot again, he says. The animal does not look as if it was about to die of this wound. It occurs to us that the animals might have escaped from a passing circus. It is too late to make inquiries. We cannot possibly live with them. We cannot kill them, either. They will not leave our kitchen voluntarily. We stand there, eye to eye with the mute wild beasts, and know: it is a hopeless situation.

Berlin, December 18, 1980   The material I am piling up around me has gotten out of control. I am no longer reading in order to provide a credible, physically perceptible environment for the inner formation of the Cassandra character, which is my real concern. I am reading because I can no longer free myself from ancient history, mythology, archaeology. Marx had no way of knowing what archaeology would (literally) unearth in Crete, Greece, and Asia Minor since the end of the nineteenth century. If he had known, no doubt he would scarcely have described the Greeks as the "children," the "normal children" of our culture, whose artistic productions continue to fascinate us for precisely that reason. Greek culture is a late and advanced culture compared to the Mycenaean, and Mycenaean culture in turn succeeded other advanced cultures, for example, the Minoan, which the Greeks still knew something about. But in Troy, I firmly believe, the people were no different from us. Their gods are our gods, the false gods. Only our devices differ from theirs.

Berlin, December 30, 1980   Stalemate beneath the dense sky of moratorium agreements: the best we can hope for Europe. The domestication of conflicts on all sides. Not the defusing of conflicts, but their trivialization in the face of (and by means of) our fear of total catastrophe, which seems to be the alternative to the status quo. The border between East and West Germany, by dividing our former country, just separates the two world systems and—it is hoped—keeps them at a distance. So apparently (or ostensibly) we must want the status quo, further its preservation, because to breach it would or could mean war (what am I saying, war? It would mean annihilation). So changes within the two German states are unthinkable. So the young intellectuals on both sides of this border are wearing themselves out working for something impossible; but that is their life. And so the older, clarified members of my generation have already recognized for a long time now: There is no scope for change. There is no revolutionary situation.

Or is that not how things are at all? Could the foundation for peace be laid (after all, what we have now is not peace but only non-war, an "atomic stalemate") precisely by setting in motion processes for productive change?

Berlin, January 2, 1981 The story of Cassandra as it now presents itself to me: Cassandra, the eldest and best-loved daughter of King Priam of Troy, a vivacious person interested in society and politics, does not want to be confined to the house, to get married, like her mother Hecuba, like her sisters. She wants to learn a profession. For a woman of rank, the only possible profession is that of priestess, seeress, which was practiced only by women in remote antiquity, in the days when the chief deity was a woman, Ge, Gaea, the earth goddess. (Men contested women's right to this profession in the course of struggles which seem to have gone on for thousands of years, as the gods pushed their way into the places of the goddesses. The Oracle of Delphi, which the god Apollo took over directly from Gaea, is a striking example.) She is assigned this profession, a privilege. She is expected to fulfill it in the traditional way. This is precisely what she must refuse to do—at first because, in her way, she believes that that is the best way for her to serve her people, to whom she is warmly and intimately attached; later, because she understands that "her people" are not her people. A painful process of separation ensues, in the course of which she is first pronounced mad for "speaking the truth," and then thrown into the dungeon—by her beloved father Priam. The visions which overwhelm her no longer have anything to do with the ritual decrees of her oracle. She "sees" the future because she has the courage to see things as they really are in the present. She does not achieve this alone. Cassandra makes contact with minorities among the socially and ethnically heterogeneous groups in and around the palace. By doing so, she consciously moves off the beaten track, strips herself of all privileges, exposes herself to suspicion, scorn, persecution: the price of her independence. No self-pity; she lives her life even in war. Tries to lift the decree that has been pronounced over her: that she is to be turned into an object. In the end she is alone, taken as spoils by the conquerors of her city. She knows that there was no viable alternative for her. The self-destruction of Troy met halfway the destruction inflicted by the enemy outside. A time is coming when violence and the struggle for power will dominate. But not all the cities of her known world will be destroyed.

Berlin, February 2, 1981 Most energies are used up in warding off the insane news that is coming in, especially from the United States; for instance, the outbreak of collective madness when the hostages return from Iran. The list of people here who are going away keeps growing. Daily struggle for the ability to work, not to mention for "enjoyment." Now you no longer need to be "Cassandra"; most people are beginning to see what is coming. An uneasiness, which many file under the names emptiness and loss of meaning, makes them afraid. We cannot hope that the used-up institutions, to which many were accustomed, will supply a new direction. Run a zigzag course. But there is no escape route in sight. You feel you are standing at bay. Australia is not a way out.

Meteln, February 22, 1981 In the news, both sides bombard us with the need to make preparations for war, which both sides call preparations for self-defense. Emotionally it is unbearable to see the state of the world as it really is. The motivation to write, any hope of "having some effect," is decaying at a breakneck pace that may parallel the speed of missile production on both sides. To whom should one say that modern industrial society itself, idol and fetish of all governments, stamped with absurdity, is turning against those who built, exploit, and defend it? Who could alter that? At night the madness goes for my throat.

In the morning a radio lecture by a Western economist who has since died. His theses: In all the industrialized nations the mass of workers must labor at monotonous jobs that destroy them as people, in the name of "prosperity," that most sacred of all today's sacred cows. Our present prosperity is (he says) unthinkable without monotonous assembly-line labor, and for the most part satisfies "false" needs that have been artfully manufactured. The amalgamation of masses of people for production purposes is making working conditions increasingly baffling, increasingly dehumanized for the individual. Sociologists have learned that effective work groups—groups in which the individual could develop meaningful relationships—should not exceed twelve people. Bureaucracy, which arises out of the amalgamation of masses into large apparatus, unfailingly makes "inhuman" decisions—not because all its executives are inhuman monsters, but because their private morality is set aside in favor of the laws of the apparatus. (It is at this point that the doubts of literary men, moralists, and moral philosophers arise, about the effectiveness of their productions: The individual *cannot* introduce his insights and attitudes into the societal process if they run contrary to those of the prevailing major institutions.)

The lecturer felt that man was meant to strive for the good, to serve his neighbor, to realize himself. All this, he claimed, was impossible in the modern industrialized society, whose chief trends were gigantism, overcomplexity, capital-intensiveness, and violence. These trends were not inevitable, but neither imagination, developmental technology, nor money was being expended on counterplans.

Meteln, March 26, 1981 Reading matter: Thomas Mann and Karl Kerényi, *Gespräch in Briefen* (Dialogue in Letters). Envious joy at the way each feels enhanced by the other. The two show trust in the meaningfulness of intellectual labor done with integrity, and trust in each other as intellectual laborers—things which have never gone unchallenged and which seem to belong to an earlier age. I was almost infected by the feeling that possibilities could still open up for us, after all. Despite the fact that these two correspondents, whose middle-class, humanistic background did little to prepare them for the ghastly grotesqueness of a Fascist Germany—despite the fact that the novelist and the classical philologist were also undermined by self-doubt. Not only the self-doubt which naturally arose in the spreading darkness that in the end eclipsed almost all Europe, climaxing in World War II, but also that caused by the acrid disappointment of the postwar years: the fact that people "do not want to learn."

The subject is humanistic studies, a fascinating dialogue. Mann, the German author, outside the borders of his fatherland but not yet in exile, is working on the Joseph novels and hence reliant on knowledge and institutions of religious history and mythology. And Kerényi, the Hungarian mythology researcher and religion scholar, dedicates to the "highly esteemed" Mann, as an opening gift, the idea of the "wolfish," the "dark" Apollo. This, by Mann's own admission, touches on the "roots" of Mann's "intellectual existence." The two men have in common their burning interest in the "deeper psychic reality" behind myth (a word which among the Greeks meant nothing other than "the true word," "the facts," later "the facts about the gods"). So, there was a "dark" underground and background to the "god of light." This claim plainly contradicts the received opinion about Apollo, the Greek god who was pushed farthest of all into the realm of the "bright" and the "spiritual." It removes him from the unfruitful antinomy of the pair of opposites, "Apollonian" and "Dionysian." It also confirms the ambivalence which Thomas Mann seems to feel in his urge to identify origins: "Who can say where the stories originated, above or below?" At the same moment that these two are corresponding, and unbeknown to them (even if they did know, they would not have referred to it), the Marxist George Thomson in England, in the western corner of Europe, is working on the totemistic origin of the Greek deities. The gods begin with the cult of the dead, a clan cult in which the dead were revered as heroes. Given the important role of animals and plants in pre-deistic ritual, the clan cult of the dead probably had a totemistic character.* Apparently the authorities of Thomson's day refused to countenance this supposition on the grounds that it was "indelicate." "Apollo Lykeios is admittedly a wolf-god, but, if this wolf-god was ever a wolf"—that is, the totemistic sign of a clan—"it was so long ago that there is no need for him to poke his nose into the picture." But he pokes his nose in anyhow, and we (along with Thomson) bump into the serpent, the sacred animal which used to be fed on honey cakes in the most ancient and in the most recent of Apollo's known temples. Thousands of years earlier the snake was venerated as the snake-goddess, the "protector of the house," at the domestic altars of Minoan homes. For she embodies the spirit of the dead, represents the double of the dead. She who sheds her skin is a symbol of their eternal life: "In snake-worship the clan totem has been replaced by a generalized symbol of reincarnation." Tens of thousands of years before that, in the primal nomadic tribe and the early clan system, when man was a gatherer and, in a primitive, unsure way, a hunter, he identified with the totem animal or totem plant and created the taboo: "Thou shalt not eat the totem!" At that time he used to represent the behavior of the totem animal in a mimetic ritual, a magical act. Initially, it may be, this was done to enable him to capture the animal; for Thomson believes that the totem had not always been inviolate but may actually once

---

* Thomson quotations here and on following pages are from *The Prehistoric Aegean* (Woodstock, N.Y.: Beekman, 1978): Chapter IV, p. 120; Chapter I, p. 38; and Chapter I, pp. 44–45, respectively.—Trans.

have been the only or principal food source of the clan. Later, perhaps, he did it in order to harness all his energies for the hunt, an "illusory technique complementary to the deficiencies of the real technique." Thomson gives evidence of an early society which men entered by marriage into the women's clan —that is, evidence for a matrilinear structure. He also summarizes how totem magic, "springing as it does from the very moment—the advance from appropriation to production—at which man parted company with the animals, is the matrix of all human culture." His discussion leads directly back to the Thomas Mann–Kerényi dialogue.

For both men are concerned with the way to the "Mothers."* Both; but especially the author is nagged at times by his intellectual conscience, when he engages in "mythologizing," which he connects "with the material sphere of nature." He explains this scruple to the deeply sympathetic scholar in a letter written from Küsnacht-Zürich on February 20, 1934.

> One finds in European literature of the present day a kind of rancor against the development of the human cerebrum, a rancor which has always struck me as a snobbish and ridiculous form of self-negation. Permit me the confession that I am no friend of the anti-intellectual movement. . . . I feared and fought it early, because I saw through all its brutally antihuman consequences before they became apparent.
>
> The "return of the European mind to the highest, the mythic realities," of which you speak so impressively, is truly a great and good cause in the history of thought, and I may claim to have contributed something to it by my work. But I trust you understand when I say that the fad of irrationalism frequently involves a sacrifice and a callow throwing over of achievements and principles which not only make the European a European, but the

* See Christa Wolf's discussion of the "Mothers" in Goethe's *Faust*, Part Two, in Essay 4 of this book.—Trans.

human being human. That sort of thing is a "back to nature"
movement of a far more ignoble sort, in human terms, than the
*movement which prepared the way for the French Revolution.**

Worth pondering even today: how the criticism of one-sided
male rationalism runs the risk of being wrongly interpreted as
irrationalism, hostility to science, and also put to wrong use.
This is particularly so in restorational eras, when the way to
the Mothers becomes a relapse into resentment, an escape route
from the analysis of circumstances, an idealization of more
primitive social conditions, perhaps a lead-up to blood-and-soil
myth. This in turn raises the question of what today could
possibly still represent "progress" (given the postulates of our
civilization), now that the masculine way has almost run its
course—that is, the way of carrying all inventions, circumstances, and conflicts to extremes until they have reached their
maximum negative point: the point at which no alternatives
are left.

Meteln, Thursday, April 2, 1981 A young man snared in a
delusional love for an actress he has never met attempts to
assassinate the American President as compensation for his
unrequited "love." On television you see a companion of the
President who sticks close by his side and is carrying a small
black suitcase. After the assassination attempt, he dives into the
armored presidential limousine as it drives away. The next day
you learn that the small black case contains the code the
President would need to trigger an atomic strike.

Meteln, April 3, 1981 A deep-seated fear of the threat from
the "Mothers" also shines through the Mann-Kerényi dialogue—
namely, when Kerényi mentions that the Greek goddess Aphro-

---

* Quoted from Richard Winston's translation of *The Letters of Thomas
Mann*, Vol. I, 1887–1942 (New York: Alfred A. Knopf, 1970).—Trans.

dite is nicknamed "the Black One," and quotes D. H. Law-rence: "She is the gleaming darkness, she is the luminous night, she is the goddess of destruction, her white cold fire consumes and does not create." The accompanying explanatory text sug-gests to me that Kerényi identifies the feminine with "essen-tially mute Nature," whereas he identifies the masculine with "mind" as well as with "conscious humanity." Not without amusement I read how he assures his highly esteemed corres-pondent that among the greatest and most human achievements of Mann's *The Tales of Jacob* is the fact "that we become aware of the terrible effects on a man of wasting his love on the 'wrong woman.'"

The murderous effects on a woman of giving her love to the "wrong man": Ingeborg Bachmann,* the *Franza* fragment.

But what causes Kerényi to identify with Lawrence's char-acterization of Aphrodite as a "goddess of destruction" whose "white cold fire consumes and does not create"? Is he perhaps alluding to the fantastical tradition in Hesiod by which Aphro-dite, born of the "sea-foam" (or the sea?), shaped herself out of the "immortal flesh" of the sexual organs of the oldest god, Uranus, whom his son Kronos had castrated at the behest of the raped (Earth-) Mother Gaea? Whereas, on the contrary, Thomson, in his studies of ancient Greek herbal magic, says that myrtle and lilies, flowers sacred to Aphrodite, were actually used to assist in childbirth. According to this view, what shim-mers forth behind Aphrodite, the goddess of love, as behind Hera, the wife of Zeus, and behind Artemis and Demeter, is by no means an uncreative principle but rather Eileithyia, the ancient Cretan goddess of birth. Eileithyia in turn, who like

---

* Contemporary German woman writer, 1926–73. *Der Fall Franza* (The Franza Case) is a novel fragment from a projected trilogy left uncompleted by Bachmann at her death. The trilogy, which was to have been called *Todesarten* (Types of Death), also included the novel *Malina*, to which Christa Wolf alludes later. For a more thorough discussion of both novels, see 4 "A Letter" in the present volume.—Trans.

Aphrodite was also symbolized by the dove, probably comes from Anatolia, where she is called Cybele; there are terra-cotta figurines from Cyprus which depict the "dove-headed Aphrodite." And here the myth touches on the legend-cycle of Troy. The Hittite Aphrodite-Astarte may have entered into the myth of Helen, one of whose variants states that Helen never came to Troy with Paris but met Paris in a temple of Aphrodite on Cyprus, where she may have been a prostitute of Aphrodite. As Herodotus describes it:

> Every woman who is a native of the country must once in her life go and sit in the temple of Aphrodite and there give herself to a strange man. . . . Most, however, sit in the precinct of the temple with a band of plaited string around their heads—and a great crowd they are, what with some sitting there, others arriving, others going away—and through them all gangways are marked off running in every direction for the men to pass along and make their choice. Once a woman has taken her seat she is not allowed to go home until a man has thrown a silver coin into her lap and taken her outside to lie with her. As he throws the coin, the man has to say, "In the name of the goddess Mylitta"—that being the Assyrian name for Aphrodite.*

Afterward the ancient Oriental Helen fled to Egypt, perhaps "abducted" by Paris, who, according to one tradition, was at first made a captive by King Proteus and then sent back to Troy. Meanwhile, he, Proteus, the King of Egypt, kept the beautiful Helen, and so the struggle for Troy was fought for an illusion: a figure invented by poets. The way to the Mothers leads into this kind of puzzle, this kind of nearly inextricable mesh, into ever deeper abysses. The division of labor among the highly diversified goddesses, who solidify into a finished product

---

* Quoted from Book I, p. 94 of *The Histories* (New York: Penguin Books, 1954), tr. by Aubrey De Selincourt.—Trans.

only in Greek statuary, reflects the development of human culture. It becomes the fate (*moíra*) of Aphrodite to arouse love.

> *Aphrodite, enthroned in splendor, immortal,*
> *Zeus's child, illusion-spinner, I beseech you:*
> *Do not, exalted one, torment*
> *my heart with sorrow and anxious care.**

Sappho's "Ode to Aphrodite," circa 600 B.C., which many scholars declare is the earliest example of the Western lyric poem. The love which the female poet wants her goddess to help her attain is the love of a woman. Early poets, even male poets (Homer, Hesiod), could still pray for the assistance of female deities without embarrassment. Lawrence, a late poet, feels threatened by the goddess of love.

Meteln, April 7, 1981 Cassandra lived between two disasters: the volcanic eruption of Thera/Santorin circa 1500 B.C., and the invasion of the Dorians (northern seafaring races) circa 1200 B.C. In the interval, perhaps in the middle of the thirteenth century B.C., came her personal disaster: the fall of Troy. It is not unthinkable that a gradual—even a swift and violent—shift took place in the morality of the Mediterranean region, which discredited the more peaceable Minoans of Crete, whose concern was trade, and benefited the violent Achaean princes, who relied on plunder: the kind of men Homer describes. Was there really such a thing as a "Pax Cretiensis," a "Cretan peace," as many scholars assume (perhaps giving way to wishful thinking)? Was there an order of peace in the eastern Mediterranean which was destroyed by the Achaeans? This would place Cassandra in the position of having to sepa-

---

* All quotations from Sappho are translated directly from Christa Wolf's German version.—Trans.

rate from a utopia that was no longer valid, and of finding no tangible place to live.

Can the psychologizing of myth be a matter of concern to us today? Thomas Mann, 1941, in a letter to Kerényi: " . . . and what ought my element to be at present, if not myth plus psychology? I have long been devoted to this combination; for in fact psychology is the means to take myth out of the hands of the Fascist obscurantists and to 'reconvert' it to a humane function. For me this alliance represents nothing less than the world of the future, a humanity that is blessed by the mind from above, and 'from the deep-lying abyss.'" The embryo outline of a utopia. What can all this mean today, when those who are planning the annihilation of entire continents are, in the general understanding, neither obscurantists nor Fascists, and do not go to the trouble of trimming a Germanic or Roman pantheon to size, to serve their ends? To be sure, they too need myths, in the sense the word has meanwhile acquired: in the sense of a false belief. An example of such a myth would be that we are living in a peace that has a future in it.

Now the year is 1947, and for Thomas Mann "exile" is (as he predicted in 1941) "no longer a waiting state aimed at homecoming," but instead, paradoxically, has become a kind of anticipation, the anticipation of a future, more universal locatedness that points to a "dissolution of nations and the unification of the world." Thomas Mann, in fact, is still in Pacific Palisades, California. But now he is occupied with "the most personal, the most daring in more than one sense," and "most exciting" of his books, the Faust novel, and within it, with the composition of the symphonic cantata "The Lamentation of Dr. Faustus." "Now," he writes to the classical philologist and humanist whose name, to be sure, is not Zeitblohm* but is still Kerényi: "Lamentation is very much a topical

---

* The humanist-narrator of Mann's novel *Doctor Faustus*, and friend of its protagonist.—Trans.

theme, don't you think? Things look bad. . . . Though I believe fundamentally that, all in all, humanity has been nudged a good piece *forward*, despite all appearances to the contrary. Moreover, it is a cat with nine lives. Even the A-bomb does not make me seriously anxious for its fate. Isn't it proving itself tough in us? What a strange rashness, or what gullibility, that we continue to produce *works*! For whom? For what future? And yet a work, even one of despair, can never have anything but optimism, faith in life, as its final substance, for despair is a strange thing: it already carries within it the transcendence to hope."

Longing for rashness and gullibility. For unconstraint and spontaneity. The precondition for that would be to forget what is, or to free oneself from it.

Meteln, Sunday, April 26, 1981   News report: A conference of peace researchers, scientists of various disciplines, physicians, and former high-ranking NATO military officers has been held in the Dutch town of Groningen. All the participants are said to view the future fate of Europe with great skepticism, because in the opinion of the assembly the United States, ensnared by the notion that the development of weapons technology would make it possible to "win" the next war even if it is an atomic war, is aiming to make Europe the theater of this next war, and including the annihilation of hundreds of thousands of Europeans and Russians in its calculations; so that the Soviet Union would be weakened without the United States having to fear any losses. We are told that if Europe does not begin to alter its policies completely, it has only three or four years left.

An announcement that changes the way I look at things. All the objects around me fuse inside a second: nature crumbles to ash at the same moment that I myself crumble. Then already I become aware that we would arrange to live even these three or four years if we had to. Already I am hating myself for the absurdity of my inner calculation: what I could still "get done" by that time. I hate everyone who could go on living, go on working after this announcement, and at the same time I know that those in power urgently need this very self-hatred.

I know that the knowers have never been able to do anything to prevent the threatened fall of their culture/civilization; know that in the last decades we Europeans have several times looked on at wars in other parts of the globe which threatened the peoples concerned with annihilation; know that now the other parts of the globe will form "the world" that looks on at us. That this is conceivable and possible.

"We are sitting here," says T., "we enjoyed our meal, and we are chatting comfortably instead of running through the streets screaming." "Australia: Shouldn't we at least try to save the children?" says someone who is still very young himself. But another remonstrates: "Would you want to look on from the outside while Europe is being destroyed? And survive yourself?" M. asks whether there isn't something "hopeful somehow" about groups and movements which no longer get involved with the destructive systems; which infiltrate institutions that have turned destructive; which do not get mixed up in useless battles with them, but try to ignore them; which try to live "differently." I hear myself saying, "Yes, yes," but inside me is a voice that says, It would take time to neutralize the self-destructive trend of today's megasystems gradually, nonviolently: time that we do not have. "Perhaps," says M., "we should proceed like the South Africans when they tried to free themselves from the racist regime: they got things absolutely clear in their own minds and accepted the knowledge: Our situation is hopeless. Maybe freedom can come out of that, after all." "So can resignation," says T. "And besides, the racist regime, powerful as it may be, cannot be compared with this encompassing umbrella we call 'atomic annihilation.'" "And it's no accident that it's getting so critically dangerous right now, when the ideologies have lost their hold, when the ruled are less and less interested in the press releases issued by their rulers. . . . The only thing that always grabs people in most Western countries is anti-Communism. So are they thinking of liberation by annihilation?" For the first time I think the line: Hitler has caught up with us. I keep it to myself. G. and I are the eldest in the circle. More than the young ones, we are oppressed by the knowledge that we are not the first. Or is this a source of hope? I read aloud a few lines from the diary of Stefan Zweig. Date: May 28, 1940, after German forces have begun the invasion of France. Zweig is living in England, where "nothing was happening" to prepare the country for a possible invasion and where he notes on May 22: "The old Cassandra feelings have come alive again." "If this war is continued, it will turn into the most ghastly thing human beings have ever known, the total finishing off of Europe. And yet—is it from inertia, courage, or loyalty?—I don't have any real desire to flee. . . . Ought one not to kick the bucket along with Europe? . . . We who live on and in the old concepts are lost; I have already provided myself with a certain little phial."

How can you teach younger people the technique of living without alternatives, and yet living? When did it begin? we ask. Was this course of events inevitable? Were there crossroads and turning points where humanity—that is, European and North American humanity, the inventors and carriers of technological civilization—could have made different decisions, whose resultant course would not have been self-destructive? Was the foundation for future development laid down with the invention of the first weapons for the hunt, with their use against groups competing for food; with the transition from matriarchally structured, less effective groups, to patriarchal, economically more effective ones? When proportions still commensurate with human experience were exceeded? Is the pursuit of products, more and more products, the root of destructiveness? Would our countries have had any chance of dropping out of this race if we had been oriented by different values?

M. says that he believes a lot of it has to do with the fact that we live so shortsightedly, that we want to have everything right away, that we want everything for ourselves, want to reap even what we have not sown. Christianity is becoming more important to him again, he says, because he can see that people today live without transcendence. I say that even if I agreed with that thesis, it could not dissolve my reservations about Christianity, reservations which had derived fresh nourishment from the work I had been doing recently. It made me realize how, in the Semitic-Christian religions, women had for centuries been assigned the role of slaves, and how these same religions supplied a serviceable background ideology to the manufacturing and factory system of early capitalism, in that they justified the discipline, industry, subordination, and self-denial which this system needed. We talk about words which encourage people to prepare for war. "The words you immediately recognize as warmongering are not the only dangerous ones," R. says. "The dangerous thing would be if the words we cherish most—'freedom,' on the one side; 'socialism,' on the other—were used to justify the preparation for war." Then S. of all people surprises us by saying that he wonders what course is left open to a country which knows for certain that it cannot defend itself against the kind of threat being imposed on it? "There will be nothing left of us," he says. "In a situation like that, is there any value higher than life?" He wonders what would be the counter-slogan to the West German catch phrase you often hear these days: "Better Red than dead." Radical thinking is being required of us now, but of what kind? What meaning would we need to ascribe to the word "Red" in order to choose it in preference to everything, including the lives of all our descendants? Or have the alternatives been other than "Red" and "dead" for a long time?

That people like him should be thrusting their way forward to such questions (I think). On the other hand, A. says that there is nothing one can do. We who call ourselves "freelance artists" know nothing about how the man with a fixed job is eroded and divided from within. A. says he is *one* kind of man at work in his institute; another kind of man in the assembly; a third kind of man in "private life," when he comes home at night. And he also uses different kinds of words in his three unconnected lives: scientific words, political words, private words—the last being the ones he regards as genuinely human. What we are discussing, what we want, is utopia, he says. Which part of this divided man would we address with our vision of peace, a vision which of course would also demand courage? Fear—yes, that's the best tack. For even fear—provided it is not the neurotic fear of nothing—is a manifestation, which implies a person standing behind it. A. sees only that the person is disappearing. "But that applies to us 'freelancers,' too," E. interpolates. "We think differently than we speak, we speak differently than we write." She for her part has recognized that censorship and self-censorship promote war; she has realized that we do not have the time to postpone writing our "real" books until later; so, she says, she has stopped speaking with a forked tongue . . .

We talk into the night. A utopian assembly. I picture hundreds, thousands, millions of such assemblies all across our continent . . .

Meteln, April 28, 1981 I want to gather together all the things that make me, make us, into accomplices of self-destruction; and that enable me, enable us, to resist it.

Daily pleasures: The morning light that falls precisely through the little window I can see from bed. Fresh eggs for breakfast. Coffee. Hanging up fragrant wash in the breeze coming from the sea. Reading about my Minoans, which unites the confusing mass of details I have accumulated in my head over the last few weeks. The good soup at noon. A short nap. Pleasure at an electric hot plate which I am finally able to buy, and which makes me independent of the bottles of propane gas. A friendly saleswoman. The young woman in the antique shop who for a long time cautiously twists a blue glass bottle in her hands so that the glow falls on her face. Nothing diminishes my enjoyment, although the thought of the three or four years of grace that remain continues to preoccupy me. What is the point of the hot plate if there should be no electric currrent, nothing to eat, no one to eat it? What is the point of beauty anymore if it is already given up for lost? Why add yet more books to the many I have not yet read? The photos from last year, which I finally had developed. The faces of the children hurt me. In the evening I enjoy the good cheese. The red wine. Now the tiredness. Writing is also an attempt to ward off the cold.

Meteln, April 28, 1981   And to what extent is it also an attempt to get used to the idea? Is it perhaps the *memento mori* of Christian doctrine, too, or something akin to it? Several times a day, if only for a few seconds, I try to picture what annihilation would "look like," how it would feel—how it *will* feel. Why only for a few seconds? Because the inner images are unbearable? That's one reason. But above all, because a deep-rooted dread prohibits me from "bringing on" the misfortune by imagining it too intensively, too exactly. By the way: Cassandra's "guilt" is precisely this, that she first brought about the doom with her prophecies. For this she feels she is justly "punished," that is, forced to suffer the misfortune of her countrymen in an intensified form. It is a law that people are not *allowed* to believe her as long as they cannot change anything, above all themselves. So what does Cassandra want when, before the war begins, she breaks into great cries of lamentation? Does she want the Trojans to give back Helen, the abducted wife of Menelaus, in response to her warning? In Homer's poem they might possibly be able to do that, and then there would be no motive for the war; but not in reality. For they controlled the access to the Hellespont, and the Achaeans wanted to have free access. So the Trojans would have been massacred no matter what. Or is this precisely what Cassandra is lamenting: that her people have no alternative? And that she is the only one who knows it? For otherwise how could they fight?

The picture I see out of my attic window at this moment is the picture I would like to see at the moment of my death: the sky dominating the landscape, blue-primed. Cumulus clouds. Streaks of cloud above them, at another level. The far horizon, broken by treetops which no longer have the look of a graphic showing bare branches, but are "picturesque": rounded, bright green. The infinitely many nuances of green which compose the picture under the blue of the sky: ranging from the rich green of our meadow—riddled with yellow dandelions since a few days ago—to the medium green of the nearby shrubbery, to the extremely delicate green of those trees in the background. But the dominant feature is the cherry tree in the middle of the meadow, I do not know another one like it. It is entirely covered with blossoms despite the bitter cold of the last few weeks. To the left in my field of vision, under the birch tree, P.'s red picture-book house. The soft, serene light, indescribable. At noon, during my nap, once again the noise of passing armored tanks on the road to M. Immediately I go to plant the last flower seeds for this year.

How do you suppose the people of Troy behaved during the siege? Allegedly there was a ten-year naval war, but not ten years of strict siege. Cassandra has many other brothers besides Paris, who was given away as a child on account of an unfavorable prophecy and, instead of being killed as ordered, was raised by a shepherd—among them Helenus. When they were both children, he, her twin brother, was sitting with her in the grove of Apollo; snakes licked their ears, thus conferring the gift of prophecy on them *both*. Snakes, the insignia of the ancient mother goddess Gaea. This, undoubtedly, was the earlier layer of the tradition, and only later the other part was added, which said that Apollo desired Cassandra after conferring the gift of prophecy on her . . .

Meteln, April 29, 1981 My interest in the Cassandra figure: to retrace the path out of the myth, into its (supposed) social and historical coordinates.

Television: program about the storage of American poison gases in the West German Federal Republic. The giant depot at Pirmasens.* A small amount of the gas is said to have already escaped in an uninhabited area of one of the U.S. states and killed thousands of sheep. You see pictures of the paralyzed animals dragging themselves forward on their knees. Rabbits are kept as measuring devices in the underground poison depots . . . (What difference is there between them and the sacrificial animals of the ancients? The progress it meant when people switched from human to animal sacrifice.) A new poison-gas rocket is being developed in the United States. The American says it is intended for the potential battlefield; and that happens to be Europe.

After that we see the protest actions of Protestant Christians, to whom politicians reply by pointing out that the Sermon on the Mount is not, after all, a guide to concrete political action. A young woman says: "I would not like it if later on my children had to ask me—the way we ask our parents and grandparents—Why didn't you speak up at the time?" She is one of a human type that has come into being, alike or identical in East and West: a slim hope.

In Priam's day, when kings ruled smaller realms (and enjoyed the additional protection of being considered divine), perhaps they were not screened off from normal everyday life as totally as today's politicians, who arrive at their decisions not on the grounds of personal observation and sensory experi-

* Center of the West German chemical industry in the Rhine Palatinate. —Trans.

ences but in obedience to reports, charts, statistics, secret intelligence, films, consultations with men as isolated as themselves, political calculation, and the demands of staying in power. Men who do not know people, who deliver them to destruction; who by inclination or training can endure the icy atmosphere at the tip of the pyramid. Solitary power affords them the protection they have not received, and could not receive, from everyday life, where they would rub shoulders and skins with normal people. Banal, but that's how it is.

The carefully filtered, serviceably built, and abstracted image of reality that is assigned to these politicians. Is it "realistic" to try to neutralize the hierarchical male reality principle—or is it, though necessary, an unrealistic endeavor? Moreover, to what extent can the man of letters, and can literature, go on supporting this "reality principle" by its total remoteness from the sensory experience of everyday life?

Air-defense exercise in X. The windows are lined with strips of paper, food is wrapped in plastic bags, the bathtub has to be filled with water and then covered. The phrase "air defense" releases in me a strong prewar feeling, from the days before 1939. The young woman actress who, horrified by this feeling, which she is experiencing for the first time, wants to put together a program of texts on peace for children, for her child's class. The man who is converting an empty house in his former village, who spends the weekends here and has begun to look after the animals and plants in the area. He records the old, solitary trees and wants to have them placed under a conservation order. Now he is fighting a plan to improve the land by filling in the little water holes which give this landscape its special character and play host to dozens of bird species. He has gotten a rare species of bird to breed in these little ponds; a sensational event for this area. We just ran into him at the water holes opposite Brehmer's house, he warned us not to stand at their edge for very long because the birds had not yet hatched their eggs and the eggs could get cold if the brooders left their nests for too long, out of fear of us. At the edge of the village we meet the von Sch. boy, who was carefully cupping a swan's egg in his hands and intended to take it to the conservationist. Tractor drivers found it while cultivating the fields and sent it to the man. He will know what to do, the boy says. For a long time we bend over the egg; it is very large, symmetrical, a light gray-green, beautiful, covered by a layer of wax. It has not yet gotten cold, the boy says; surely it can be saved.

Meteln, April 30, 1981 Yesterday, the pictures the Americans took when they liberated Dachau concentration camp. Piles of bones, piles of corpses. Germans from Dachau energetically throwing the corpses onto the farm wagons that are taking them away to be buried. The faces of well-nourished Americans underneath their helmets—figures from another world. This constellation—conquerors and conquered, the humiliated and the triumphant—is a basic constellation in human history. The conquest of Troy is one of the first cases we know of, and was itself an artist's composite of the conquests of dozens of cities which took place in those times. But no doubt it has happened only once that the victors came across stigmas like Auschwitz, like Dachau. A word like "inhuman" says nothing because it covers up rather than reveals. Aren't the emotional insensibility and antlike industriousness which signalize such frenzied atrocities also symptoms of a leaning to self-destruction that stems from a malignant, long-term frustration of the ability to act? Isn't it inevitable that a dearth of action such as that imposed on progressive forces over vast stretches of German history will lead to atrocities? Must it not turn on its head the contrasting pair "empty of deeds and full of thoughts"?

Meteln, May 1, 1981 To prevent wars, people must criticize, in their own country, the abuses that occur in their own country. The role taboos play in the preparation for war. The number of shameful secrets keeps growing incessantly, boundlessly. How meaningless all censorship taboos become, and how meaningless the consequences for overstepping them, when your life is in danger.

About reality. The insane fact that in all the "civilized" industrialized nations, literature, if it is realistic, speaks a completely different language from any and all public disclosures. As if every country existed twice over. As if every resident existed twice over: once as himself and as the potential perceiver of an artistic presentation; second, as an object of statistics, publicity, agitation, advertisement, political propaganda.

As for turning things into objects: Isn't that the principal source of violence? The fetishizing of vital, contradictory people and processes, within public notifications, until they have rigidified into ready-made parts and stage scenery: dead themselves, killing others.

To what extent is there really such a thing as "women's writing"? To the extent that women, for historical and biological reasons, experience a different reality than men. Experience a different reality than men and express it. To the extent that women belong not to the rulers but to the ruled, and have done so for centuries. To the extent that they are the objects of objects, second-degree objects, frequently the objects of men who are themselves objects, and so, in terms of their social position, unqualified members of the subculture. To the extent that they stop wearing themselves out trying to integrate themselves into the prevailing delusional systems. To the extent that, writing and living, they aim at autonomy. In this case they encounter the men who aim at autonomy. Autonomous people, nations, and systems can promote each other's welfare; they do not have to fight each other like those whose inner insecurity and immaturity continually demand the demarcation of limits and postures of intimidation.

Shouldn't an experiment be made to see what would happen if the great male heroes of world literature were replaced by women? Achilles, Hercules, Odysseus, Oedipus, Agamemnon, Jesus, King Lear, Faust, Julien Sorel, Wilhelm Meister.

Women as active, violent, as knowers? They drop through the lens of literature. People call that "realism." The entire past existence of women has been unrealistic.

Meteln, May 7, 1981 But why do I feel uneasy when I read so many publications—even in the field of archaeology, ancient history—which go under the title of "women's literature"? Not just because I know by experience the dead end into which sectarian thinking—thinking that rules out any points of view not sanctioned by one's own group—invariably leads. Above all, it is because I feel a genuine horror at that critique of rationalism which itself ends in reckless irrationalism. It is not merely a dreadful, shameful, and scandalous fact for women that women were allowed to contribute virtually nothing to the culture we live in, officially and directly, for thousands of years. No, it is, strictly speaking, the weak point of culture, which leads to its becoming self-destructive—namely, its inability to grow up. But it does not make it any easier to achieve maturity if a masculinity mania is replaced by a femininity mania, and if women throw over the achievements of rational thought simply because men produced them, in order to substitute an idealization of prerational stages in human history. The tribe, the clan, blood-and-soil—these are not values to which men and women of today can adhere. We Germans, of all people, should know that these catchwords can supply pretexts for hideous regressions. There is no way to bypass the need for personality development, for rational models of the resolution of conflict, and thus also for confrontation and cooperation with people of dissident opinions and, it goes without saying, people of different sex. Autonomy is a task for everyone, and women who treat their femininity as a value they can fall back on act fundamentally as they were trained to act. They react to the challenge which reality poses to them as whole persons with a large-scale evasive maneuver.

Meteln, May 10, 1981 The archaeology of the last hundred years offers an opportunity to observe the manufacturing process of a so-called historical truth. Take the example of Troy: A man, Heinrich Schliemann, takes Homer's epic literally, while everyone else regards it as pure invention. At the end of the last century, he finds the remains of superimposed layers of fortress buildings at the spot designated by Homer: on the hill of Ate by the river Scamander. To be sure, he is mistaken in identifying a certain layer as the Homeric Ilium, and is corrected by his later collaborator Dörpfeld. All the same, he opens the eyes of science to the fact that ancient Greek history is not a myth, or more properly, that the myths mirror "truth." Sir Arthur Evans, who at around the same time is busy with the Palace of Knossos in Crete, tries to date Minoan culture by linking it to the already-existing Egyptian timetable; later the attempt will be made to incorporate the dates of Troy into the Minoan scheme as well. Contradictions, lacunae, discrepancies persist until today; but a certain school is gaining acceptance. This builds on the idea that we can perceive reality, historical reality, only within a system of space-time coordinates, so that an isolated expression like "Late Minoan III B" (approximately the time to which "Troy VII A" is dated) may be considered to mean virtually nothing on its own. How is history to be recalled among peoples without a written language— history which, as Fritz Schachermeyr says, unfolds "sequentially and at the same time simultaneously"?

The essential and the inessential, the gradual and the abrupt, the tedious and the diverting, flowering time and fallow time, crises and catastrophes, succeed each other by turns. As a rule history is also tiring, involved, and complex. In the form in which it really happened, it is often unsuited to preservation in the untrained memory and in naïve recollection. Thus history as it really was cannot be remembered by non-specialists, but only written up.

In cultures which have no written language or at least no written history, there are (Schachermeyr says) only two ways to make the past accessible, at least to a limited degree, to human perceptual faculties: the formation of lists and concentration on what the poetic imagination perceives as essential. This concentration process—which, if one were lucky, could lead in the end to a Homeric epic—simplifies the quantity of human figures, reducing them to just a few vivid and vital, ideal figures. It replaces the crowd of phenomena with a few symbolic acts. Vast stretches of time are fused together. People have had no memory for the prosaic, but they have effortlessly retained thousands of lines of verse.

What meaning does this observation have for a literature which no longer wants to create large-scale, vital, ideal figures; no longer wants to tell coherent stories held together by war and murder and homicide and the heroic deeds which accrue to them? What kind of memory does the prose of Virginia Woolf require and endorse? Why should the brain be able to "retain" a linear narrative better than a narrative network, given that the brain itself is often compared with a network? What other way is there for an author to tackle the custom (which no longer meets the needs of our time) of remembering history as the story of heroes? The heroes are exchangeable, the model remains. Aesthetics developed on this model.

Meteln, May 11, 1981 A West German politician says that a universal change of consciousness has taken place in the last decade, comparable to that which took place in the Renaissance. What could be the substance of this change? Perhaps renunciation? A renunciation of the domination and subjection of nature, a renunciation of the colonialization of other peoples and continents, and also of the colonialization of woman by man? So that it is a pleasure to be alive—provided that one is *not* master of the world and is not trying to be?

It occurs to me that literature is judged to be unrealistic, just as the peace movement is, and by the same people. A "realist" today is one who stands on the ground of facts—but in the plans of today's "realists," the ground is already contaminated. What effect does this concept of realism have for aesthetics?

Meteln, June 16, 1981 Lewis Mumford's *The Myth of the Machine* proceeds from the idea that the chief invention of early peoples was not the tools of production but symbols—for example, ritual—by which they channeled the burden of their dreams, of the unconscious; and that their greatest intellectual achievement was the invention of language. A grand-scale polemic against a vulgar-materialistic interpretation of man and history.

Meteln, June 16, 1981 Difficulty in linking interpretatively the individual elements of the Cassandra story. Several possibilities flash to mind, namely: Her "madness" could be real madness, a regression to undifferentiated stages of her personality (and of human history), triggered, for example, by the demand to break a taboo: let's say to offer a human sacrifice in her role as priestess—perhaps a boy, in memory of the alleged practices at the courts of queens. She is unable to do this. Could this event be related to the advent of Penthesilea, who embodies the doomed line of the matriarchy? But she is not imprisoned on account of madness. She is locked up in the dungeon because of the *content* of her visions. For purely pragmatic reasons she is betrothed to Eurypylos, who brings an army of Mysians as reinforcements to the Trojans. She plumbs to the depths what it means to be turned into an object ex-

ploited by others. She withdraws increasingly from her service
to her own family, from the social machinery she is built into,
and associates with people who like her are outsiders—either
voluntarily or because they have no choice. Her inner history:
the struggle for autonomy.

To show how the historical Cassandra, whom I take as my
basis, and her historical surroundings are guided by ritual, cult,
faith, and myth; whereas for us the material is "mythic" *in its
entirety*.

The character continually changes as I occupy myself with
the material; the deadly seriousness, and everything heroic and
tragic, is disappearing; accordingly, compassion and unilateral
bias in her favor are disappearing, too. I view her more soberly,
even with irony and humor. I see through her.

Then her environment crowded in on me: her women friends,
her family. I must get to know them. I realize: I have "known"
them for a long time. More and more the abstractions are filled
with flesh and blood, with faces, gestures. I will need much
more time for the narrative—which increasingly I am coming
to regard as a *roman à clef*—than I had estimated for that
instructive piece which I must have envisaged to begin with.

Meteln, June 30, 1981 Recently a scientist talked on television
about the fact that many people are withdrawing from destructive institutional structures on all sides; so there is hope, after
all, he says; though on the other hand, deep down he nevertheless believes that a large part of the human race will one day be
annihilated by atomic war. All the necessary means to this end
lie ready to hand . . .

Lewis Mumford: *The Myth of the Machine*. After eight
hundred pages describing and analyzing the origin and nature
of the organizational form of megatechnology today; after
drawing a comparison between today's ruling power systems and
the power bloc of the Roman Empire, which in its time was
technologically advanced and seemingly invincible but which

was gradually undermined and crumbled by the Christian minority, Mumford writes:

> If such renunciation and detachment could begin in the proud Roman Empire, it can take place anywhere, even here and now: all the more easily today after more than half a century of economic depressions, world wars, revolutions, and systematic programs of extermination have ground the moral foundations of modern civilization to rubble and dust. If the power system itself seemed never so formidable as now, with one brilliant technological feat following another, its negative life-mutilating counterpart has never been so threatening. . . . Yes: the physical structure of the power system was never more clearly articulated: but its human supports were never more frail, more morally indecisive, more vulnerable to attack. . . . All this has happened so suddenly that many people are hardly aware that it has happened at all, yet during the last generation the very bottom has dropped out of our life; the human institutions and moral convictions that have taken thousands of years to achieve even a minimal efficacy have disappeared before our eyes: so completely that the next generation will scarcely believe they ever existed. . . . The first evidences of . . . a transformation will present themselves in an inner change; and inner changes often strike suddenly and work swiftly. Each one of us, as long as life stirs in him, may play a part in extricating himself from the power system by asserting his primacy as a person in quiet acts of mental or physical withdrawal—in gestures of non-conformity, in abstentions, restrictions, inhibitions, which will liberate him from the domination of the pentagon of power. . . .
>
> Though no immediate and complete escape from the ongoing power system is possible, least of all through mass violence, the changes that will restore autonomy and initiative to the human person all lie within the province of each individual soul, once it is roused. Nothing could be more damaging to the myth of the machine, and to the dehumanized social order it has brought into existence, than a steady withdrawal of interest, a slowing down of

*tempo, a stoppage of senseless routines and mindless acts. And has
not all this in fact begun to happen?**

Meteln, July 21, 1981 Narrative techniques, which in their
closedness or openness also transmit thought patterns. I experience the closed form of the Cassandra narrative as a contradiction to the fragmentary structure from which (for me) it is
actually composed. The contradiction cannot be resolved, only
named.

Meteln, August 12, 1981 On the sixth of August, the anniver-
sary of the day the bomb was dropped on Hiroshima, the American President made the decision to build the neutron bomb;
the Secretary of Defense revealed that the first warheads have
been mounted and could be in Western Europe in a few hours
in case they were needed there. This could be our death sentence, I thought; but what did I really feel? Helplessness. I
put breakfast on the table in the yard. Talked with the others.
Laughed.

On the evening of August 6, a documentary film about a
Japanese family in Hiroshima. The wife was pregnant when
she was exposed to radiation, gave birth to a handicapped
daughter, and in 1979 died miserably of the delayed effects:
bone cancer. The camera showed the stages of disintegration.
The husband who is a barber. The face of the helpless daughter, who does little things to help out when her mother can
no longer do anything for herself. The doctor who tells the wife
that her spine has been "affected." The neighbor woman who
comes to visit her regularly. The two women's heartrending
goodbye. Every time the sick woman's position is shifted, she
has to be afraid that one of her brittle bones will break. Her
face weeping. Her emaciated arms, imploring hands. The daughter weeping. She refuses to separate from her dead mother at

* Quoted from *The Pentagon of Power* (New York: Harcourt Brace
Jovanovich, 1970), pp. 431–33.—Trans.

the funeral. Weeks later she asks to go to the cemetery. Kisses the smooth stone on her mother's grave. A class of school-children who have seen this film are taking an interest in the family's fate. Most young people in Japan know nothing about the effects of Hiroshima.

No document could be more moving. It would not have the slightest effect on those in charge of weapons deployment, even if they should see it. Why not? Would it not, in this case, be better to be moved than to make a move? What if no one who works with weapons would lift a finger anymore? Then they would all be unemployed. So what? you think. Better unem-ployed than dead. But that is not how they think, for they fear certain societal death more than uncertain physical death. These are what I call false alternatives. Their number is in-creasing.

Meteln, August 17, 1981　Discussion with an economic official, a likable man. His feeling that we have "passed the zenith"; he feels sorry for those who are young today. Great skepticism regarding the future. But his conviction that nations and their economy can be governed only by the yardsticks of competition and performance remains incontestable. It amazes me, though, that even the realization that we are unable to solve life-critical problems does not bring such people to reflect on the relation-ship that exists, for example, between the arms race and patri-archal structures of thought and government.

A woman doctor tells me about a civil-defense training ses-sion at which the speaker demanded that we must all learn to "think with war in mind"; suddenly the room became com-pletely still.

Meteln, August 21, 1981　I am reading some writings of Hans Henry Jahnn,* who stated on May 6, 1949, when the first

---

* German author, 1894–1959, among many other things a pacifist and campaigner against nuclear energy.—Trans.

cracks appeared in the Allies' Anti-Hitler Coalition: The program has been laid down for World War III. He recognized immediately the devastating significance of the atomic bomb. He declared: There is no such thing as an armed peace. Peace is unarmed or it is not peace—regardless of what one thinks one has to defend. Twice in this century, war has arisen out of "armed peace," each war crueler than its predecessor. Brecht said exactly the same thing in the fifties: If we do not arm ourselves, we will have peace. If we arm ourselves, we will have war. I do not see how anyone could think differently about this.

Meteln, August 23, 1981 "Knowledge which has not passed through the senses can produce none but destructive truth" (Leonardo da Vinci). There could truly be a new renaissance of consciousness if this insight were to bear fruit again, after the long dangerous experiment with abstract rationality, which resulted in thinking that everything is a means to an end. What speaks against this possibility? The fact that the senses of many people—through no "fault" of their own—have dried up, and that they are justifiably afraid to reactivate them. The fact that perhaps they are no longer capable of doing so. What loss would mankind suffer if it were deprived of "European man" as is now being contemplated? What can we plead in our own favor? The fact that it was Europeans who, by subjugating and exploiting other peoples and continents, learned—or confirmed —that consciousness of mastery and race which determined the direction of technological development (including development of weapons technology), as well as the structures of the economy and of nations? The fact that we ourselves brought into the world the forces which threaten us? That the megamachine, in its destructive irrationality, represents the final end product of our culture?

The debate about the origins and definitions of culture is of course a highly explosive, ideologically charged theme among archaeologists. Marie E. P. König resists the view that the beginnings of culture must be sought where written language began, that is, among the advanced cultures of the Orient, because this view would deny to culture its full intellectual depth. It would imply the loss of our historical origins, the knowledge of all the earlier generations, which is the precondition of progress. In Europe, she says, the country population always kept in touch with past ages. The Celts, for example, preserved the knowledge of all the past generations. In no other part of the world does the soil conceal such rich treasures of past culture, and nowhere else do we have such an unbroken record of the past, reaching back into the Paleolithic. "As long as we do not have analogous documents from other regions of the world, we must assume that the cradle of civilization lay in the West."

Without knowing König, Hans Georg Wunderlich engages in an imaginary dialogue with her. His book advocates the strongly contested thesis that the large palaces of the Minoan culture on Crete are not centers of secular rule but places for worship and burial of the dead. At the end of it he poses the question: Why did the cradle of European civilization lie in Greece, of all places? Why not in Etruria, in Gaul, in northern Germany, or elsewhere? . . . Western culture, whose beginnings go back to the Minoan and Mycenaean heritage, has held out for over 3,500 years already (Wunderlich says) and is at present expanding to become the acknowledged world culture, so that its destruction would be tantamount to the end of mankind—a questionable thesis. It seems to me that one concept of his is worth discussing: The formative process, spanning many generations, that leads to the highest cultural achievements, unfolded, initially, via "language spoken and heard" rather than via written notations. Moreover, the point of origin for early Greek language development was the hero cult, "originally a cult of the dead which kept alive the memory of the people's great dead in a profusion of hero tales." People of the pre-Christian millennia were preoccupied, in a way inconceivable to us, with the cult of the dead, which was a way of warding off their fear of the beyond; and it led, too, to the architectural monuments of Near Eastern and Egyptian culture, stone memorials for individual heroes which united the labor and energy of whole peoples. The strife-torn, relatively poverty-stricken, small early Greek tribes were incapable of such achievements, hence their brilliant solution, born of necessity: Instead of raising stone monuments they would hold festival games for the dead heroes. Here they could not only measure their physical prowess but also identify with the hero's life history in the heroic epic modeled on his life that was played out in the theater; so the theater became a kind of "alternative setting." In this way (Wunderlich claims) the hero cult, and knowledge of the heroes, became common property. In this way Greek theater was born, one of the roots of European culture. In this way the incredible became reality. The Oriental potentates sealed "for all time" in sumptuous but, intellectually speaking, sterile palaces for the dead were forgotten; but the spoken word concerning the Greek heroes remained vital, and preserved our memory of them down to the present day.

Is it possible to set such a thing as "the living word" against the contemporary necrophilia, which manifests itself in steel, glass, and concrete (and which, by the way, does not fail to affect the theater)? This word would have to be subversive, carefree, "im-pressive," in the literal sense of the word, and it may not ask whether it achieves its "aim"—indeed, it must not even have an "aim." Max Frisch has said that the situation of contemporary authors is unique in that they no longer count on having any posterity. Such a word as I have described might draw from this situation a conclusion which could help to create a posterity again, perhaps even a future. This word would no longer produce stories of heroes, or of antiheroes, either. Instead, it would be inconspicuous and would seek to name the inconspicuous, the precious everyday, the concrete. Perhaps it would greet with a smile the wrath of Achilles, the conflict of Hamlet, the false alternatives of Faust. It would have to work its way up to its material, in every sense, "from below," and if that material were viewed through a different lens than in the past, it might reveal hitherto unrecognized possibilities.

4 ❧ A LETTER,

ABOUT UNEQUIVOCAL AND

AMBIGUOUS MEANING,

DEFINITENESS AND

INDEFINITENESS; ABOUT

ANCIENT CONDITIONS AND

NEW VIEW-SCOPES;

ABOUT OBJECTIVITY

For the facts that make up the world need the non-factual
as a vantage point from which to be perceived.

—INGEBORG BACHMANN, *The Franza Case*

Dear A.: When I have moved from Berlin to Mecklenburg,
as I always do at the end of the winter; when I have finally
unpacked my suitcase and emptied out the sacks of books in
the workroom I love best—a room that smells of wood; from
one of whose round "bull's-eye" windows I look out at our
grassy yard, the home-planted willows by the pond bank, the
pond, neighbor O.'s manure pile and stable wall, Edith's washing (today is her housekeeping day), my two oak trees, inter-
woven, bare and full of promise, and the village houses which
later in the year will be hidden by the foliage of these oak trees;
from whose other bull's-eye window, before which my desk
is standing on a wooden platform, I have that view which I

would like to see in the hour of my death: the big meadow, still dun-colored, in the middle the mighty cherry tree, a sign of coming spring, diaphanous, surrounded by smaller apple trees, bramble bushes; P.'s red crofter's cottage right beside the pond, which is almost completely concealed behind a billow in the earth; and then far off, the low horizon with its shallow undulations, plowed land, pasture, groups of trees; then I feel my expectations rise. I will not even begin to talk about the colors, or the skies either—for now that I have reached the end of the sentence which began with the spilled-out books, I still have the duty of listing a few of the titles which lie, perfectly legible, on top of the book-mountain, or half hidden farther down: *The First Sex. Mothers and Amazons. Goddesses. Patriarchy. Amazons, Warrior Women, and He-Women. Women—the Mad Sex? Women in Art. God-Symbols, Love-Magic, Satanic Cult. Male Fantasies. Female Utopias—Male Casualties. Women and Power. The Sex Which Is Not One. The Secret of the Oracle. Utopian Past. Outsiders. Cultural-Historical Traces of Repressed Womanhood. Mother Right. Origin of the Family, Private Property, and the State. Woman's Wild Harvest. The White Goddess. Woman as Image. A Room of One's Own. Womanhood in Letters.* And yet this list, even if I were to continue it, would not give you a proper idea of the remarkable blend which has made up my reading for the last year; for the archaeology, ancient history, and classical authors are still inside another suitcase.

It began harmlessly, with a question which I felt I had to ask: Who was Cassandra before anyone wrote about her? One effect of this, for the time being, is that I suddenly feel that I understand a poem by Ingeborg Bachmann which I have known and loved for a long time—and that (not coincidentally) I have come to understand it right now, while I am raking the lawn, clearing flower beds, trimming the hedge in the front yard: "Explain to Me, Love." Probably you know the penultimate stanza by heart the way I do.

Explain to me, Love, what I cannot explain:
Should I, for the short dreadful while,
be friends with thoughts only, and alone
know nothing sweet, do nothing dear?
Must someone think? Isn't he missed?

Missed—by whom? Missed in what connection? Maybe missed from these simple activities, carrying wood indoors, hanging up wash, grilling herring, which I enjoy only when I am here. These are things which the thinker is accustomed to avoid, which thus do not influence his thought, cannot even color it, for his profession is thought, has been from time immemorial. Not touching. Not doing. Because work with his hands does not belong to the vocation of the free citizen of the polis: a minority in the state, of whom the philosopher forms an even smaller subgroup. But he *does* find time to listen to the rhapsodists who take turns psalmodizing (among other things) a certain epic by a certain Homer, which extols, above all, the wrath of a hero named Achilles, and the murderous fighting of numerous other heroes of olden times. Yet the names of women also appear in it, as seductresses, as wives, as mothers (that is, of course, in relation to a man); and also the name of a prophetess of doom, Cassandra. I can see the impressive gallery of thinking male heads, reaching back through two and a half millennia, beginning with that one ancient thinker, who educates himself, who composes writings; for written language has handed down their names to us. "Must someone think" may perhaps mean: must a man—or a woman—think like *that*? So—exclusively? In a way that excludes love, and what is lovely: "be friends with thoughts only, and alone / know nothing sweet, do nothing dear." "Explain to me, Love": How do you read that? Whom is she addressing? Love—a personified abstraction —or a woman whom she calls "Love"? Is she speaking as a woman, is she speaking as a man? "You say another spirit counts on him . . ." Is "Love" the male lover with whose

thoughts the "I" of the poem is supposed to "be friends only"
—and in consequence the "I" can "know nothing sweet, do
nothing dear"—and thus misses him, the thinker? Is "Love"
she herself who, thinking in this exclusive way, is forced to miss
herself, and is missed?

The "you" of the poem is equally ambiguous. "Your hat lifts
gently, greets, floats in the wind, / your bare head has captivated
the clouds, / your heart has business elsewhere, / your mouth
is annexing new languages." Whom is she addressing? Herself,
addressed as "you"? The woman whom she later calls "Love"?
(Assuming that this "Love" is a woman.) Do you have the same
experience with this poem that I do? The deeper I get into it,
the closer to its ground (which however I cannot feel underfoot), the more I am caught by the puzzle to which it bears
witness, and which it does not undertake to resolve, as it
describes love-play in nature in images that reinforce, intensify,
and outbid each other ("The peacock in solemn amazement
spreads his tail"). Even water, wave, stone are called to bear
witness ("The wave takes the wave by the hand" . . . "One
stone knows how to soften another!"). Then the poem sinks
back to personal deficiency, to irreparable personal loss. "Should
I, for the short dreadful while . . ." What do you think about
the word "dreadful"? To be abused by the person, the people,
one loves most. To be not allowed to be I, not allowed to be
you, but "it": the object of others' purposes. To be friends
only with purposefully directed thoughts, not with the man
who is doing the thinking (and not thinking about me). "You
say another spirit counts on him . . ." Certainly this is not the
spirit of love. No, the spirit which counts and measures and
evaluates and rewards and punishes according to deserts.

> *Explain nothing to me. I see the salamander*
> *go through every fire.*
> *No shudder pursues him, and nothing gives him pain.*

To be without feeling: this is the price of invulnerability, which, it seems to me, the I and the you of the poem (I like to think of them conjointly) do not want to pay. The thinker, the one who for hundreds of years has thought in order to toughen himself up: He is now missed. He now lacks the fraternity, naturalness, guilelessness which he got rid of by thinking them away. Steeled and armored as he is, does he still notice whether he is walking through fire or frost? He will take instruments along to measure the temperature, for his surroundings must be unequivocal. Reflecting on this, regretting it, even lamenting it, the poem itself gives an example of the most precise indefiniteness, the clearest ambiguity. Things are this way and no other way, it says; and at the same time (this cannot be thought logically) things are that way, a different way. You are I, I am he, it cannot be explained. The grammar of manifold simultaneous relations.

Explain to Me, Love

Your hat lifts gently, greets, floats in the wind,
your bare head has captivated the clouds,
your heart has business elsewhere,
your mouth is annexing new languages,
the quaking grass is taking over the country,
the summer blows star-shaped flowers alight and out,
you raise your face blind with flakes,
you laugh and cry and die of being you,
what more can happen to you—

Explain to me, Love!

The peacock in solemn amazement spreads his tail,
the dove fluffs up his feather ruff,
the air stretches, glutted with cooing,
the drake screams, the whole land

eats wild honey, even in the staid park
a golden dust borders every bed.

The fish blushes, catches up the shoal
and bursts through grottoes into coral beds.
The scorpion dances shyly to the music of silver sand.
The beetle smells the Glorious One from afar;
if only I had his senses, I too would feel
that wings are gleaming under her armor,
and take the road to the distant strawberry bush!

Explain to me, Love!

Water knows how to talk,
the wave takes the wave by the hand,
in the vineyard the grape swells, bursts, and falls.
So guilelessly the snail steps from its house!
One stone knows how to soften another!

Explain to me, Love, what I cannot explain:
Should I, for the short dreadful while,
be friends with thoughts only, and alone
know nothing sweet, do nothing dear?
Must someone think? Isn't he missed?

You say: Another spirit counts on him . . .
Explain nothing to me. I see the salamander
go through every fire.
No shudder pursues him, and nothing gives him pain.

Dear A.: It's witchcraft. Ever since I took up the name
Cassandra and began to carry it around like a sort of credential
and watchword; ever since I entered these realms where it now
leads me, everything I encounter seems to be related to it.
Things that in the past were separate have merged without

my realizing it. A little light is falling into previously dark, unconscious rooms. Underneath them or previous to them (places and times flow together), further rooms can be sensed in the dim light. The time of which we are aware is only a paper-thin, bright strip on a vast bulk that is mostly shrouded in darkness. With the widening of my visual angle and the readjustment to my depth of focus, my viewing lens (through which I perceive our time, all of us, you, myself) has undergone a decisive change. It is comparable to that decisive change that occurred more than thirty years ago, when I first became acquainted with Marxist theory and attitudes; a liberating and illuminating experience which altered my thinking, my view, what I felt about and demanded of myself. When I try to realize what is happening, what *has* happened, I find that (to bring it down to the lowest common denominator) there has been an expansion of what for me is "real." Moreover, the nature, the inner structure, the movement of this reality has also changed and continues to change almost daily. It is indescribable; my professional interest is wide-awake and aims precisely at description, but it must hold back, withdraw, and it has had to learn to want and to bring about its own defeat. (Now who was it who taught us to enjoy being disconcerted!) An intelligent and cultivated poet told me he does not understand me; why should I no longer wish to accept the authority of the literary genres? After all, they really are (he said) the objective expression of laws filtered out of centuries of labor, the laws of what is valid in art, and by which we can recognize and measure it. I was so stupefied that I could not answer him.

I set to work on Aristotle. "The mimetic artist depicts human beings in action. These people are necessarily either good or bad."* These are more or less the same criteria most of our newspaper reviewers still apply to books today, I thought in surprise. Swiftly—and I ask you to do the same—I reviewed my

* Passages from Aristotle are translated directly from Christa Wolf's German version, which differs slightly from the standard English translations. —Trans.

family, friends, acquaintances, and enemies, as well as myself, subjecting us to the test "good" or "bad." By Aristotle's standards there would be no suitable models for the imitator-artist to represent. But Aristotle knows how to defend his case: "Homer, for instance, depicts people with higher qualities than average." (Whereas comedy "portrays people who are inferior.") Yes, I thought: Homer. I cannot resist the temptation to quote to you the passage I underlined in the fifteenth book of the *Iliad*. Homer, justly famed—*very* justly famed for his metaphors and similes—describes as follows the flight which Hera, Zeus's wife, undertakes to the other Olympian gods at Zeus's behest.

> *Safe home the seasoned traveler names*
> *A foreign town—"Ah," he exclaims,*
> *"That charming spot! I wish I were*
> *No longer here, but once more there."*
> *Then other towns he calls to mind,*
> *His thoughts run swifter than the wind*
> *And, though his body does not move,*
> *Revisits every scene they love.**

In the same way, Hera needed merely to think of Olympus, and there she was: entering the banqueting hall of Zeus's palace.

But the facts—that is the myth—about Hera are these (and please bear with the following, perhaps longish digression from Aristotle): Like the other goddesses Artemis, Aphrodite, Athena, she had already been incorporated by the Greeks into their patriarchally structured pantheon by Homer's time—that is, the eighth century B.C., when they were (once again) taking over a written language from the Phoenicians. That is, Hera too, the wife of Zeus, has a long prehistory which can only be

---

* This simile about Hera as man's thought is quoted from the Robert Graves translation, Book XV of *The Anger of Achilles: Homer's Iliad* (London: Cassell, 1959).—Trans.

interpreted in matriarchal terms. This prehistory, I believe, still shines through the seemingly abstruse Witches' Multiplication Table in Goethe's *Faust*:

> *See, thus it's done!*
> *Make ten of one,*
> *And let two be,*
> *Make even three,*
> *And rich thou'lt be.**

Goethe—like all his contemporaries—considered history to have begun at the point arbitrarily fixed by the Greeks, in the year of the first Olympiad, 776 B.C. Yet Goethe knew the triformity of the ancient mother goddesses (the very first trinity, from which all the later trinities derived). In this trinity "three" were "even" (the same), in that one goddess appeared in three manifestations corresponding to the three tiers that composed the world. First she was a bright young maiden-huntress of the air (Artemis). Then she was the mature woman goddess at the center, dispensing fertility, ruling land and sea, an erotic divinity (Demeter, Aphrodite, Hera, who earlier was called Era = *Erde*, or earth, whose other names are Gaea and Rhea: the Great Earth Mother of Crete and the Near East). And finally she was an old woman who lives in the underworld, the goddess of death who at the same time effects rebirth (Io, the Cretan cow-goddess, one aspect of Hera, and of course Hecate-Hecuba). Their/her colors are red, white, black, corresponding to the phases of the moon which is their/her symbol and whose goddess they are (do you notice how we have to struggle with ourselves in order to speak of many as one? The convolutions of our brains, and our linear speech, resist the Witches' Multiplication Table).

---

* Quoted from the "Witches' Kitchen" section of *Faust* (London: R. Warne, n.d.), p. 76.—Trans.

And now read in *Faust*, Part II, that passage in the classical Walpurgisnacht where Anaxagoras and Thales debate the world's underlying substance. Here Anaxagoras, an adherent of the catastrophe theory, causes a mountain to grow which is inhabited by Pygmies. They immediately get into trouble through their own wickedness and vengefulness, so that the philosopher, "after a pause, speaking with solemnity," feels compelled "in this to raise his hands to heaven":

> *Ageless on high, and evermore the same,*
> *Threefold in nature and threefold in name,*
> *Out of my people's woes I cry to thee,*
> *Diana, Luna, Hecate!*
> *Thou deep of heart, the soul's endower,*
> *Thou outward peaceful, yet of inmost power,*
> *Reveal thy fearful gulf, profound as night,*
> *And, without magic, show the ancient might.**

Diana (in the above verse) is the Roman form of the Greek Artemis, the maiden-huntress. Luna corresponds to the Greek Selene, goddess of the moon, whose other aspects were Artemis and Hecate. It is claimed that Luna bore a strangely scintillating relationship to the mythical Cassandra—not the literary Cassandra!—and indeed was identical with her. For originally the twin brother and sister, Helenus-Cassandra, were one person, namely the Argive moon goddess Selene, who was fused into the Trojan Helen and the Greek Helen. So Cassandra remained as Paris's sister, a "Hellenized version of the Trojan Helen": beautiful (like Helen), endowed with the gift of prophecy like the Greek Helen and the Trojan Helenus. By the way, prophetic power was once closely linked to the moon deity. It was not exercised in the service of Apollo, the god of light

---

* All passages from *Faust*, Part II, on this and succeeding pages, are quoted from the Philip Wayne translation (New York: Penguin Books, 1959).
—Trans.

and the sun. *He* is much younger than Hecate, Selene, Helen, Helenus, and Cassandra, and is a mythological reflex of the patriarchal revaluation of values, as is Aristotle's *Poetics* in the realm of art legislation. Goethe's predecessors and Goethe himself, as a young member of the middle classes, rescinded the *Poetics* along with the rules and other lumber of the French aristocracy. But never, as far as I know, did they argue against the passage from Chapter 15 of the *Poetics* about "Characters," where Aristotle asks authors to take care that their characters possess "goodness." He goes on: "Woman, too, and even a slave can be good, although in general woman is perhaps an inferior, and the slave a worthless being." For this reason it was logical that women never attended Greek tragedy, not even as actresses. Iphigenia, Antigone, Clytemnestra, Electra, Medea, Hecate, the Trojan women, were all men in women's dress, wearing buskins, slender-limbed no doubt, pretty, possibly homoerotic—but men. This whole earthy-fruitful hodgepodge, this undisciplined tendency to merge and change into each other, this thing which it was hard to put a name to, this throng of women, mothers, and goddesses which it was hard to classify and to count, was brought under control, along with the right of male inheritance and private property, after what appear to have been long, difficult centuries, which now are described as "dark" and have been forgotten. The prohibitions of that day still tell us what things made people feel threatened. Aristotle: "For example, character is good when a man has courage; but in general it is not appropriate for a woman to be brave and manly or even alarming." Alarming to whom—to the man, who has deprived her of all education, of all public activity, of course of the right to vote? Yes, precisely *because* he has done so. We know from our own experience that the things we exclude and ban are the things we have to fear. This is what happens to Goethe's Anaxagoras, who, you will remember, has recklessly invoked the moon goddess and learns to his horror: She is coming!

Lo, ever mightier, candescent, clear,
With orbed throne the goddess, looming near,
Brings terror to the eyes, a portent dire,
And gulfs of gloom now redden with that fire.
Thus far, no further, globe of threatening power,
Lest we, earth, ocean, perish in this hour.

A rock has fallen out of the moon and crushed the race of Pygmies. So this was what Anaxagoras had intended as an example of the "ancient might" "without magic"! Surely his plight is an anticipation of the significant, painful insight voiced by the aged Faust in the ghostly presence of the "four gray Hags" (Want, Guilt, Need, Care—if there were only three of them the analogy to the three Moirae, the Parcae, the Norns, the weavers of fate would be complete):

Could I but break the spell, all magic spurning,
And clear my path, all sorceries unlearning,
Free then, in Nature's sight, from evil ban,
I'd know at last the worth of being man.

Magic, though, was once exclusively the art of women (who, when driven to lovelessness, revert, not without reason, to magic spells). It was the art of the female tribal elders in the early agricultural societies; then, for a long time, of the priestesses, from whom the first priests could entice away the ritual only by pushing their way into the magical clothing of women. It would seem comical to me to point out these things in a tone of indignation, for humanity could not stay at the level of magic and sorcery. But what I ask myself and you is: Was it necessary that the man should come to stand "alone" before Nature—opposite Nature, not in it?*

* Cf. the original line in Goethe, *Stünd ich, Natur! vor dir ein Mann allein* (lit. "If, Nature, I stood before you a man alone"), in Act 5 of *Faust*, Part II ("Midnight" scene).—Trans.

Recently I was discussing the problems of modern science with a company of younger scientists, and we also talked about the history of woman in the West. One of the young men—evidently determined to come clean at last, declared: "People should stop complaining about the lot of woman in the past. The fact that she was subordinated to the man, took care of him, served him—that was the precondition for the man's ability to concentrate on science or on art, and to achieve peak results in both fields. Progress was and is possible in no other way, and all the rest is just sentimental twaddle." A murmur arose in the room. I agreed with the man. The kind of progress in art and science to which we have grown accustomed—extraordinary peak achievements—*is* possible only in this way. It is possible only through depersonalization. I suggested that a kind of Hippocratic oath should be introduced into the mathematical sciences which would forbid any scientist to collaborate in research that served military ends; and the debaters declared that this was unrealistic. If scientists here did not break the oaths (they retorted), they would in any case be broken somewhere else; there could be no taboos on research. "For me," I said, "the price is now too high for the kind of research that science as an institution has been producing for some time." Later I heard that some of the participants had detected in me a trend of hostility toward science. A ridiculous misunderstanding! I thought in the first moment. Then I paused. Could I be "amicably" disposed toward a science which has moved so far from the thirst for knowledge it derives from, and with which I still secretly identify it? I believe we have to stop taking seriously the labels that people throw at us.

Where did we leave off? At women's magic, Goethe, the question of what is the meaning of "progress" today. At the way to the Mothers. At the beautiful Helen, whom Faust longs for unspeakably, and whom Mephisto is not able to produce for him, as he has produced everything Faust wanted in the

past, by means of "witches' cranks" and "ghostly gossamers."
"Yet aids there are."

> FAUST: *Then quick, let these be told!*
> MEPHISTO: *Loth am I now high mystery to unfold:*
> *Goddesses dwell, in solitude, sublime,*
> *Enthroned beyond the world of place or time;*
> *Even to speak of them dismays the bold.*
> *These are the Mothers.*
> FAUST: *Mothers?*
> MEPHISTO: *Stand you daunted?*
> FAUST: *The Mothers! Mothers—sound with wonder haunted.*
> MEPHISTO: *True, goddesses unknown to mortal mind,*
> *And named indeed with dread among our kind.*
> *To reach them, delve below earth's deepest floors;*
> *And that we need them, all the blame is yours.*

Mephisto tries to describe the indescribable emptiness, the
nothingness, which Faust must traverse (and where Faust hopes
to find "the All"). Then he hands him a key. "Follow it down,
'twill guide you to the Mothers."

> FAUST (shuddering): *The Mothers—still I feel the shock of fear.*
> *What is this Word, that I must dread to hear?*

Mephisto's presence is designed to trivialize this shudder of
awe—a shudder which Goethe, by his own confession, also
experienced when he came to this passage and wrote the word
"Mothers," and which Faust loyally affirms:

> *And yet in torpor see I no salvation:*
> *To feel the thrill of awe crowns man's creation.*
> *Though feeling pays the price, by earthly law,*
> *Stupendous things are deepest felt through awe.*

One cannot marvel enough that the word "mothers"—long since debased into an everyday term—should have not yet spent all its radiance, that it still possessed a mythical, "awesome" element in Goethe's time. For in his time this element could not be pinpointed rationally. Nothing was actually known about the background of the Mothers, nothing was known about archaeological digs, field research, the time strata of Greek mythology, its localized features. People *knew* only about a race of gods sprung from Uranus, who hid in the womb of the earth all the sons born to him by the primordial mother Gaea, so that they could not become rivals to his throne. They also knew how the father was castrated by Kronos, his son by Gaea, at Gaea's instigation. They knew about the relationship between Kronos and Rhea—a sibling marriage, for both were the children of Gaea and the incest taboo was not invented until much later. They knew about Kronos's anxiety to hold on to his power, which caused him to devour his sons "to Rhea's unspeakable grief" (Hesiod); he even wanted to devour Zeus. In order to rescue Zeus, who is destined to become the father of men, Gaea gives her son Kronos a stone wrapped in swaddling clothes instead of the newborn infant, whereupon he coughs up the stone along with all the children he has devoured. No idyl, that's for certain. But it would not have occurred to Goethe's contemporaries that this myth might reflect struggles which had actually taken place. Moreover, they had no way of knowing the function of the hero in matriarchal societies, who once a year had to unite with the tribal mother, the priestess, the queen, in a "sacred marriage," and then was sacrificed in a solemn ceremonial—a circumstance which, like the castration of Uranus, could very well justify male fear of women's rituals. German classicists committed an act of self-deception that in historical terms was understandable, even necessary, when they viewed Greek classicism as an example of the successful bonding of the individual (male) to the community ("They are what we were; they are what we shall become again": Schiller). This encouraged them to smooth over the unharmonious aspects of conditions in classical Greece. So what, if not personal experience, is the source of Goethe's reflex of fear at the "Mothers"? This same fear is also reflected in the traditions about Medea and the Amazons, and made Goethe particularly detest Kleist's *Penthesilea* . . .

Awe is composed of reverence and dread. I often think that people today have nothing left but the dread.

I must ask you not to lose patience. Don't think I have lost sight of the question I am really trying to get at: Who was Cassandra before people wrote about her? (For she is a creation of the poets, she speaks only through them, we have only their view of her . . . This, too, is one of the trails I must follow up, until another trail branches off that I must follow, until the third compels me to let go of the second.) What I would like is to communicate to you the feeling which has induced my restlessness—a restlessness which this letter no doubt reflects. It is the feeling that everything is fundamentally related; and that the strictly one-track-minded approach—the extraction of a single "skein" for purposes of narration and study—damages the entire fabric, including the "skein." Yet to put it in simplified terms, this one-track-minded route is the one that has been followed by Western thought: the route of segregation, of the renunciation of the manifoldness of phenomena, in favor of dualism and monism, in favor of closed systems and pictures of the world; of the renunciation of subjectivity in favor of a sealed "objectivity."

The achievement of objectivity was one use to which German classicism put the "ancients." The "objective" aesthetic norms which Goethe developed, when he was not yet forty, after viewing the copies/originals of Greek artworks in Italy, are also subjective symptoms of the way he was foundering in public life in the grand duchy of Weimar: "On this trip I hope to pacify my mind with regard to the fine arts, to imprint their sacred image in my soul and preserve it for quiet enjoyment, so that then I can address myself to the trades and, when I come back, study chemistry and mechanics. For the time of the beautiful is past, our days call for privation and harsh necessity." For me it does not tell against Goethe's theory of art forms that a subjective component was brought into it along with his new philosophy of renunciation—renunciation in political and, partly, in human matters, too. This concept showed that he had a need for certainty, uniformity, tightness, and security; a longing for unshakable, "true" laws and for compliance with them. "These exalted artworks are at the same time the highest works of nature, being produced by men in accordance with true and natural laws. Everything capricious, imaginary wastes away; there is necessity, there is God." There is restraint, control, strictness of form, even in the depiction of ghastly subjects. Schiller wrote a "Cassandra," after all; a poem which begins:

> Glad they were in halls of Troy
> Ere the feast that fell that day,
> All hear hymns of heartfelt joy
> Resound in strings that golden play.
> Weary of battles lost and won
> All hands rest from sad adieus
> Because Peleus' splendid son
> Priam's lovely daughter woos.

This situation derives not from the *Iliad* but from other traditions. The Greek hero Achilles, in reality a libertine, has fallen in love with Cassandra's sister Polyxena; she has lured from him the secret of his vulnerable heel, along with the promise to end the siege of Troy if she consents to marry him. He comes barefooted and unarmed into the temple of the Thymbraian Apollo—whose priestess is Cassandra—to seal this treaty. Here Paris pierces his heel with a poisoned arrow. Thus there is no question of any genuine marriage, and the evil outcome of this day is predictable. No prophetess is needed to foresee it, since its events have already been planned. Schiller changes the suppositions in order to set Cassandra in opposition to the general mood:

> *Joyless in the midst of pleasure,*
> *Alone and unsociable did rove*
> *Cassandra with a silent measure*
> *In Apollo's laurel grove.*

In smooth and evenly flowing stanzas we meet a Cassandra who laments her lot as a seeress—a figure from the age of sentimentality who would rather be conventionally married than continually to groan under the burden of her visions.

> *My laments they ever chide,*
> *And they mock my pains that tear,*
> *To solitary deserts wide*
> *I my tortured heart must bear.*
> *Shunned by those that happy be,*
> *Mocked by those of cheerful mien!*
> *Hard the lot you gave to me,*
> *Pythian god, to vent your spleen!*
> *Into the city of the blind*
> *Why did you set me who could see,*
> *With an ever-opened mind*
> *To proclaim your prophecy?*
> *Why did you give me sight, alas,*
> *Of what I cannot turn away?*
> *What is ordained must come to pass,*
> *What is feared, we cannot stay.*

And so forth. The almost unsurpassable simplemindedness of this view of Cassandra, which gives full justice to the popular bourgeois abhorrence of greatness, especially greatness in a woman, surely springs not only from Schiller's ideal of woman but equally from his classical ideal, which does not allow him to impute to a heroine a long, contradictory historical development. And this brings me back to Goethe's Mothers and Mephisto's instruction to Faust to take their tripod and bring it back with him when he leaves them.

> *A burning tripod bids you be aware,*
> *The deep of deeps at last awaits you there.*
> *And by that glow shall you behold the Mothers.*
> *Some of them seated, some erect, while others*
> *May chance to roam: Formation, Transformation,*
> *Eternal Mind's eternal re-creation.*
> *Around them float all forms of entity;*
> *You they see not, for wraiths are all they see.*
> *Pluck up your heart, for peril here is great:*
> *Go to the tripod well resolved, and straight*
> *You touch it with your key.—*
>   *Ay, that's the style!*
> *You it will follow, be your slave the while;*
> *Calmly you rise, and follow Fortune's track,*
> *Before they know it, you and your prize are back.*
> *And once you have it here, you hold the might*
> *To call heroic spirits from deep night. . . .*

The tripod, which Faust does in fact use to conjure up the apparition of Helen, is an ancient sacred object. We see it on Cretan seals next to representations of the most ancient goddesses. It is used in cult practices. In Act 3 of *Faust*, the Helen act, Phorcus-Mephisto lists the tripod among the objects needed to prepare a sacrifice. The most famous oracle of Greece, the Pythia at Delphi, is known to have sat upon a tripod. Apparently she had done so since the most ancient times, long before the multifaceted god Apollo took charge of the cults and the myths in the course of patriarchalization, and took over the temple at Delphi, too. In the process of taking over the temple he became the first dragon-slayer. Oh yes, he had to kill the dragon Python, the offspring of Gaea, with an arrow shot— which can only mean that he had to disinherit the women oracles (predecessors of Cassandra), with their female pedigree, in order to install his male oracle priests, who allegedly came from Minoan Crete. Beyond any doubt this same Apollo, son of Leto, brother of Artemis—Phoebus, "the radiant"— evolved gradually out of the matriarchal cults of Artemis in Asia Minor. He jumped via Delos (where he was supposedly born as the son of Zeus!) onto the Greek mainland circa 1000 B.C. Then he rose to become not only the supreme, the "most clear-sighted" god of the oracles, but also the *"musagete,"* leader of the Muses (his attribute, the seven-stringed lyre, signified his entitlement to that position) and the *moiragetes,* leader of the Moirae, the weavers of fate. These, it is claimed, were originally "the Moirai," the elderly female relatives and midwives who helped the newborn infant into the world, and who wove into his first clothes those magic signs which distinguished him from all others, so that his relatives, members of his clan, could recognize him—just as the exposed king's son is recognized by a sign in countless fairy tales. Fascinating, the way these female ancestors were transformed into goddesses of fate when the clan evolved into a tribe and the tribe into a kingdom; their relationship to the Cretan Erinyes; the way they merged into the Horae, who, in that they embody law and order, peace and justice, appeared only with the advent of a class society, with the formation of city-states.

Aeschylus is still conscious that, in the beginning, the world was ruled "by the tri-form Moirae and the fidelity of the Erinyes." Even Zeus—whose figure appears only with the existence of kingdoms governed by male succession—could not long override the dictates of the Moirae, the elder goddesses of fate. Two processes ran parallel: the formation of nation-states and the overcoming of ancient tribal goddesses by the new, state-recognized gods. It was in these same centuries that the god Apollo annexed the shrine at Delphi. Initially the mountain nymph Daphne ("laurel"), once installed by the earth mother Ge as a soothsayer-priestess, used to perform her duties at Delphi in a simple hut of laurel branches. This was in the second millennium B.C.—the time of the "historical" Cassandra! At Delphi, too, there was a purely matriarchal cult of priestesses who accompanied every important public occasion of their clan, their tribe, with choral chant, dance, ritual sacrifices, and the pronouncement of oracles. Later came a "temple of wax and feathers," which had allegedly been built by bees (these creatures which belong to female clans). Finally, these cults gave way to the first great Bronze Age temple, which arose in seventh-century Delphi and now was unequivocally dedicated to Apollo, and which is said to have borne the "golden singers" only as figures adorning the pediment. These were the so-called keledones, shouting women, who used to go to the crossroads once a month and invoke the moon—a cult linked to Demeter and Artemis, the sister of Apollo . . .

The women were incorporated into the pediment frieze of the male god. But down below, in the temple of Delphi itself, was the soothsaying Pythia, the only woman left in the otherwise exclusively masculine cult of the oracle. Now she was nothing more than a medium in the control of the powerful priests, placed in a trance by narcotic vapors, by the chewing of laurel, perhaps by autosuggestion or hypnosis. Stammering, writhing, she uttered the incoherent words of her oracle, whose interpretation and, to some extent, poetic formulation once again devolved upon men—priests, the first poets. At first men had identified with women, mimed the birth process, castrated themselves so they could become priests (it is claimed that even Apollo did this); wormed their way into the office of priestess dressed in women's clothing (Apollo is said to have done this, too). At Delphi later this relationship is more than simply reversed—the woman becomes a tool in the hand of the men. Here, in the profession of poet, prophet, priest, which derives from a magical root, you can detect it most clearly: The woman, once the executant, has either been excluded or turned into an object.

Centuries have passed since then. At one seam of these conflict-ridden happenings stands Cassandra. Daughter of a royal house in which patrilinear succession seems secure; but in which the queen, Hecuba—who, many scholars believe, comes from the matriarchal culture of the Locrians—has not yet sunk into insignificance on that account. Moreover, here the transitional custom by which a suitor steals a princess because only the woman could confer the throne on the man is still a familiar phenomenon (witness Paris's abduction of Helen). In this house, the ancient matriarchal cults may well be practiced alongside the young cults of the new gods; especially, no doubt, by the rural population, especially by the lower classes. In this house a young woman can become a priestess, but there is no chief priestess anymore. In this house she can be a "seeress" overwhelmed by visions, and qualify as such, but she cannot be the official oracle. It is men who read the future out of the flight of birds, the entrails of sacrificed animals. Men like Calchas, Helenus, Laocoön. She lives in a culture which perhaps was no match for the strictly patriarchal culture of the Mycenaean Achaeans, for their harsh determination to conquer. Perhaps Cassandra was not "really" a priestess of Apollo at all? (Please don't protest, she actually did exist!) Or at least perhaps she was the priestess of a different Apollo from the "radiant" god of the classical Greek pantheon, he who "strikes his mark from afar"? Was she priestess of an older Apollo who appropriately bore the designation "Loxias," "the dark one"; whose wolfish ancestry, whose dual identity with his twin sister Artemis, were still present in the people's minds? In the same way the Athena who is honored in another of Troy's temples cannot have been the classical Pallas Athena but a cult symbol. Her qualities lie somewhere between those of the chthonic female ancestor-idols, and of that later virginal, dominating goddess who sprang from no mother's womb but from the head of her father Zeus. This latter Athena sprang forth like thought, which Greek men—intellectuals of course—are taking charge of during this period, in order to drive it to astonishing heights, to an admirable level of abstraction. Thought too, indeed, has no mother but only fathers. Does it seem misguided to you to believe that if women had helped to think "thought" over the last two thousand years, the life of thought would be different today? (We forget too easily: Woman as an intellectual has existed in appreciable numbers only for the last sixty or seventy years. We know stories of her and about her, but *her* history—a history of incredible exertion and courage, but also of incredible self-denial and renunciation of the claims of her nature—has still to be written. It would be, at the same time, the history of one of the undersides of our culture.)

So, ought we to go "back to nature," or—what many people take to be the same thing—back to early stages in human history? Dear A., we cannot want that. "Know thyself," the maxim of the Delphic oracle, with which we identify, is one of Apollo's slogans; it could not have occurred to any goddess in the undifferentiated age. But this god, one of whose many other nicknames is "Hekatos," the "ever-distant"—a term that refers to his "radiant purity" and to his "eternal distance from terrestrial things"—this god of noble intellectual freedom, who by definition does not come in contact with the earth, is unable to attain the self-knowledge he strives for. The thin regions whither he and his disciples retreat, fearing to be touched— thinking, yes, and writing—are cold. They need cunning little devices to avoid dying of the cold. One of these devices is to develop women as a power resource. In other words, to fit them into their patterns of life and thought. To put it more simply, to exploit them.

I will not refrain from skipping over two and a half thousand years to copy out for you a few lines of dialogue from *Tiefsee-*

fisch ("Deep-Sea Fish") by Marie-Luise Fleisser: a dialogue between Wollank, a former cycling star, and Tütü, the head of a literary clique. Time: the twenties. Place: Berlin, capital of the Reich.

> WOLLANK: *These women are dreadful, the way they swarm around you and each one dies performing a different service.*
> TÜTÜ: *I don't see why I shouldn't take what I can get. I have turned it into a system. Everything that is able to stimulate me is brought to me without my having to lift a finger. I am spared all the painstaking work which wears out the nerves unnecessarily.*
> WOLLANK: *Doesn't it make you afraid?*
> TÜTÜ: *Afraid of what?*
> WOLLANK: *Man, you'll shrivel up this way.*
> TÜTÜ: *Quite the contrary, I'm developing faster. The high points in my life become concentrated so that I experience it more intensively. My energies are freed for what is essential. . . . I can devote myself completely to pursuing my instincts, bright ideas, my appetite for action.*

Dear A.: Do you believe that this is the kind of objective thinking which gives rise to an "objective" aesthetics? Recite all the great names of Western literature, forget neither Homer nor Brecht, and ask yourself with which of these mental giants you, as a woman who writes, could identify. We have no authentic models; this costs us time, detours, mistakes; but it does not have to be purely a disadvantage. Few, very few women's voices have reached our ears since Sappho sang circa 600 B.C.

> *The moon has set*
> *and the Pleiades too. Mid-*
> *night it is; the hour goes past.*
> *But I sleep alone.*

or:

One man praises horsemen as the most beautiful treasure
of the dark earth, another foot soldiers,
another fleets of ships, but I say it is
what a lover longs for.

In Sappho's time Lesbos was one of the five places in Greece where there were still schools for girls; Sappho presided over one of them. She was an independent professional woman. Then that kind of thing stopped. In the wake of the prophetess her successor, the woman poet, grew silent for thousands of years. Men took exclusive charge of what had been the office of women. They extolled the moon and love, lamented the increasing coldness of the world, not infrequently had to put up with the chiding of more realistic members of their own sex who called them "emotional," "sentimental," "womanish," and, above all, "cut off from reality." I believe that it became increasingly difficult to be a man. "It is good to be a woman and no victor" (Heiner Müller,* *Quartett*). We hear some men say that today with conviction.

On the other hand, only people with conflicts have stories to tell. The choral song of the priestesses, completely embedded in the unfolding seasons among a largely undifferentiated group of human beings, is a hymn; there is no narration. Only the advent of property, hierarchy, and patriarchy extracts a blood-red thread from the fabric of human life, which the three ancient crones, the Moirae, had in hand; and this thread is amplified at the expense of the web as a whole, at the expense of its uniformity. The blood-red thread is the narrative of the struggle and victory of the heroes, or their doom. The plot is born. The epic, born of the struggles for patriarchy, becomes *by its structure* an instrument by which to elaborate and fortify the patriarchy. The hero is made to serve as a model, and still does so down to the present day. The chorus of female speakers

* Contemporary East German author, b. 1929.—Trans.

has vanished, swallowed up by the earth. The woman can now become the object of masculine narrative, in the role of heroine. Helen, for example, who, rigidified into an idol, lives on in the myths.

"Helen, much admired, and blamed as much": For the last time I will quote *Faust*, but unfortunately only a part of the speech of Helen. Now back in Sparta, whence Paris had abducted her, restored to the hands of her husband, Menelaus, after the fall of the fortress of Troy—Helen no longer knows who she is.

> *You have, in rough, unseemly wrath,*
> *Evoked the frightful forms of images unblest,*
> *Which hem me in, with fear lest Orcus and the shades*
> *Snatch me away, in mockery of the fields of home.*
> *Looms this from some past life? Or am I seized and crazed?*
> *Was all this me? Is still? And ever shall I be*
> *The phantom scare of them that lay proud cities waste?*

The stations of her peregrinations through men's beds are reeled off from memory; she was indifferent throughout, an object that was desired, married, kidnapped, fought for. In theatrical presentations of *Faust*, the character of Helen is always misacted; directors see her as a coquette who ruins men, instead of as a ball tossed back and forth. No one reads what Goethe makes Helen herself say, and no one seems to believe that he (and she) mean it seriously. The last man who joined with her "in burning passion" was Achilles.

> HELEN: *Then was I but a wraith, and with a wraith was joined.*
> *It was a dream, the very words declare this true.*
> *And now—I swoon, becoming to myself a wraith.*

The word "wraith" = "idol," from the Greek *eidolon* = image. The woman is deprived of her living memory, and an image which others make of her is foisted upon her in its place: the hideous process of petrifaction, objectification, performed on living flesh. Now she is classed among the objects, among the *res mancipi*—like children, slaves, property, livestock—which their owner can turn over to someone else via the legal procedure of *mancipatio*. The recipient in turn has the right to *manū capere*, grasp her with the hand, lay his hand on her. For a long time *emancipatio*, release from the power of the *paterfamilias*, was provided only for sons. And when the word "emancipation" was finally applied to women (today it still is often used pejoratively: "I guess you must be an emancipated woman?"), both men and women used this concept of release in the sense of "equal rights," played down its importance, and misunderstood its meaning; for its revolutionary, radical meaning was and is disturbing.

Now, dear A., this is a wide field, but I think we had to come to the edge of it if we were to follow the lead of the watchword "Cassandra." Do people suspect, do *we* suspect, how difficult and in fact dangerous it can be when life is restored to an "object"? When the idol begins to feel again? When "it" finds speech again? When it has to say "I," as a woman? We see a landscape generations wide where the writing woman still tends to get lost: lost in the man, the male institutions, federations, churches, parties, states. We have eyewitness and earwitness documents of how men and women talk to each other. Let's take the things the man Elnis says to the woman Ebba in Fleisser's *Tiefseefisch*: "A woman who loves a man can do anything." "I am so tender inside." "My sufferings are your sufferings. We are one body and one flesh." "You shall have no will. You shall no longer be there. I want to absorb you." "You must become completely my slave, and I must become completely your slave." "I have seized on you the way a male animal corners his mate. I defend my prey. I will think about you so rigorously that it will keep you at my side, spellbound." "You will forget that you are being sacrificed." "I am a magician."

"You must trust in me blindly. Naturally I cannot have someone near me who doubts." "Put an end to yourself if you feel sorry for yourself. Hang yourself, walk into the water! Then there'll be one less woman." "I will make a human being out of you yet."

And what does the woman say in this forlorn landscape? What can she reply to this man who is diseased in himself? She says things like this: "I cannot see my way in my life anymore. Am I not a human being who feels things?" "You will not be a slave, not you." "It is terrible." "You would not illtreat people if you were not handsome." "Mine is a nature that sees ahead. I can renounce things." "I am always forced to see the abyss. I could scratch the eyes out of my head." "I want to become different." "His eyes accuse me. I could wipe myself off the face of the earth."

Dear A.: You know as well as I do that you cannot argue against such sentences, using other sentences that begin, shall we say, with "But." I claim that every woman in this century and in our culture sphere who has ventured into male-dominated institutions—"literature" and "aesthetics" are such institutions—must have experienced the desire for self-destruction. In her novel *Malina*, Ingeborg Bachmann has the woman disappear inside the wall at the end, and the man Malina, who is a part of her, serenely states the case: "There is no woman here."

The last sentence reads: "It was murder."

It was also suicide.

Dear A.: I have notified you that it is hard to define the limits of the theme which my thoughts are orbiting. Nevertheless, I will not yield to the urge to talk about "the position of women," to cite observations, to quote from letters. One day, no doubt, I must do so, if only to give legitimacy to what women write about women, which critics do not want to acknowledge. Of course I see that this desire to legitimate still reflects the compulsive notion that we women have to adapt or disappear. I also see that it reflects indoctrination by that prevailing system of aesthetics that I have called up for discussion here. For women there have been three thousand years of muteness or, at best, sporadic speech. Then along comes a woman who says: "I will collect only the stories which do not come to public notice, and only stories with a lethal outcome" —*Todesarten*—"Types of Death."* Dear A., I cannot prove my assertion—or can prove it only in isolated cases, which prove nothing in favor of the kind of summary declaration I am about to put forward so coolly—*but*: Aesthetics, to the extent that it is a system of categorization and control, and especially where it advocates certain views about the subject matter of the various genres, namely "reality" (I notice this word appearing between quotation marks more and more often in my writing, but I can't help it)—aesthetics, I say, like philosophy and science, is invented not so much to enable us to get closer to reality as for the purpose of warding it off, of protecting against it.

Do you think that Bachmann did not know how Goethe wrote novels, as well as Stendhal, Tolstoy, Fontane, Proust, and Joyce? Or do you think she was unable to foresee that a creation like the one she presented in the guise of a "novel" would dumbfound all duly qualified rules and categories of aesthetics —even if they were interpreted with great latitude!? And that encountering no net, however thin, to break its fall, it would catapult straight to the ground? "I am Madame Bovary." Flaubert said that, as we know, and we have admired this remark for more than a hundred years. We also admire the tears Flaubert shed when he had to let Madame Bovary die, and the crystal-clear calculation of his wonderful novel, which he was able to write despite his tears; and we should not and will not stop admiring him. But Flaubert was *not* Madame

---

* The "woman" is Ingeborg Bachmann. "Types of Death" is the title of Bachmann's projected novel trilogy, left uncompleted at her death. The quotation about "stories with a lethal outcome" is also taken from Bachmann, Vol. III of *Werke* I–IV.—Trans.

Bovary; we cannot completely ignore that fact in the end, despite all our good will and what we know of the secret relationship between an author and a figure created by art. But Ingeborg Bachmann *is* that nameless woman in *Malina*, she *is* the woman Franza in the novel fragment *The Franza Case* who simply cannot get a grip on her life, cannot give it a form; who simply cannot manage to make her experience into a presentable story, cannot produce it out of herself as an artistic product. Lack of talent? This objection does not apply, at least not in this case. To be sure, it is hard to understand that one sign of her quality as an artist is the very fact that she cannot kill the experience of the woman she is, in "art." A paradox, yes indeed. An ability to be "authentic"—to use another literary term—that comes only by renouncing the detachment afforded by definite forms. A frenzy driven to find words, that cannot adhere to the subduing ritual, that cannot adhere to anything, that is untamed, wild. A wild woman, you can only raise your arms in perplexity. It is a different kind of logic that comes from her, who perhaps better than any woman knows the male thinking process: the If this/Then that; Because/Therefore; Not only/But also. A different way of asking questions (no longer the murderous who did what to whom). A different kind of strength, a different kind of weakness. A different friendship, a different enmity. Whichever direction you look, whichever page you open the book to, you see the cave-in of the alternatives which until now have held together and torn apart our world, as well as the theory of the beautiful and of art. A new kind of tension seems to be struggling for expression, in horror and fear and tottering consternation. There is not even the consolation that this is still capable of being given form; not in the traditional sense.

"This"? What is "this" exactly? The sacrificial victim becomes aware of her sacrificial function and refuses to serve in the ritual; but her ecstasy can be self-destructive all the same, because she has misunderstood her slayer, loved him and regarded him as a lover. The victim breaks out, instead of accepting her lover's offer to collaborate with him, to become just like him but as anonymous as possible: and at all events to remain an object. What could have destroyed her in this way? That is the question her brother asks himself in the *Franza* fragment, where he is the only male being, the only human being, to whom his distracted sister can appeal for help. As far as I can see, that is the question around which the material is organized: a question which unfortunately—yes, unfortunately—cannot be answered objectively, in the manner of the old or the new novel, not even of the most avant-garde. Neither of the siblings—neither the mortally ill sister nor the brother, who understands at least that he must stay by her side—neither, up to the end, can give a straightforward accounting; at least not in the words we have at our disposal. And we, too, will experience terror rather than an answer. Or are we meant to come up against the fact that terror is the answer for our times, nameless horror; and that we—men and women—will not make progress, not liberate ourselves, not emancipate ourselves, if we try to dodge this dread?

"It's just that it is hard to tell about it" (we are told at one point; the voice has difficulty breathing; is that all?) in "words that do not exist" and in "words that exist because they are insisted upon." The thing that then is nevertheless narrated, compiled, woven together, is a tissue formed of the most extraordinary, partly farfetched threads. You can guess how it is when two lines from Musil's poem "Isis and Osiris" sound between the siblings as a recognition slogan and password, and as an assurance of unconditional mutual reliability.

> Among a hundred brothers him I greet
> who ate my heart and I his heart did eat.

Musil has "*of all* my hundred brothers," and whoever remembers the history of the Egyptian royal brother-and-sister couple—the history of the propagation of their cult, the significance of the ritual "eating" of the members of human sacrificial victims—will not expect any brother-and-sister idyl. And yet their meeting, their brotherly, sisterly way of entering into each other's feelings and of missing the mark with each other, forms the present moment which is being narrated and in which the narrative takes place. Whereas the completely different, insanity-breeding, unbearable time, ambiguously called "Jordanian time," is not experienced, can at most be remembered, and even that not immediately and not always. Professor Jordan, to whom Franza was married, is a famous psychiatrist, a higher morality, an authority, a standard which she wanted to make her own. This is the very point where the emancipation of woman must take a stand in all the systems I know—it must dare to doubt this standard. The man to whom she devoted herself ("What a disgrace!") "could not bear to see anyone extended beyond the limit he had placed on them." "Why am I hated, no not I, the Other in me." He dissected her as he did everyone, she was the unknowing object in a "diabolical" experiment: "You call it Fascism, that's funny, I have never heard that word used to describe private behavior"; but "after all it has to begin somewhere." "Yes, he is evil, even if today one is not allowed to say evil, only sick." "He must be crazy; and there is no one who appears more rational . . ." "I was with a man, separated from society, in a jungle in the middle of civilization, and I saw that he was well armed and that I had no weapons." He let her see the notes he was making about her: a scientific voyeur like the many artist voyeurs. "He hounded me into a trap," into what she (and certainly he, too) called her "mannerisms," into compulsions which overwhelm her more and more and for which there are "phrases" as for everything in this civilization, scientific designations which she now casts off along with everything which the intellect of the white man wanted to impose on her. "I am talking about fear. Shut all the books, the abracadabra of the philosophers, these satyrs of fear who busy themselves with metaphysics and do not know what fear is."

I ask you now, what is the status of fear—not the anxiety in the psychiatry textbooks, but the naked, bare fear with which a woman is alone, limbs trembling and sleepless, and which no one believes she feels. What status has this enduring fear in the textbooks of artifact-aesthetics, where the concern is with control of self and material?

The woman who calls herself Franza must acknowledge that she has been colonized. "I am of a lower race . . . He is the exemplar that rules today, that is successful today, that has today's cruelty, that attacks and therefore lives." She might have known that; but because she was excluded for so long from his activities, she is caught unprepared when she enters the scene as his colleague, collaborator, partner—his rival, competitor. Here follow the key sentences which unite all the women I have talked about today—seeress, poetess, priestess, idol, subject of artworks:

> You can really steal only from people who live magically, and for me everything has meaning . . . In Australia the aborigines were not exterminated, and yet they are dying out, and the clinical investigations are not able to find the organic causes. There is a deadly despair among the Papuans, a kind of suicide, because they believe that the whites seized all their possessions by magical means. . . .
>
> He has taken my possessions from me. My laughter, my tenderness, my ability to feel joy, my compassion, my ability to help, my animality, my radiance; he has stamped out every sprout of all these things, until they stopped sprouting. But why does someone do that, I don't understand.

The magical trimmings of her life are at the same time its realest part. She approaches another kind of storytelling when she introduces these trimmings into her narrative, and when she encircles her irrational, deadly grief with words whose magical significance is unmistakable. This is most apparent in those chapters which invoke magical, prehistoric worlds in

Egypt, in the burial chambers robbed of their magic by the whites; indeed, even in her almost magical death from terror— terror of a recurrent event,* struck into her by a man who is himself sick and who needs to be able to frighten a woman to death. "Let the whites be cursed": Those are Franza's last words, and I, dear A., and no doubt you too, believe in the efficacy of such a curse, and we must do everything we can to see that it is lifted. By writing, yes; but how can we write under the glowing sun of reason; in this rigorously cultivated, arrogant, and deciphered landscape, robbed of our possessions, including our words, which could have the power to cast spells? This, too, is a question which can only be approached by asking further questions. If only we could buy time. What is Cassandra's message today, when of course she is mocked, unheard, described as abnormal, exposed, consigned to death? She says:

The whites are coming. The whites are landing. And if they are repulsed again, they will return again once more. No revolution and no resolution and no foreign currency statute will help; they will come in spirit if they can no longer come in any other way. And they will be resurrected in a brown and a black brain; it will still always be the whites, even then. They will continue to own the world in this roundabout way.

---

* The man who terrorizes Franza on the Egyptian pyramid recalls an earlier attack by her husband.—Trans.

ALSO BY CHRISTA WOLF

NO PLACE ON EARTH
Translated by Jan van Heurck

In this haunting novel, Christa Wolf contemplates an imagined meeting between the now long-forgotten though in some ways very 'modern' poet, Karoline von Günderrode (1780-1806) and the celebrated writer Heinrich von Kleist (1777-1811).

It is the summer of 1804. The French Revolution lies fifteen years in the past, the talents of women writers are beginning to emerge in Germany; it is a time of transition. At a gathering of literary friends in a small town on the Rhine, the two writers slowly come together. They talk of ambition and creativity, love and hate, self-esteem, and the tragic impossibility of life: neither can accept the world in which they must live. This powerful and bittersweet meeting, pure conjecture, is pieced together from extracts of actual letters written by Kleist and Günderrode. In real life, both committed suicide some years after the events of this book.

Despite its historical setting, *No Place on Earth* is a novel of astonishing immediacy, reflecting Christa Wolf's extraordinary talent for illuminating the psychological and moral issues of our own times. It is, as Joyce Crick says, 'a duet on the importance and vulnerability of creation in dark times, of male and female sensibilities, of death, friendship and hope'.

'*No Place on Earth* is exalting work by a writer who can do almost anything' – *Susan Sontag*

ALSO BY CHRISTA WOLF

A MODEL CHILDHOOD
Translated by Ursule Molïnaro and Hedwig Rappolt

'What is past is not dead; it is not even past. We cut ourselves off from
it; we pretend to be strangers.' Thus begins Christa Wolf's A *Model
Childhood*, an account of the author's years growing up in Nazi
Germany, as seen through the prism of a brief trip in 1971 back to
her native town, accompanied by her husband, her brother and her
daughter, Lenka, who inevitably asks certain unavoidable, probing
questions about the past. After the trip, Wolf returns home to write
about the experience, about her childhood (adopting the role of an
external narrator), and about the difficulties of writing her story with
any sort of objectivity or clarity.

In 1933, the child Nelly is four years old and lives in Landsberg,
now Grozów Wielkopolski. Nelly's family believes in Hitler's new
order: her father joins the party, and she, as a matter of course, joins
the Nazi youth organisations. In school Nelly learns of racial purity
and the Jewish threat, and when the local synagogue burns, she feels
not pity, only fear of an alien race. No voice of objection is raised,
not even when the euthanasia programme dooms Nelly's simple-
minded Aunt Dottie. It is only much later, when her family is
fleeing westward before the advancing Russian army, that Nelly,
now in her teens, tries to come to terms with the shattering of the
fundamental values of her childhood.

The adult Nelly, who must answer her daughter, tries to explain
the passion for Hitler, what was and was not known at the time, how
it was possible to not know, to not admit you did know, how it is still
possible for some. Looking through the eyes of her younger self,
Christa Wolf explores the experience of Nazism as it was lived by
ordinary people in an ordinary town. In doing so she has created a
great novel which is also a plea to remember and to learn from the
past.

'A powerful and finely sustained novel' – *The London Review of
Books*

THE QUEST FOR CHRISTA T.
Translated by Christopher Middleton

Christa is a young girl in Hitler's Germany; she survives to embrace the new order but her enthusiasm and idealism wither as crass materialists corrode its splendid dreams. A teacher in a village school, a student at Leipzig University, a wife and a mother, the life of Christa T., here recalled by her friend, is the life of an ordinary, intelligent, sensitive woman. But this famous novel is more than that. Christa's is the story of a whole generation, and a moving celebration of the unique value of each human being and all human life.

'A sensitive writer of the purest water – an East German Virginia Woolf' – W. L. Webb, *Guardian*

'Undoubtedly one of the few great novels in the German language since the war', – *The Times*